'Englishness'
in Music

from Elizabethan times
to Elgar, Tippett and Britten

JAMES DAY

Thames Publishing
London

Printed and bound in Great Britain
by Lonsdale Press, London

Contents

For Jennifer, Jane, Shelagh and Will

I held it truth, with him who sings
To one clear harp in divers tones,
That men may rise on stepping-stones
Of their dead selves to higher things.

– Tennyson

Preface

This is not a history of English music, or even of music in England. If it were, it would have to devote much more space to great medieval musicians such as Dunstable and to the music of such masters at the early Tudor court as Cornyshe, Fayrfax, Tye, Tallis and Taverner, to mention a few names out of many. It would also have to deal with the contributions to English musical life of those composers of the present age and the one immediately preceding it who, even if they did not reach the highest pinnacles of achievement, none the less merit close attention. Such composers, for example, as the Berkeleys, father and son, as Burgon, the Matthews brothers, as the present Master of the Queen's Musick, as Oliver Knussen, Mark-Anthony Turnage, Judith Weir or Thomas Adès are either not mentioned at all or referred to only cursorily. This does not mean I consider them of little or no significance as musicians. I am not setting out to devise a league-table of musical merit thinly disguised as narrative.

My aim has been conditioned by the courses out of which the book arose. These were delivered on the International Summer Schools run by the Cambridge University Board of Continuing Education in collaboration with two colleagues, Dr Michael Stenton and Charles Stephens. Our intention was to identify, if we could, certain peculiarly English characteristics to which the attention of our students might be drawn in various aspects of English history, literature and music. We should have liked to involve a further colleague well-versed in English pictorial art and sculpture as well, but our course was limited to eighteen lectures; and we had therefore to restrict ourselves each to six aspects of our chosen area. In music, our choice fell on the Elizabethans, Purcell, Handel, Elgar, Vaughan Williams and Britten.

At the suggestion of John Bishop (Thames Publishing), I have tried to integrate what were in fact and in origin six discrete lectures into a continuous narrative by adding an introduction, five linking chapters and an epilogue. These fill-in chapters attempt to show how social and economic attitudes in England to music as an art fluctuated and changed over the generations separating my six chosen figures. The linking chapters are no more comprehensive than the main ones. They consciously omit any reference to a number of figures of some significance in English musical life, especially among executant musicians and administrators. They are simply an attempt to set out some of the reasons why I think the history of music in our country has been such a chequered affair.

My thanks are due to John for encouraging me to undertake the work, to various colleagues employed by the Cambridge University Board of Continuing Education and particularly Sarah Ormrod, who was in charge of the courses when the lectures were delivered; and above all to our students from all over the world, who may have felt mentally a little punch-drunk after our several harangues, but who certainly asked some stimulating questions and offered some valuable and searching comments.

1 – What is 'Englishness?'

Speculating on what is specifically English about some aspects of English life and culture is not all that difficult. There are certain features of our way of life that operate in ways that differ markedly from those found in parallel features of other cultures; and in these cases it is possible to draw general conclusions from specific examples. Our unwritten constitution can be cited as one such case, with its Queen in Parliament, its elected House of Commons and its selected and/or hereditary House of Lords. We may reasonably claim that the way in which the system has developed demonstrates a suspicion of absolute, eternally valid, cut-and-dried theoretical schemes in preference for letting the way in which our laws are made and administered develop organically out of the social and historical context.

Similarly, our common law has little to do with the orderly system, based at some remove on ancient Roman principles, that Napoleon imposed with varying degrees of success and permanency throughout his conquests in Western Europe. The Anglican church is certainly a further case in point. It is, in fact, possibly an even more 'typically English' institution, even though it has been exported to so many other cultures that the parent body now forms a mere fraction of the world-wide communion into which it has developed. Yet it still acknowledges the Archbishop of Canterbury as its spiritual head. Catholic, evangelical, liberal, broad church, high or low, it embraces an extremely wide range of beliefs[1] and practices as long as they can be accommodated to the Thirty-nine Articles set out in the *Book of Common Prayer*. It is cited by its admirers as an example of English tolerance and derided by its detractors as one of English apathy.

---

[1] You don't have to be an atheist to be an Anglican bishop, it is sometimes maliciously (and erroneously) asserted, but it helps.

Then there is our language itself, with its complex and amazingly flexible and expressive blend of structural and lexical elements derived from Celtic, Latin, Germanic, and many other sources. It provides the native English speaker[2] with an instrument of communication capable of expressing a wide range of shades of meaning, a superb vehicle for the display of poetic imagination. Because of its complex roots it can easily absorb all kinds of new influences; and because it is possible to integrate new elements so effortlessly and apparently so casually into the already existing lexical and structural stock, it can expand its expressive resources to a degree unrivalled in other Western European languages that happen to derive almost exclusively from only one of its various sources. The words 'mortal', from Latin, 'deadly', from Anglo-Saxon, and 'lethal' from Greek overlap[3] in meaning to some degree, yet each of them has different nuances. All men may be mortal, but they may not necessarily be lethal or deadly. Two brothers may be deadly, though not necessarily lethal enemies. Another example: the French national motto appears in quite a different light if it is translated 'Freedom, fairness and brotherhood' rather than 'Liberty, equality and fraternity'. Anyone who has ever taught English as a foreign language will know the difficulties experienced by overseas learners, even of high intelligence and linguistic skill, when they try to master the English tense system, with its network of simple, progressive and perfect forms. It is neither here nor there that the overwhelming majority of native English speakers misuse this wonderfully flexible instrument of communication. What matters is that it exists for their use; and it is the product both of their ancestors' imagination and of their surliness and laconism.

Our rural landscape, with its neat enclosures of hedges or dry-stone walls, and certainly some of our townscapes, with their often dreary and

---

[2] And, to an increasing degree, those working within multi-national organisations.

[3] Can one be in *lethal* peril, for example? One certainly cannot be in *lethal* or *mortal* earnest: the accepted collocation is *in deadly earnest*. And it makes quite a difference to one's meaning if one refers to a person one dislikes as *mortal* rather than *lethal*.

monotonous rows of terraced slate-roofed houses, each varying only very slightly in matters of detail according to the taste of the occupiers, might also be considered to express an aspect of our national character: a love of privacy, say, or lack of imagination, of individual self-expression within a framework of regularity, or a feeling of cosiness. If this is the case, then any representative art, such as painting, that involves using our rural or urban scenes as ikons or images is likely to evoke a different atmosphere than similar art developed in other cultures. Even our food, with its tendency towards weighty pies, puddings and meat dishes (and our often unnecessarily unimaginative treatment of sauces and vegetables), might be included; and if, as the Germans say, 'man ist, was man ißt[4], then surely that will affect our national character.

But music? What could possibly be English about that? Studies of the intricate non-harmonic musical cultures of other continents, with the microtonic subdivisions of the octave of some of them, the wide and exciting varieties of rhythms of their dances, the intricate melismata of their melodies, have enabled scholars at any rate to pinpoint features characteristic of the music of other regions and continents than western Europe. Bela Bartók used to refer to certain rhythms as 'Bulgarian': they distinguished music cast in them from the Magyar folk-music in which he was primarily, though by no means exclusively, interested. As far as he was concerned, national culture, if not national character, could be distinguished in certain types of traditional music. Indeed, even within the culture of the British Isles, one national instrument, the bagpipe, differs in the intonation of the scale it uses from other wind instruments such as the oboe or the clarinet.

If there is anything 'national' or 'characteristic' of England about the music of the country, how can it be expressed or differentiated when the fundamental conventions of musical procedure – the scales, rhythms and intervals that composers use, the interplay of themes and harmonies that they have been trained to exploit, and the resultant large-scale structures in which the music itself is cast – have been the common

---

[4] 'One is what one eats'.

property of all West European nations since at any rate the last quarter of the sixteenth century? True, English composers might of course use these elements – the mechanism[5] of music, as it were – differently from other musicians trained in other traditions. There certainly used to be differences between the manner in which German-trained musicians approached innovations in musical conventions and forms from that in which French or Italian do.

To take an example from military music, the 'feel' of a march like *Colonel Bogey* differs quite markedly from that of, say, *The Stars and Stripes forever*, or from *Marche Lorraine*, to say nothing of the different sound-palette of a French, an American or a British regimental band and the style and swagger that each imparts to the music it performs. These surely reflect national differences in their attitude to military ceremonial and the ethos it projects. Such differences between what may be called the balance of emotion in music and its effect on the listener surely depend on canons of taste accepted by the social and musical establishment of different societies, especially when the music is part of a larger theatrical spectacle or state ceremonial. Things, for example, that a Parisian public of the Second Empire would welcome with glee from Offenbach might not be considered quite acceptable by a Victorian audience wishing to be entertained by Gilbert and Sullivan. And, *mutatis mutandis,* that same Parisian public would probably be bored to tears by Sullivan's erudite fugal passages characterising the Lord Chancellor's legal learning in *Iolanthe*. Nor would it find much to laugh at in the ponderous mock-Handelian music associated with King Gama's three dim warrior sons in *Princess Ida*. Yet the musical styles as such are not specifically English (or Irish, bearing in mind Sullivan's origins). What may be legitimately regarded as English is the manner in

---

[5] So powerful is the force of national tradition in some centres that the conductor Erich Leinsdorf, visiting his native Vienna after many years' residence in the U S A, was amused to discover that at the Conservatoire there the curriculum still virtually ignored any music, such as that of the French impressionist composers, whose harmonic conventions lay outside the Germanic tradition.

which the mechanism of music is exploited to convey a specific message – an emotional or ethical attitude.

The examples mentioned above, of course, all deal with music wedded to a vernacular text. But is there a 'national' element in the purely abstract type of music? What is it about Elgar's *Enigma Variations*, for example, that caused a Swiss violinist to thank Sir John Barbirolli after he had conducted a performance with the Basel Symphony Orchestra for bringing them Elgar, because he was so *English?* Why did Ralph Vaughan Williams (rightly) single out the fifth variation of the set as being part of an Englishman's heritage rather than, say, *Nimrod*, with its elegiac associations of Westminster Abbey tributes[6] to the distinguished departed? Is it just the majesty and the feeling behind the words that causes a mass audience to sing Parry's setting of Blake's *Jerusalem* with such fervour? Or does Parry's noble tune have a quality that strikes an emotional as well as a musical chord among English people? Is it just the feeling of belonging to a politically powerful community that induces the audience at the last night of the Proms to burst out with *Rule, Britannia* or *Land of Hope and Glory?* Jingoism? Nostalgia for a lost empire? Wishful thinking? Or does the music mean something to an English audience that is independent of the words? Could the same be said of a tune like *Fairest Isle?* – Dryden's words are a gentle hymn of praise of the sensual delights of the England in which he lived, projected back on to the legendary England of King Arthur. Why does one feel, again and again, with such combinations of words and music that they seem to have been made for one another?

Against that, however, it can certainly be argued that even such a sturdily 'English' tune as that of our national anthem can be perfectly well associated with other words relating to other societies: the Swiss

---

[6] *Nimrod*, as is well known, was a portrait of August Jaeger, who was not English at all, but German; and the variation that bears is name was, by the composer's own account, more the record of a conversation about Beethoven's slow movements than a character-study of Jaeger himself. Moreover, the original metronome mark and tempo indication were much faster (*Moderato*, 66 crotchets to the minute) than those that have become traditional (*Adagio;* 52 crotchets to the minute).

know the tune as *Heil Dir, Helvetia!* and the Americans as *My Country, 'tis of thee.* Nor should we forget that *The Star-spangled Banner* itself, like *Land of Hope and Glory*, is a poem set to a previously-composed tune. How many Americans know that a performance of what they know as their national anthem always prefaced the meetings of a London glee club, the Anacreontic Society, from the 1760s onwards? The original words were *Anacreon, Rise!* until Frances Scott Key wrote the stirring poem that is now inseparable from John Stafford Smith's tune. Even so rampantly 'English' a tune as *Come if you dare* in Purcell's *King Arthur* shows an obvious relationship with the ceremonial style of the introduction to a work like Charpentier's *Te Deum*; and with the fine music for the entry of the ill-fated Zempoalla in Purcell's *The Indian Queen*, the relationship with the Charpentier tune is so close as almost to constitute an unconscious crib. As for our fine school of madrigalists, their output was at least in part the consequence of a great surge of cultural interest in all things Italian that arose in the last fifteen years or so of the Virgin Queen's life.

A further case that might be mentioned is that of the main theme of Smetana's *Vltava*. What, one imagines, might be so Bohemian as this tune? It seems in fact that Smetana picked it up when he was in Sweden, before he could even speak a word of Czech. And Christopher Hogwood has pointed out[7] that something suspiciously similar to the theme occurs in a Trio Sonata by Marini (*c* 1587-1663). Is the tune Swedish, Italian, or Czech? Or is it just an attractive tune that has acquired Czech character through association?

We are on slightly safer ground, as the Bartók example quoted above would suggest, when we consider the rhythms of popular dances. What determines the nature of the polka, the furiant, the mazurka, the courante, the galliard, the fox-trot or the tango are essentially rhythmic characteristics. In this case, one is slightly more justified in saying that a polka rhythm gives a piece a Czech feel, or a tango rhythm a Latin-American one. Certainly in both *Vltava* and in other movements of *Ma Vlast*, Smetana played on the national associations of Czech dance-

---

[7] In his BBC monograph *The Trio Sonata*, pp 27/8 and 36

rhythms. And William Walton brilliantly played upon this association with national characteristics in *Façade*, where he sent up the waltz, the tango, the yodel, the polka, the tarantella, the Scottish reel and (*pace* the late Frank Howes) the pastoral kind of English folk-song. But is there a genuinely English dance rhythm that differentiates it from that of other nations? The gigue, perhaps, might serve: English jigs certainly, whether by Purcell, Boyce, Sullivan, Parry or Elgar, have something more robust and earthy about them than those from other lands. But that is not a lot to go on.

So is it really worthwhile considering what is specifically national about the musical culture of a nation, let alone one whose products have continuously been denigrated not just by foreign critics unable to see the trees for the wood and their English counterparts, who take pride and pleasure in dismissing our major composers either because they are allegedly too technically gifted (Britten), technically incompetent (Vaughan Williams), vulgar jingoistic upstarts (Elgar) or mercenary money-spinners who ought not to have succumbed to the lure of the entertainment world (Sullivan). If there has been a specifically English strand in the contribution made by such musicians to our culture, we have to look beyond mere tricks of style and technique. I believe that despite all the signs to the contrary, there is.

The national character of a people, if such a thing exists, is surely conditioned by the language, its institutions and social environment. And one of the features most often overlooked when dealing with the history of music in England is that from 1660 onwards, in contradistinction to almost all the other countries of Europe, the Swiss Confederation and some of the German and Italian cities excepted, England was, to however limited a degree, a constitutional democracy. This meant that the Crown did not have unlimited control over its revenues and expenditure. The King could not do just as he liked, whether politically or in terms of the splendour of his court (and that included the splendour of his musical establishment). Thus opera, which flourished under the auspices of the despotic rulers of other countries, became essentially a commercial enterprise in post-Restoration London. It could not rely on a generous subsidy from the Crown; it had to be viable in the market. Handel's Italian operas were; and Handel was the first great composer who was a business-man as well as a courtier. His income from the Crown was limited; that from his commercial ventures was such that he left more on his death in real terms than Arthur Sullivan did a century and a half later, and a greater actual sum, even in terms of £s sterling, than Elgar did a third of a century years later still[8]. This aspect of English musical life had a crippling effect on the development of a national opera, simply because the kind of opera that succeeded in England was bound to be of the most popular kind. Art is all too often considered from the point of view of the producer (or perhaps, as so many critics are failed composers, from that of the would-be producer) rather than that of the consumer. It is because they evoked a response not just from the cultured few but from a much wider range of social orders that Purcell, Arne, Elgar and others can be considered as English not only by birth but by character.

I believe that there are qualities discernible in our music that are related to our national heritage and outlook and that speak with particular intensity to our fellow-countrymen. Hence it is wrong to consider Byrd as a kind of minor Palestrina, Purcell as a mini-Charpentier, Boyce or Arne as a would-be Handel, Elgar as a reach-me-down Brahms patched up with shreds of Franck, Wagner or Richard Strauss, or Vaughan Williams as a rather less refined and subtle Debussy. It is perfectly possible and indeed legitimate, if not essential, to *relate* these great British composers to their continental contemporaries, simply because the idiom in which they composed in many ways resembles stylistically that of the great composers with whom they are compared. It is always dangerous to consider any work of art out of context; and it is especially so to consider a national culture outside of the context of that of the countries with whom its inhabitants had their closest trading and political relationships. Britain may be an island; but the British should not weakly consider themselves prisoners of their island position.

In his striking description of the bonfire-makers of Egdon Heath in *The Return of the Native,* Thomas Hardy writes of 'the permanent moral

---

[8] The actual sums were: Handel £20,000 (not to mention a considerable collection of valuable paintings), Sullivan £55,000 and Elgar £14,000.

character' of those faces sporadically illuminated by the flickering flames. He therefore assumes that an individual person's physiognomy gives some indication of the permanent and basic traits of his or her character: what the ancient Greeks called ἔθος, as opposed to his or her sudden outbursts of feeling or emotion, which they called πάθος. Is there perhaps a set of attitudes that constitute what might be called an English 'ethos', using the word as the Greeks did? And are there certain types of 'pathos' that reveal themselves in English music at the expense of others that might be found more consistently in Spanish, French, Italian, Russian or German music? If there are, which of these attitudes are characteristic of English society and values at a given period and which are more permanent? What are the images, tricks of style and so on used by English composers to express them? Or do they? – can they? – evade the issue and take refuge in superficial pattern-making: a kind of sonic solid geometry conveying nothing but an ordered and ultimately sterile sequence of sounds?

The 'ethos' of a people can perhaps be checked against its attitudes to number of important issues that confront every sensitive human being at some stage or other of his/her life. It is not just a sense of community – that can be tribal, class-based or economically motivated. It is a shared attitude towards certain basic human experiences: a sense of values. Whether this sense of values is regarded as innate or acquired is of little relevance here. The 'important issues' referred to above can perhaps be tentatively summed up under five headings: love, death, character, ceremony, and God. I have chosen 'ceremony' rather than what it usually symbolises – power and authority – because the march or dance of life and human relationships (which, after all, are involved in the power game) have so often been expressed down the ages in terms of ceremony and ritual. Attitudes taken by English composers to these themes will be discussed later.

Before we start, however, it may be amusing (and, I hope, instructive) to see how various commentators have judged the English character down the ages.

'Grave, like the Germans; lovers of show ... Active and lively ... good sailors, and better pirates, cunning, treacherous, and thievish ... powerful in the field, ... impatient of anything like slavery; vastly fond of great noises that fill the ear, such as the firing of cannon, drums, and the ringing of bells' (Paul Hentzer, a German traveller, writing in 1598). 'A nation of shopkeepers' (Napoleon). A nation who 'think of an opinion as something which a decent person, if he has the misfortune to have one, does all he can to hide' (Margaret Halsey). 'A country infested with people who love to tell us what to do, but who very rarely seem to know what's going on' (Colin MacInnes). 'The paradise of individuality, eccentricity, heresy, anomalies, hobbies and humours' (George Santayana). A people who are 'always dull and usually violent' (Oscar Wilde). Or who 'think incompetence is the same thing as sincerity' (Quentin Crisp). A nation 'who think . . . they are moral when [they are] only uncomfortable' (G.B. Shaw). A people who 'may not like music, but . . . absolutely love the noise it makes' (Sir Thomas Beecham). A country that is little: 'little music, little art. Timid. Tasteful. Nice' (Alan Bennett). One where a single individual waiting for something forms a queue (George Mikes). 'The most class-ridden country under the sun . . . a land of snobbery and privilege, ruled largely by the old and silly' (George Orwell). A nation for whom 'the past was always sacred and inviolable and who prided themselves on their obstinacy' (Tom Sharpe). One which 'has come to rely on a comfortable time-lag of fifty years or a century intervening between the perception that something ought to be done and a serious attempt to do it'. (H G Wells).

There is more than a grain of truth in most of these generalisations, though not all of them can be universally applied to all ranges and classes of English society at all times. National character, or at any rate our perception of its most obvious characteristics, may change and change radically over the ages. So can the definition of the 'nation' as such. In the Middle Ages, for example, the 'nation' could be defined in terms of the 'political' nation, that is, in terms of the attitudes and values of the small band of rich and powerful noblemen who determined the fate of their vassals and liege men. Those values were not always consistent, nor were they consistently noble. Falstaff is at least as typically English as his antipode and drinking companion, Price Hal, as we shall see when we come to consider Elgar. Squire Western and Sterne's Uncle Toby are as English as Mr d'Arcy or the Lady Catherine de Bourgh; the flamboyant Nelson as revered a national hero as the phlegmatic H M Stanley, with his 'Dr Livingstone, I presume'; Oliver Cromwell as much God's Englishman as Henry VIII, Defender of the Holy Catholic Faith and founder of the Protestant and Reformed Church of England (who came of Welsh stock anyway). Sometimes the colourful and the cool co-exist and form complementary aspects of one and the same person: the *sang-froid* of Sir Francis Drake, claiming that there was time to finish a game of bowls and to defeat the Spaniards too, is counterbalanced by his feckless unbridled piracy.

The family and social environment, experience and upbringing of an artist will certainly affect his style. Among the generation born between 1842 and 1872, for example, we have the Italo-Irish Englishman Arthur Sullivan, born to poor but musical parents and educated at the Chapel Royal, the Royal Academy of Music and the Leipzig Conservatoire, co-opted into social 'respectability' and popular among the great and the good to an extent than his tart, prickly and much less lowly-born collaborator W S Gilbert never was. We also have the highly-strung yet outwardly conventional English country squire Hubert Parry, son of a successful painter, educated at Eton and Oxford and swept off his feet, musically speaking, by the impact of the first-ever cycle of *The Ring* at Bayreuth. We have the volatile and irascible Dublin protestant Charles Villiers Stanford, from an upper-middle-class professional family, organ scholar first at Queens' and then at Trinity College, Cambridge, and great admirer of Brahms, yet wanting somehow or other to show within the confines of a Brahmsian idiom that he was really Irish. We have the nervous and self-taught Elgar, from a 'trade' background, who married into and adopted the *mores* of the respectable English country gentry from which his wife was descended, yet who felt himself an outcast among the academically-trained musicians of his age because he was neither a 'gentleman' by descent, an academic by training nor a protestant in faith. And, finally, we have the cultivated, serious-minded agnostic Ralph Vaughan Williams, who none the less loved the cadences of the Bible, cherished a life-long admiration for the works of Bunyan and Blake and responded eagerly to the liberalising influence of Walt Whitman, to the quiet contours of his native English landscape and the folk-songs of its fast-vanishing peasantry, yet who also believed that for all the grandeur of the Niagara Falls, the mid-western plains and the

Grand Canyon of the Colorado River, there was nothing in the whole American Union as thrilling as the skyline of New York City. All of these to a greater or lesser degree composed music that had their own personal (and in some cases unmistakably English) style stamped upon it.

The comments enumerated just now suggest a people that is highly conservative and deeply suspicious of innovation; unimaginative, conformist and matter-of-fact, yet individualistic and quirky; not particularly worried by rough and ready craftsmanship or technical flaws as long as something 'works'; pragmatic and eclectic rather than formalistic in their approach to style and layout; not always articulate, despite the supreme expressive qualities of their language; relying to an almost excessive degree on custom and a kind of sleep-walking intuition rather than on planning or careful thought; quietly self-confident and therefore regarding boastfulness and ostentation as indicative of lack of breeding; self-disciplined, with a strong sense of fair play and of law and order; ribald and at times scurrilous in their attitude to rigid authority, but rarely malicious or merciless; suspicious of self-importance and pedantry, yet respectful of the correct observance of ceremony and ritual – above all, in fact, moderate.

If there is any truth in these claims, we should expect these characteristics to be reflected both in the forms and in the substance of our music. The English might well prefer to work in miniature forms rather than large-scale ones. Emotional expression would be kept well under control, understated but not inhibited in expression. Fun, parody and even ribaldry would be given free rein, but not at the expense of good taste. Majesty and rhetoric would not degenerate into pomposity and bluster. Power would not become violence or brutality. These are *post hoc ergo propter hoc* conjectures; and there is always the danger when looking for evidence that one would become ensnared in a circular argument. About formal and technical matters: harmonic and rhythmic formulae, structural or developmental procedures such as sequence, canonic imitation and so on, we cannot be quite sure; but perhaps there is something typical to be found there. We shall start our investigation with a look at the great composers of the so-called 'Golden Age' of English music: that remarkable period from roughly the defeat of the

Spanish Armada in 1588 to the accession of Charles I in 1625, when this 'nest of singing birds' produced at least five masters of outstanding quality in three different fields: William Byrd in that of sacred music, John Dowland in that of the lute song, and Thomas Morley, Thomas Weelkes and John Wilbye in the field of the madrigal. But it was the Virgin Queen who was popularly held to symbolise the virtues of her compatriots; and perhaps the best way to begin our investigation is to examine the way in which musicians, led by Thomas Morley, paid tribute to her in the series of madrigals called *The Triumphs of Oriana*.

2 – The Fair Oriana and the 'Golden Age'

The English excel in dancing and music, for they are active and lively.
Paul Hentzer: *Travels in England (1598)*.

It cannot be too strongly emphasised that for every one of those who produce music – the composers – there are also far more of those who consume it: the listeners. There are also, of course the performers who interpret the product for the consumers. They in their turn may either be the producers themselves, or, in the case, for example, of the 16th-century madrigal, the consumers. Nor should it ever be forgotten that for most civilisations, and for the overwhelming majority of cases in that of the West, most music has had an extra-musical function. Sometimes it has been that of creating a suitable atmosphere for the celebration of the holy miracle and mystery of the mass: the transubstantiation of the bread and wine by the priest into the Body and Blood of Christ. Since the Reformation, much church music has been the vessel for the presentation of doctrine: the cantatas and passions of Johann Sebastian Bach and of countless of his musical inferiors are cases in point. The earliest operas and dance spectacles, such as masques, were meant either to form part of a much more extensive programme of entertainment for some kind of celebration at a court or to edify and glorify the prince or patron before whom they were performed. Even abstract instrumental music was considered as a stimulant to or a mirror of the feelings of those before it was performed:

If music be the food of love, play on,
Give me excess of it; that, surfeiting,
The appetite may sicken, and so die...
That strain again! it had a dying fall...

These words from *Twelfth Night* are all too familiar; but we should not forget why the music is being performed. First of all, it is intended to soothe the lovesick Orsino, who is clearly listening intently. (Imagine a production that opened to the strains of *Colonel Bogey* or *The Stars and Stripes for Ever!*). It is also there to establish the mood of the opening of the play and to help establish in the mind of the audience the kind of man that Orsino is. And thirdly, of course, it is there to attract the attention of the audience and remind them that the play has begun.

At least until the time of Newton, music was also believed in some way to reflect the unheard music of the cosmic spheres in motion, as the famous passage from *The Merchant of Venice* makes abundantly clear:

> How sweet the moonlight sleeps upon this bank!
> Here will we sit, and let the sounds of music
> Creep in our ears. Soft stillness and the night
> Become the touches of sweet harmony.
> Sit, Jessica. Look how the floor of heaven
> Is thick inlaid with patens of bright gold.
> There's not the smallest orb which thou behold'st
> But in his motion like an angel sings,
> Still choiring to the young-eyed cherubins.
> Such harmony is in immortal souls,
> But whilst this muddy vesture of decay
> Doth grossly close it in, we cannot hear it.

Lorenzo is here drawing attention the difference between the music that we hear on earth and the unheard music that holds the cosmos itself in harmony. Only once he has done this does he summon the musicians to '. . . wake Diana with a hymn.' He then goes on to explain to Jessica why it is that she is never merry when she hears sweet music and to conclude:

> . . . Since naught so stockish, hard, and full of rage
> But music for the time doth change his nature.
> The man that hath no music in himself,
> Nor is not moved with concord of sweet sounds,
> Is fit for treasons, stratagems, and spoils.
> The motions of his spirit are dull as night,
> And his affections dark as Erebus.
> Let no such man be trusted. . .

15

Being an indispensable component of the dance, music was not merely essential to the enjoyment of a pleasant pastime, it was also part of the court ceremonial and, among the common people, tied up with the seasonal round of spring, the sowing and reaping of crops, fertility, hunting and harvesting.

But there was a further consideration. At the time when our first examples of Englishness in music were active, it was becoming more and more a vehicle for conveying the emotions expressed by the English language. It is no coincidence that the so-called Golden Age of English Music coincided almost exactly with the Golden Age of English Drama and the first flowering of English lyric verse. As part of their training, musicians were expected to be able to compose texts as well as music; and if so many of our verse and lyric forms derived from Italian models, why should not Italy be the source of our musical styles as well? This was certainly so in the case of one of the most celebrated of all English musical products of the late Tudor era: the madrigal.

Yet a number of fallacies have for too long been extant about the music of the Golden Age. First and foremost of them is the fallacy that the English madrigal in particular thrived because there was so much magnificent poetry for musicians to set. This is nonsense. There was plenty of magnificent poetry and some of it was set to music; but very little, if any, of it found its way into madrigals. The truth is that the first genuine madrigals to be performed in England were imported from Italy in the late 1580s, with their text translated into English by musicians such as Nicholas Yonge; and although English musicians were trained in the art of composing for the church according to current techniques, there was no tradition of writing English madrigals.

There was, however, a tradition of composing songs for solo voice and a consort of viols or other instruments; and some of the works published as madrigals by composers such as Byrd were in fact arrangements for 'vocal consort' of music composed for voice and instruments. (The delightful *Though Amaryllis dance in green* is a case in point. Gibbons's magnificent *What is our life?* is another). The texts of these songs ranged over a wider and often more philosophical field than those of the madrigal proper, whose sentiments were usually restricted to pastoral conventions that can be traced back to the time of the ancient

Greeks and had been developed by the poets of the Italian Renaissance. It was thus natural that when the madrigal caught on in the 1590s, the moods and emotions expressed and the literary and musical conceits used to express them should be borrowed largely from Italian models. Much of the quality, therefore, of English madrigal verse derived from the fine Italian and other texts of which it was either an adaptation or a direct translation. It was the quality of the Italian originals that gave the quality to English madrigal verse rather than any direct connection with the masters of English poetry active at the time when they were composed. As far as we know, there were no English Petrarchs, Ariostos or Tassos for English composers to set; and if there were writers of the calibre of Marlowe, Spenser and Shakespeare, the best of their lyrics to attract composers' attention were set as part of a dramatic spectacle rather than as lyrics in their own right in madrigals or lute songs. Moreover, it cannot be taken for granted that the madrigal and the consort-songs were aimed at the same public. One was presumably a listening public, assuming, that is, that the instrumental backing was provided by professional viol-players. The other was surely to a large extent a performing one, though one cannot imagine that no audience ever listened to their singing. The publics must surely have overlapped; and it is clear that neither form can be defined as 'English' in the sense that an anonymous folk-dance or a battle-cry could be. Both were 'art-music' aimed at a public that was to a high degree musically and poetically literate and could appreciate not just a good tune and a sturdy rhythm, but even to some extent musical and poetic wit. Yet to be part of an English identity, both would also surely display some kind of stylistic features that betrayed their country of origin.

There is one important clue, however, to what some of those stylistic features might be: the nature of English speech-rhythms and the manner in which they were taken up by English musicians. There was much debate among what we should nowadays call the intelligentsia about how the English language might be used and scanned in verse. The elegant verse-forms, such as the sonnet, that had come to us from the continent were eagerly taken up and exploited by our poets; and there was some uncertainty as to how verse pieces written in English should be scanned. Should they be scanned according to the stress, and thus the spoken rhythm, of the words? Or should they be scanned in the 'academic' manner, following the example of Latin, according to the 'quantity' of the syllables? In English, as in French and German, experiments were carried out in both kinds before the former course was adopted.

Most 'serious' music had up till the mid-16th century been composed to Latin texts: after all, the Church had used Latin from time immemorial as its liturgical language. But during the Middle Ages the roving scholars and clergy who had composed verse in Latin had often resorted to a system of scansion that paid more attention to the spoken stress of the text than the approved academic system. The famous sequence from the Mass for the Dead, for example, which dates from the 13th century, is a case in point:

> Dies IRae, Dies ILla
> SOLvet SAEclum IN faVILla
> Teste DAvid CUM SyBILLa

And so on. With the Reformation, and the consequent emphasis on the importance of the music projecting the word of God rather than simply adding a mystical atmosphere to the solemn liturgy, texts, whether in English or Latin, tended to be set more syllabically. And in England, this meant that composers set them according to the way English people would naturally stress them rhythmically. And if this meant that the natural rhythm of the words danced, as it were, rather than falling into a solemn, measured gait, then so be it.

The moods reflected in the text were to be reflected in the music, and particularly in its rhythms and harmonic progressions. And the rhythms, which determined at least in part the shape of the 'points' or melodic themes that the composer developed, were conditioned by the natural spoken rhythms of the words. It was these rather than the intrinsic appeal of the verse that gave the Elizabethan madrigal its 'English' qualities, though as we shall see, certain conceits do turn up from time to time in madrigal texts that seem to have no parallel in the models from which they derive. Basil Patterson[9] pointed this out half a century ago:

> The Elizabethans clearly realised the difference between metre and rhythm. In poetry there is a regular pattern that continues in the mind throughout the reading – the metre; but this implicit pattern is not always evident in the actual sound of the verse, which gains its interest from innumerable tiny variations from the fixed metre. The metre is subconscious most of the time, once the poet has set the mind ticking the right pattern; the rhythm is the tune counterpointed on that subconscious pattern by the natural stresses and quantities of the words. The madrigal, too, has metre behind its rhythmic fluidity.

Morley himself expressly states[10] that when setting words, due care should be paid to their natural rhythm, which he clearly regards as to be scanned according to stress, not quantity:

> We must also have a care to applie the notes to the wordes, as in singing there be no barbarisme committed: that is, if we cause no sillable which is by nature short be expressed by manie notes or one long note, nor no long sillable be expressed with a shorte note, but in this fault do the practitioners erre more grosselie, then in any other, for you shall find few songes wherein the penult sillables of these words, *Dominus, Angelus, filius, miraculum, gloria,* and such like are not expressed with a long note, yea many times with a whole dossen of notes, and though one should speak of fortie he should not say much amisse, which is a grosse barbarisme, & yet might be easilie amended.

It is clear from the examples cited that Morley is thinking of the 'English' (stress-timed) manner of scanning these words rather than the 'classical' (quantitative) one. This was to have a marked influence on the declamation, and hence the rhythmic phrasing, of vocal music of the Golden Age.

---

[9] Basil Patterson, *Music and Poetry of the English Renaissance,* London, 1948.

[10] *Plaine and Easie Introduction to Practicalle Musicke,* 1597, OUP, 1937, p 177.

One problem with setting English to music, however, is the tendency English speakers have to diphthongise their vowels. English actually has half as many true vowels again as Italian – twelve as against eight – but the facts that we do not pronounce many of our vowels purely and that far fewer English words than Italian end on a singable vowel means that in some respects English is at a disadvantage as a 'singable' language compared with Italian. But the sharp, often syncopated, rhythms of English bisyllabic words give our verse a strong rhythmic freedom, a firm kick and immense tensile strength if a line is set to music according to the stresses of the text rather than according to a quantitative scansion based on a syllable count. Whereas an Italian speaker would tend to draw out the length of an emotive vowel that he wished to stress, an English speaker would tend to pronounce it in a more clipped and forceful manner., though of course the 'Italian' manner of drawing attention to the vowel is by no means unknown in English. By the end of the sixteenth century the argument as to whether English verse should be scanned quantitatively, like French and Latin, or syllabically and timed according to the stresses, had been decided in favour of the latter; and any composer sensitive to the natural speech-music of his native language ignored the fact at his peril, at any rate until the advent and consequent influence on musical style of Italian *opera seria* in the early 18th century. The existence of so many weak or unstressed syllables in a verse-line offered all kinds of rhythmic opportunities; and it is worth noting that during the 'doldrum' period of English music, composers often forgot how to set their own language. Ironically, it was in the 'frivolous' operettas of Arthur Sullivan that they were provided with an example of how to approach the problems of setting English with true regard to its real spirit and nature; and this we owe to his librettist W S Gilbert rather than to anyone else.

There is more to expressing nationality in music, however, than just skill in setting one's native language. There is also the matter of accepting and developing traditional forms and procedures and of showing awareness of and the ability to profit from new and fruitful developments taking place abroad. Just because they are foreign does not necessarily mean that they are bad (nor that they are acceptable without question); and English composers of the Elizabethan age were skilful indeed at adopting and adapting what they learned from foreign models, especially from Italy. On the face of it this was somewhat surprising, in view of the rift between Catholic and Protestant faiths, yet the willingness of English musicians to learn from their continental contemporaries was as marked in music as it was in literature.

Compared with her successors, Elizabeth I is traditionally thought of as a resolute monarch and a generous patron of the arts in general and of music in particular. She was nothing of the kind. Compared with the first two Stuart monarchs, she was notably stingy in the money she was prepared to lay out to encourage musical spectacles. She was also, even in weighty matters of state, appallingly volatile in her decisions, rescinding them in all too many cases hardly a few hours after she had taken them. This did not help her ministers and servants to decide important matters of policy. Yet she retained their affection and their loyalty: what mattered was not her generosity but her position as the Virgin Queen, admired, feared and respected by her subjects because she was a shrewd politician, a woman and because she could command authority. Stingy, indecisive, volatile or no, however, Elizabeth I was undoubtedly highly musical. She was a competent performer on the keyboard and a passionate and accomplished devotee of the dance. Her successor, James I, enjoyed none of these attributes. His two sons, Henry and Charles, were both quite probably the most gifted musicians that any British royal line has ever produced, but one of them died before he could inherit the throne and the other was wilful, devious and a poor judge of men. There is no necessary connection, of course.

The sense of linguistic unity, of common institutions, of generally agreed attitudes and standards of values are all of course part of the sense of nationality. But there is also a shared sense of the symbols that represent those things. The pageantry of a national commemorative ceremony, the kind of urban and rural environment to which a community is accustomed and the role-model figures that feature in the community's mythology also resound very strongly in a community's sense that however diverse the individuals that comprise it, there is an underlying unity that is worth preserving. Those symbols were potently summed up in the scathing denunciation of things as they were under

Richard II, rather than as they ought to be, that Shakespeare magnificently put into the mouth of the dying John of Gaunt:

> Methinks I am a prophet, new-inspired,
> And thus, expiring, do foretell of him.
> His rash, fierce blaze of riot cannot last,
> For violent fires soon burn out themselves.
> Small showers last long, but sudden storms are short.
> He tires betimes that spurs too fast betimes.
> With eager feeding food doth choke the feeder.
> Light vanity, insatiate cormorant,
> Consuming means, soon preys upon itself.
> This royal throne of kings, this sceptred isle,
> This earth of majesty, this seat of Mars,
> This other Eden, demi-paradise,
> This fortress built by nature for herself
> Against infection and the hand of war,
> This happy breed of men, this little world,
> This precious stone, set in the silver sea,
> Which serves it in the office of a wall,
> Or as a moat defensive to a house
> Against the envy of less happier lands;
> This blessed plot, this earth, this realm, this England,
> This nurse, this teeming womb of royal kings,
> Feared by their breed and famous by their birth,
> Renowned for their deeds as far from home
> For Christian service and true chivalry
> As is the sepulchre in stubborn Jewry,
> Of the world's ransom, blessed Mary's son;
> This land of such dear souls, this dear dear land,
> Dear for her reputation through the world,
> Is now leased out – I die pronouncing it –
> Like to a tenement or pelting farm.
> England, bound in with the triumphant sea,
> Whose rocky shore beats back the envious siege
> Of envious Neptune, is now bound in with shame,
> With inky blots and rotten parchment bonds.
> That England that was wont to conquer others
> Hath made a shameful conquest of itself.
> Ah! Would the scandal vanish with my life,
> How happy then were my ensuing death.

Most readers will know this famous passage, not least through Hubert Parry's fine tune to fit the bowdlerised and squared-up version of it familiar from his unison song *England*, which was composed, significantly enough, during the First World War. But let's look at Shakespeare's original more closely: remember – this was contemporaneous with the great songs of Dowland and Danyel, the Oriana madrigals and some of the noblest church music composed by any English composers. So it is reasonable to assume that these attributes and symbols were dear to the great musicians as well as to Shakespeare's audiences.

First of all, John of Gaunt is railing against the manner in which England has been compromised by 'inky blots and rotten parchment bonds', dominated by others who are not part of the community that holds the same scale of values deemed worthy of Englishmen. And what are those values? John of Gaunt is above all extolling the military virtues such as chivalry and Christian service, and presumably valour in combat. These were the virtues prized, if not always practised, by the ruling aristocracy – the 'political' nation – in the age of chivalry. The nation is an 'earth of majesty' and a 'seat of Mars'. Notice the historical and social references: the resonance of the crusades, the country seen as a 'nurse' and a 'teeming womb of kings/ Feared by their breed and famous by their birth'; as a 'royal throne of kings' and a 'sceptred isle'. The note of pageantry, royal pride and ceremony is struck again and again. And underlying this is the moral sense that all these things are symbols of service to 'the world's ransom, blessed Mary's son.'

The land itself, however, is also celebrated. The 'precious stone' is set in a silver sea; the sea itself is a barrier, a wall, a moat, a protection against 'the envy of less happier lands'. It is an island of innocence: another Eden, with all that that implies in terms of tranquil beauty and undisturbed innocence. It is a garden – again the idea of a walled, enclosed safe haven: from what? The shore itself is rocky – once more the idea of a kind of wall, protecting it against 'infection' (of what kind?) and the hand of war. Even Neptune himself is described as 'envious'. England is not only protected by its island situation; the island situation is a privilege and a challenge as well as a protection.

The community that inhabits it is intended to dwell in harmony and independence, but its harmony has been shattered and its independence 'leased out/ Like to a tenement or pelting farm'. It is, as already pointed out, the 'envy of less happier lands'. The passage is in fact celebrating an England that, at least in the viewpoint of John of Gaunt, was losing its heritage of unity, harmony and brotherhood. It was not just the 'political' nation that was suffering from the loss of its prestige and its values; it was the populace as a whole. The contrast is drawn between the England that had been and that ought to be and the present England, riven with strife, pettifogging quarrels and litigation. And all because of a King who was not worthy of his throne. It is certainly true, if the *Agincourt Song* is anything to go by, that Englishmen, musicians among them, felt a sense of national unity[11] and pride long before the days of the Virgin Queen. What is perhaps surprising is that the *Agincourt Song* did not produce any progeny in the time of the Tudors.

Or did it? The embodiment of all the abstract qualities inherent in this complex image of security, family bonds and national integrity was of course the monarch. More than this, however, she was God's viceroy on earth, responsible for the welfare of her people and the secular head of His church in her domains. Could a descent into the abyss of civil strife happen again after the death of the Virgin Queen? Whether or not, as has sometimes been claimed, Shakespeare conceived his history plays as a cycle leading up to the glorious days of Henry V and then collapsing into the treachery and anarchy of the Wars of the Roses, and was warning his audience that the same thing might happen again, that is in effect what they *seem* to tell us. At present, the subtext of John of Gaunt's speech implies there was no insurmountable problem; and Englishmen should count themselves lucky that this was so. The might of Spain had been beaten off – and the Queen herself was happy enough

---

[11] The growing sense of some kind of political bond between England and Scotland, determined by geographical factors, is attested by the Earl of Moray's reference in a letter to Elizabeth's minister Cecil (14 October 1567). Moray refers to the two nations 'whom God hath thus from the beginning enclosed within one isle and separate from the rest of the world.' (See Jasper Ridley, *Elizabeth I,* London 1987, p 153).

to invoke divine intervention as the cause of England's victory: the commemorative medal she had struck to celebrate the defeat of the Armada bore the motto (in Latin) 'He blew with His winds; and they were scattered.' Once again, the sea and the elements had provided a defensive barrier against papist foreigners. Yet by the time that the Oriana madrigals were published in 1601, the clouds had begun to gather again; and uncertainty as to who was to succeed her added to them.

It is certainly not without significance that when the Earl of Essex was planning the rebellion in 1601 for which he was later executed, he paid the Lord Chamberlain's Players (the company to which Shakespeare himself belonged) to put on a performance of *King Richard II*. This has – almost certainly rightly – been interpreted as a preliminary attempt to influence public opinion in his favour. If this was so, the work had already[12] become a symbol in its own right. Its message is clear: it was the duty of those who had the safety of the realm at stake to depose a sovereign who could not keep order within her domains. Essex had lately been the dedicatee of a book by Sir John Hayward called *The History of Henry IV*; and the dedication pointedly but cannily and ambiguously mentions (in Latin) that under the auspices of the Earl, King Henry might 'go forth in public happier and safer'. Elizabeth was suspicious – after all, Henry Bolingbroke was a usurper – and had Hayward arrested and imprisoned in the Tower. Essex himself was arrested when his rebellion collapsed, convicted of high treason and executed on 25 February 1601.

The background to *The Triumphs of Oriana* is thus of considerable interest and no small relevance to the theme of England as a nation. Thomas Morley set up the publication of *The Triumphs of Oriana* with the intention that it should be published in 1601. There is no reason why he should have chosen that particular year. It celebrated no significant anniversary in Elizabeth's reign: she had been born in 1533 and on the throne since 1558. The years 1501, 1526, 1551 and 1576 held no immediate significance either to her or to her people. She had no

---

[12] Elizabeth herself reckoned that the play had already been performed forty times in open streets and houses. (Ridley, *Elizabeth I*, p 331).

intention of marrying and the problem of her succession had not been solved. It would seem that Morley and his collaborators wished to pay a loyal and fulsome tribute to her while they had time – she was sixty-eight years of age and older than any recorded English monarch before her[13] – rather than that they were actually celebrating any anniversary for her.

The original idea was that twenty-six madrigals (the number of stars in the constellation of Virgo) should be composed in honour of the Virgin Queen. One or two of his chosen contributors did not meet the deadline, however; and Michael East was late, so the final collection as published amounts to twenty-four pieces. The principal composers of the day (with the interesting exceptions of Morley's teacher William Byrd and John Dowland) were all invited to contribute; and the collection was modelled on *Il Trionfo di Dori,* a collection of 29 madrigals (again, all by different composers) commissioned in honour of a rich Venetian's bride in 1592.

Oriana was the – chaste, of course – maiden beloved of the hero of the Spanish 15th-century romances centred on *Amadis de Gaule.* Amadis was the flower of chivalry; and the romances were taken up in France in particular in the seventeenth century: Quinault adapted part of the story as an opera libretto which was set by Lully in 1684. In 1597, Nicholas Yonge had published a second volume of *Musica Transalpina* to complement the first, published in 1588, the year of the Spanish Armada, and the volume responsible for the introduction of the Italian madrigal into this country. Like the first volume, the music was by Italian composers and the texts had been translated by Yonge from the Italian. The final item of this volume was taken from a collection called *Il trionfo di Dori*, published in Venice in 1592, and is by Giovanni Croce, one of a number of composers Morley had recommended as models that same year in *A Plaine and Easie Introduction to Practicalle Musicke.* The English text of a Croce madrigal was in fact adapted and expanded by

---

[13] Even Henry III and Edward III, who had reigned longer than she did, had not lived to such an age as they had both succeeded to the throne in their childhood and adolescence respectively. Elizabeth was twenty-five when she came to the throne.

Morley for his own contribution to the Oriana collection, *Hard by a crystal fountain.* It ended, *mutatis mutandis*, with precisely the refrain that is employed as the pay-off line in all the madrigals in Morley's collection:

> Then sang the shepherds and nymphs of Diana:
> Long love fair Oriana.

There was certainly a degree of wishful thinking here: the fair Oriana was not far short of the traditional biblical allotted span when the collection was published. Needless to say, flattery and exaggeration abound throughout the texts; as Disraeli was to remark two centuries later, when it came to royalty, flattery had to be laid on with a trowel. The imagery is for the most part conventionally classical; and the texts themselves, *pace* Canon Fellowes, rarely rise above the level of serviceable doggerel. They are nearly all pastoral in character and the themes that they cover all relate to topics that are suitable both for expressive and for illustrative musical treatment. The pastoral convention was of course nothing new in European verse; and its employment here, though probably influenced by Italian models, goes back much earlier in time to such works as Virgil's *Georgics.* It was to persist for much longer.

Yet however much of the texts (and presumably the music) of the Oriana madrigals are designed as flattery, the flattery does have an element of genuine sincerity about it. It is thus worthwhile examining the texts of a series of madrigals designed as a tribute to the fair Oriana in order to see what kind of qualities in her make-up are praised. It is quite interesting simply to read the texts of the Oriana madrigals through without any reference to the music in order to discover exactly what 'triumphs' are being celebrated. The 'action', such as it is, marks time sporadically, but a definite progression can be discerned from theme to theme. In the collection as it was published, the first theme to be addressed after the preliminary exaggerated command to the stars to vanish and give way to the 'shepherds' star,/Excelling you by far' is Oriana's nimble and athletic skill in dancing, which (of course) arouses the envy of the nymphs and shepherds[14]. This was well attested; Elizabeth herself was not only a keen and nimble dancer, she was also not above engaging in dances that were sometimes considered daring and beneath the dignity of a Queen, such as *La Volta.* This dance is itself referred to in the text of Marson's *The nymphs and shepherds danced,* the seventh madrigal in the collection. The text of Marson's madrigal is explicit. It refers to 'the crown-graced virgin' in whose honour the dance is being performed; and when she appears, of course, her dazzling beauty stops the dancers in their tracks. Her skill in dancing and her subjects' response to it inspires a general dance of nature itself.

But as well as being a paragon of the lady courtier's accomplishments, she is after all the sovereign lady of the land. This leads naturally to the consideration of the universal dance of tribute from the natural world and of the loyalty that she commands. A particular admirer, one 'Bonny-boots', is singled out for attention. The relationship between them is close but we have no clue as to who he is:

> Thus Bonny-boots the birthday celebrated
> Of her his lady dearest,
> Fair Orian, which to his heart was nearest.
> The nymphs and shepherds feasted
> With clotted cream, and were to sing requested.
> Lo, here the fair created,
> Quoth he, the world's chief goddess.
> Then sing, for she is Bonny-boots' sweet mistress.
> Then sang the nymphs and shepherds of Diana:
> Long love fair Oriana.

Whoever he was, Bonny-boots was hardly unfamiliar with music and feasting in the royal household. Various guesses have been made as to who he was, assuming that he existed at all. He might have been a courtier; he might have been a symbolic figure; he might merely have been Elizabeth's master of revels or some other of her court retinue. It can hardly be that the reference was to Essex, coming so soon after his

---

[14] This was almost certainly because East was late in delivering his contribution and the editor decided to place it first rather than insert it elsewhere.

rebellion and execution. Yet it is interesting that whoever he is, Bonny-boots is the only other non-mythical person mentioned in the collection.

Moreover, Bonny-boots is dead by the end of the cycle, as the text of Edward Johnson's contribution, *Come, blessed bird,* tells us. And *Come, blessed bird* is, as it happens, the final madrigal in the set as it was published. Let us examine the text and its relationship to the music a little more closely:

> Come, blessed birds, and with thy sugared relish
> Help our declining choir now to embellish,
> For Bonny-boots, that so aloft would fetch it,
> O he is dead, and none of us can reach it.
> Then tune to us, sweet bird, thy shrill recorder.
> Elpin and I and Dorus,
> For fault of better, will serve in the chorus.
> Begin, and we will follow thee in order.
> Then sang the wood-born minstrel of Diana:
> > Long love fair Oriana.

The collection is not just a purely formal tribute, then. It takes account of some kind of personal loss felt by the Queen. The 'declining choir' who are performing the madrigal for their royal patron are apparently poor substitutes for Bonny-boots himself. Whether the reference is literal or symbolic, we can only guess at this distance in time.

Oriana also brings peace and prosperity, for which she is now praised (Tomkins: *The fauns and satyrs tripping;* Wilbye: *The lady Oriana/Was dight in all the treasures of Guiana*). Finally, attention is drawn to her reputation as a caring ruler:

> Fair Oriana, seeming to wink at folly,
> Lay softly down to sleeping.
> But, hearing that the world was grown unholy,
> Her rest was turned to weeping.
> So waked, she sighed, and with crossed arms
> Sat drinking tears for others' harms.
> Then sang the nymphs and shepherds of Diana:
> > Long love fair Oriana.

So runs the text of Robert Jones's contribution to the collection. A similar theme is taken up in the following madrigal, John Lisley's *Fair*

Cytherea. Again, part of the choice of imagery is surely mere convention; yet the situation was such that people would be almost bound to read some kind of reference to it into the text.

In other words, the texts of the Oriana madrigals are almost certainly a kind of collective (and, considering the political situation when they were composed, a somewhat fanciful) rebuttal of the charge conveyed by John of Gaunt's dying speech. The implication is that under Elizabeth, England had regained the condition that it had lost so long ago under Richard II. In themselves, these madrigals are charming musical tributes; taken as a whole, they are a celebration, not just of the Virgin Queen herself but of the land over which she rules. They are as significant for their sub-text as they are for the sentiments that they overtly express.

What of the music? Do any of the madrigals seem to show that the composer was deliberately, so to speak, pulling out all the stops in honour of the Queen? And, perhaps more importantly, does the style show any personal or 'national' characteristics? Certainly the musical 'points' emerge for the most part from the natural speech-rhythms of the text. The 'illustrative' motifs, such as rising and descending scales, the use of two and three voices at a time to underline nymphs descending 'two by two' and 'three by three' respectively, are part and parcel of the Western European musical stock-in-trades of the time. The texts are exploited as points of departure for musical illustration and mood-painting, not as part of a display of conscious national self-assertion; and any dance elements that occur in the music, and there are many, recall the internationally accepted courtly dances of the time rather than exhibiting any rustic and national flavour.

Pattison makes the shrewd point[15] that some of Morley's ballets and canzonets composed on other occasions fit the Italian texts from which the English ones were translated equally well. He concludes that if the volumes of Anerio and Gastoldi in which the original Italian words occur had been lost and all Morley's English works with them, leaving only his settings of the Italian poems, these would have been accepted as

---

[15] *Music and Poetry,* p 98.

the music of an Italian composer. Indeed, his own contribution to the Oriana collection, *Hard by a crystal fountain,* is based on an Italian model.

There is a difference, however. The textures and working-out of many English madrigals are altogether richer and more complex than most of their Italian models. Jerome Roche[16] mentions Morley's *Shoot, false love* and compares it with the Italian work on which it is modelled, Gastoldi's *Viver lieto voglio.* Gastoldi's treatment of tonality is much less adventurous than Morley's; so is his rhythmic and textural treatment of the 'fa-la' passages. When it comes to *Hard by a crystal fountain,* Roche comments:

> Even this work is a parody of an Italian model, *Ove tra l'herbe e I fiori,* itself published in *Il trionfo di Dori* (1592), . . . As with Gastoldi's *balleti,* Morley sets out to expand and develop an Italian piece whose style is simpler and comparatively featureless in character, by enlarging the key-range and the scope of the contrapuntal treatment, and adding many felicitous touches of tone-painting.

There is, in fact, ample evidence that in many cases, the English madrigal was often both textually and musically a more sophisticated and 'intellectual' type of piece than its Italian model and that this was not just because some of the English composers were more learned than the Italian ones.

Now Morley's treatise is not only learned, it is highly readable and of great value when trying to assess the 'Englishness' of English musical practice in this period. It would be absurd to suggest that English musicians, whether amateur or professional, sat down and read up Morley before writing or performing their pieces, but it is evident that, like most theorists, Morley was codifying what composers (and particularly Italian composers) had been practising for some time. He was in a sense 'naturalising' the sentiments and methods to contemporary English taste.

Melancholy and unrequited love, for example, are sentiments that are by no means confined either to these islands or to Italy. But the

---

[16] *The Madrigal,* London 1972, p 128-30.

expression given to them, even when the composers are closely following the models provided by the Italian madrigalists, is individual; and some of it is traceable to technical procedures adopted by English musicians. For example, it seems that the false relations of the third and sixth degrees of the minor scale have always fascinated composers, both for technical harmonic and for expressive reasons. This is not confined, as is sometimes thought, to our own composers: Mahler and Brahms, for example, exploited their potential with considerable skill. Brahms's Third Symphony is largely built up on the ambiguity of the third of the key of F. But the 'false relation' of the third and sixth is almost a mannerism in English music of this period – and it recurs in the following century, when harmonic procedures had changed markedly with the arrival of the baroque and the multifarious modal scales of the earlier era had been largely replaced in art music by the major and minor scales. Sometimes the two types of third and sixth are juxtaposed; sometimes they are sounded simultaneously, so that it sounds as if someone is singing or playing a 'bum note'.

Morley wrote that minor thirds and sixths could be introduced when the composer wished to express 'a lamentable passion' and major ones to signify 'hardnes, cruelty or other such affects' – a verdict that we might find strange, equating, as we tend to do, the major scale with cheerfulness and joy. Pieces such as Wilbye's *Draw on, sweet night* and Ward's *Come, sable night* show a structural and emotional quality that ranks them among the finest 'serious' madrigals of any country. They do so in some measure by skilful exploitation of this ambiguity.

The texts of these two fine madrigals are similar in mood and layout. It is worth quoting both in full, Wilbye's first:

> Draw on sweet night, best friend unto those cares
> That do arise from painful melancholy.
> My life so ill through want of comfort fares
> That unto thee I consecrate it wholly.
> Sweet night draw on, my griefs when they be told
> To shades and darkness find some ease from paining,
> And while thou all in silence dost enfold,
> I then shall have best time for my complaining.

And here is Ward's:

Come, sable night, put on thy mourning stole,
And help Amintas sadly to condole,
Behold, the Sun hath shut his golden eye,
The day is spent, and shades fair lights supply.
All things in sweet repose their labours close,
Only Amintas wastes his hours in wailing,
Whilst all his hopes do faint, and life is failing.

Both texts deal with a man stricken with sadness. In Ward's case it is because his hopes (presumably of gaining the favours of his lady love) have been dashed; in Wilbye's, the cause of the grief is unspecified. In both cases, the major-minor ambiguity is skilfully exploited. Wilbye's madrigal (published in 1609 and notable throughout for its smooth and soothing rhythms) starts out unequivocally in a modern major tonality. There are some piquant dissonances (bars 13, 16, 22 and 25, for example, in the Philip Ledger edition in the *Oxford Book of Madrigals*), but the first hint of a minor modality comes does not occur until the new point that introduces 'My life so ill through want of comfort fares' in bar 32. So virtually the whole first quarter of the piece (it is 129 bars long in all) has been in the major mode. But once the security of the major has been undermined, Wilbye exploits the tonal clashes for all he is worth. The final lines and the way Wilbye sets them leave us in no doubt that while the recounting of his nameless griefs cannot be explained in daylight, at least the daylight will bring some relief to them.

Ward's piece, published in 1613, is much more mournful right from the start; after all, the conventional parallel between night and (love-) death is strongly underlined in his text; and he has a superb gift for extending his long paragraphs by moving towards a close in one direction and then swerving harmonically in another. He also engages in one brief episode (2 bars in the *Oxford Book* out of 122 in all) of block harmony, which not only draws attention to the phrase 'And help Amintas') but also imperceptibly quickens the momentum of the piece. And there is no relief at the end. Both these works show a command of the long phrase, an adroit use of harmonic procedures and a fine sense of the emotive charge of the text. They also fit Sully's comment (made incidentally in 1630) that 'Les Anglais s'amusent tristement selon l'usage de leur pays'. The somewhat dour and stolid nature of the

English was well attested even in those days; yet it was also claimed that they were a people whose sadness was due to the predominance of certain 'humours' in their temperament.

These melancholy pieces – and the two works are by no means isolated, though they are among the finest of their kind anywhere in Europe – can hardly be considered after-dinner entertainment music. To counterbalance this melancholy, there is also, however, a kind of arcane verbal and musical wit found in a small number of English madrigals that corresponds to nothing that might be found in any Italian model. The wit is generated by the demands of the text; and the texts themselves are more than a little unusual. Two of the most striking examples of this are Weelkes's *Thule, the Period of Cosmographie,* which carries to an extreme the fanciful imagery defining the pangs of love, and the even more remarkable *Consture* [Construe] *my meaning,* by Giles Farnaby. Weelkes matches the imagery of his strange text with equally striking illustrative musical imagery. This is perhaps the most extreme and whimsical of all his works, but it is by no means alone.

The Italians were past masters at introducing chromaticisms into their textures to illustrate pain or puzzlement; but in *Consture my meaning* the text prompts Farnaby into taking chromaticism almost to extremes. The nearest Italian parallel seems to have been Giuseppe Caimo's *Piangete valli,* which is set to an elegiac text probably mourning the death of a much-admired lady. Both Farnaby and Caimo use 'points' so chromatic that they almost resemble dodecaphonic tone-rows. By the end of the fifth bar, in fact, Farnaby has already used nine of the twelve notes of the chromatic scale in one or other of the two parts so far involved, and by the end of the ninth bar, all twelve. Farnaby would surely have justified his procedure by pointing out the elegiac nature of his text, which challenges reader and music critic alike:

> Construe my meaning, wrest not my method;
> Good will craves favour, witness the high God.
> If I have meant well, good will reward me;
> When I deserve ill, no man regard me.
> What shall I say more? Speech is but blasting.
> Still will I hope for life everlasting.

The point of the text is that it is intentions that count towards eternal salvation, not mere professions. Farnaby makes those professions as musically ambiguous and tortuous as he dares. The entries are not predictable: the cantus and tenor parts are a fifth apart, entering on C and F respectively, but when the bass enters, he comes in on an A, a sixth below the tenor; and so does the alto (an octave higher than the bass, of course). The modality is ambivalent; the inflections of the vocal lines highly chromatic throughout; and there are plenty of harmonic shocks, though no outrageous Gesualdesque progressions or dissonances. Moreover, Farnaby – whose training as a musician took place some time after he had qualified as a craftsman in wood and instrument-maker – has here taken a text of a kind rather unusual in the field of the madrigal, which tends rather to the pastoral and fanciful than to sombre and philosophical issues of this kind. This is scarcely after-dinner entertainment in any sense, unlike most madrigals. The vocal line is so chromatic as to be almost instrumental; yet a reading through of the musical text will show that the vowels to which Farnaby appends his long notes are all eminently singable. Like Elgar three hundred years later, he seems to have been willing to venture into harmonic realms that few of his more conventional academically-trained contemporaries dared to attempt.

Mention was made earlier of the consort song that had entered the bloodstream of English secular music during Elizabeth's reign and that became blended with madrigalian technique by composers such as Byrd and Gibbons. A further development related to it was that of the solo ayre for voice and lute. This derived in part from French rather than Italian models and also from the consort song popular in the earlier part of Elizabeth's reign. It was with the ayre that the same age as produced the flowering of the English madrigal generated a magnificent harvest of lute songs, with two outstanding composers, one of whom had a reputation not only in his own country but all over Europe. His name was John Dowland. The fact that his reputation was high on the continent sparks off the question as to how well his songs, if performed to English texts, were understood in continental Europe; and if they were not well understood, how much his listeners felt that it mattered. The other was John Danyel, whose available output is much more restricted than Dowland's, yet whose contribution to the literature was of high quality and emotional intensity.

Dowland published his first collection of Ayres in 1597 and it was a runaway success. It started something of a craze for this kind of work, and as well as three further books from Dowland, collections were published by Campion, Rosseter, Danyel, Jones, Pilkington, the younger Ferrabosco, and many others. Many of the collections were published in such a format that they could also be performed as part-songs or as songs with accompaniment by a consort of viols.

Now the texts of the ayre are much more the product of the burgeoning school of English poetry than were those of the madrigal. Many of them were published, without the music, in anthologies of verse. And the line of descent of the ayre is more cosmopolitan than that of the madrigal. Its roots can be traced back to France and an older English native tradition than just to Italy. It is not just Dowland's own personal character ('semper Dowland, semper dolens') that is so striking about many of these pieces – the intense seriousness and mournful intensity that supercharges his outstanding melodic gift and raises him to the level of one of the greatest song-writers who has ever lived – but the way it parallels an aspect we have already discussed of the English madrigal. Such songs as Danyel's three-part *Can doleful notes* (1606), Dowland's *Flow, flow, my tears* and, above all, *In darkness let me dwell* betray aspects of the English character that link up directly, in emotional terms, at any rate, with the black, raging despair that is put into the mouth of some of Shakespeare's characters. It matters not whether the composers were subjectively involved in the setting of these gloomy texts. What does matter is the unparalleled intensity with which they set them. Not even Dowland could surpass the sombre intensity of the music to which Danyel sets:

> No, let chromatic tunes, harsh without ground,
> Be sullen music for a tuneless heart;
> Chromatic tunes most like my passions sound
> As if combined to bear their falling part.

in the second part of *Can doleful notes*. How much of this text and its setting is pure rhetoric and how much deeply-felt emotion is difficult to disentangle at this distance in time; yet the effect is powerful indeed. The lute texture, like so many of Dowland's, is highly contrapuntal, which adds to the intensity of the music and the projection of grief in it; yet it is clear that we are dealing here, not with an arrangement of a madrigal but of a genuine solo song.

Our concern here, however, should not be just with matters of technique and craftsmanship but with the kind of mood and emotion to which English musicians responded most intensively. The simplest answer is probably the most likely. The musical training undergone by professional English musicians was overwhelmingly directed towards the service of the church. If they got a court appointment (which Dowland, for example, managed to do only abroad in Germany and Denmark until quite late in his life), that was an added bonus. Those appointed to the Chapel Royal, indeed, served both court and church; and the Chapel Royal appointment left them a considerable number of days a year when they could accept engagements or commissions elsewhere.

But one factor was peculiar to the Reformed Church of England. The Queen was not just head of state: she was the head of the state-established church as well. This put her in a unique position vis-à-vis her musicians as compared with other monarchs. Catholic monarchs had to acknowledge (even if they chose not to submit to) the power of the Pope. Protestant ones set the tone for their subjects' religious observances but were not viewed as the supreme heads either of the Lutheran or of the Calvinist churches in their domains. This allowed Elizabeth to appoint Roman Catholic musicians to her Chapel Royal and require them to set the canticles for the Anglican liturgy in English while turning a blind eye to the fact that they were also composing Mass settings and Latin motets for their fellow-recusants. This was certainly the case with the greatest of her church musicians, William Byrd, who not only composed some magnificent canticle settings in English for the Anglican rite, but also three superb Masses and many motets in Latin for his co-religionists to perform in private. (It is noteworthy that many of the motets that have survived are to texts relating to the Babylonian exile and captivity, or some other such duress from which the Almighty is asked to deliver His people). Byrd's music for the Anglican church shows the same craftsmanship and sense of the quality and rhythms of the texts as anything that he composed to secular texts as lute-songs, madrigals or consort songs. Nor was he compromising himself in any way: the texts are all Biblical and although in the vernacular could not possibly be construed as in any way heretical. Perhaps Byrd took seriously the text of his song *I joy not in no earthly bliss*, with its celebration of the virtues of moderation:

> The Court and cart I like nor loath,
> Extremes are counted worst of all;
> The golden mean between them both
> Doth surest sit and fear no fall.
> This is my choice, for why I find
> No wealth is like the quiet mind.

This is surely archetypically English in its sentiments, yet extolling the virtues of 'the quiet mind' was already a cliché hundreds of years before Byrd or an English nation existed. It was a commonplace of classical pastoral verse.

In common with other reformed churches, the Church of England had moved away from the idea that the Mass, with its holy mystery and miracle of the transubstantiation by the priest of the bread and wine into the Body and Blood of Christ, was the central act of worship towards a liturgy that centred round the preaching of the word of God as set out in the Bible. Thus, music embellishing the liturgy had to ensure that the verbal message was clear. It did not constitute a kind of aural holy smoke intended to heighten the sense of a divine presence unless the text being set specifically implied so. This had a number of implications.

First of all, it meant that not just the function of music but its place in the context of the act of worship changed markedly. The reformed Anglican rites of Matins and Evensong allow for many places where short musical movements may be inserted. Only in one place, however, that allotted to the anthem, is a really extended musical composition called for. And the anthem, like the sermon, should at any rate in theory expound a scriptural text, only with musical rhetoric replacing verbal. This in turn meant that the successive phrases of the text should be clear to the congregation and that the 'point' or theme to which they were set should convey the inner meaning of each phrase before the composer wove it into a satisfactory interplay of parts and harmonies. The technique adopted was similar to and influenced that of the madrigal. The emotions – grief, repentance, humility, affection, longing, and so on – were often identical. Only the object of those emotions – confession, supplication and dedication to God – differed. And once again, the musical line of descent was similar. But this time, it generated two kinds of musical form: the verse anthem and the full anthem.

The verse anthem is a close relative of the consort song. The text is 'expounded' as it were, usually by a solo voice with instrumental accompaniment and then re-stated in similar, variant or identical form by the whole choir. The accompanying instrument(s) are integral to the overall musical design. In the full anthem, the instruments (if any) merely double the voices, so the piece may be performed unaccompanied without any loss of the harmonic texture. Both these forms were exploited by English musicians[17].

The musical forms, then, adopted by the great Tudor and Jacobean composers were as English as the English language themselves: a judicious compound of sturdy native elements, especially in the use of the English language, with foreign ones; and just as the English language itself demonstrated its protean flexibility, so did the alert and imaginative musicians whom Elizabeth and James I had the good fortune to employ demonstrate theirs. They did not need to demonstrate their nationality by setting xenophobic or chauvinistic texts. Even the dance rhythms that they exploited both in their solo songs and their instrumental pieces were West European rather than specifically English. They *were* able to demonstrate it by dedicating their art to the Queen, who was the all-too-human yet conventionally idealised symbol of the community in which they lived or to the God they believed to preside over both her destiny and theirs.

[17] The most thorough, readable and scholarly account of the relationship between church and musicians remains Peter le Huray's *Music and the Reformation in England, 1549–1660*, London 1967.

3 – Henry Purcell: the Complete Restoration Man

Music historians often tend to consider the development of styles and idioms without relating them over-much to the *kind* of music that was in demand at a particular time from a given society, or of the quality of the response that composers made to that demand rather than to demands made on their colleagues elsewhere. In England, the issue has for many generations been clouded by the fact that the church had a virtual monopoly of the training of 'serious' musicians for the cathedral organ loft or the university college chapel. This was in itself a consequence of the manner in which English political and social life developed after the Reformation.

People still sometimes believe that the early seventeenth century, when church and courtly musical cultures in other countries were thriving, saw a period of utter mediocrity in English music. Yet while it is true that we produced no towering and revolutionary genius of the calibre of Monteverdi, music was very much alive at the court of the first two Stuart kings. And, as we shall see, the establishment of the Puritan Commonwealth after the execution of Charles I in 1649 led to a change of direction in rather than an outright suppression of musical life in England.

One of the objections raised by Puritans about the Stuart court was that it frittered away public money on lavish and spectacular entertainments in which music played a large part. To understand why this happened, we have to consider how the relationship between monarch, state and church in early 17th-century England differed from that of Tudor times.

Unlike his immediate predecessor, James I, whose father had been mysteriously assassinated and whose mother executed as a traitor, had early developed the idea that kings were granted their position of authority by divine right. They did not govern by the will of the people, or even by that of their courtiers, but by that of God. They were therefore symbols, not so much of the community that they governed but of the God by whose grace they reigned; and the image that was projected of them related to Heaven rather than to earth. Thus in theory, at any rate, the laws that their parliaments debated and passed (or rejected) reflected their will – and hence God's – not that of the people and their political and commercial interests, great and small, whom the two Houses of Parliament represented.

In England, in particular, the monarch was also the secular head of the state church; and the first two Stuart kings were determined to exercise their authority in that direction as well as in the field of secular politics. Thus the services and the rituals, not just of the Chapel Royal but of the Church of England in general, reflected the taste and the preferences of the monarch. Not for nothing is the magnificent monument to the power and flexibility of the newly-minted English language that we know as the Authorised Version of the Bible also known as the King James version. James did not of course have a hand in the translation, but it was under his patronage, both as monarch and as head of the state church, that the great enterprise was begun and brought to a successful conclusion. From 1611 onwards, this was the version of scripture that generated the Bible-based anthems of the Anglican liturgy. Its cadences and imagery have had an incalculable influence on the diction, rhythm, idiom and style of countless English writers – and musicians sensitive to the cadences of the English language – ever since.

Further evidence of the monarch's tastes were seen in the work of the Court of Star Chamber and in the influence exerted by Archbishop Thomas Laud, whose high-church preferences in respect to the liturgy and to church doctrine were regarded by many as perilously close to the beliefs and practices of the Roman Catholic Church. Catholics still regarded their Church, and particularly its head, the Pope, as the final authority not just on religious matters but also on secular ones. For example, Copernicus's claim, substantiated by Galileo, that the earth revolved round the sun and not vice-versa was one of the few issues whereon Catholics and Protestants agreed. It was condemned, not only by Martin Luther, who held it to be contrary to Holy Scripture, but by the papacy as well. Freedom of political and of philosophical opinions was to play an ever-increasing role in the intellectual currents of the seventeenth century; and strangely enough this very freedom was to lead to a downgrading of the status of music in the cosmic scheme of things.

Yet, given their attitude to royal authority and to the ceremony that surrounded it, it is hardly surprising that James I and his successor Charles I were aware of technical musical developments on the continent; and they encouraged their court and church musicians to emulate these, while also endeavouring to maintain the traditions that had been built up in England during the latter part of the sixteenth century. James, indeed, sent his favourite composer, Nicholas Lanier, to the continent expressly to study the new developments. Walter Porter is known to have studied with Monteverdi and produced some remarkably innovative anthems showing the influence of the new style for the Chapel Royal. And although it is stretching a point to claim that any of those who served the first two Stuart kings were of the calibre of a Byrd or a Dowland, there were certain musicians whose work commands respect and shows a willingness to adapt to English conditions what was happening on the continent in general and in Italy in particular.

The major musical development abroad was the rise of opera. It is true that opera in English as such was not experimented with – surprisingly enough – until the days of Oliver Cromwell. But ironically, it was the court equivalent of opera under the Stuarts that contributed in no small measure to Puritan dissatisfaction with Stuart vanity and extravagance. We do wrong to imagine that opera as originally conceived was simply part of the theatre, *tout court*. The first operas were composed for special festivities lasting days, if not weeks, that would include banquets, tournaments and other celebrations. A component of court ceremonial that continually increased in significance, they would often pay allegorical tribute to the individual, couple, or family whose nuptials or whatever were being celebrated. The lavish and brilliantly conceived masques that were regularly performed at the Stuart court fulfilled a similar function to that provided by operas in Italy; and opera itself was eagerly appreciated by privileged English visitors who were susceptible to music. These visitors included none other than John Milton, Puritan of the Puritans, who seems to have reacted to music in a manner that would have been regarded a hundred years later as extravagant and effeminate – not at all the done thing for a gentleman of taste and breeding. Milton loved music; and he himself saw the uplifting and didactic potential of the masque and wrote the text for one – *Comus* – that was not only successfully performed, and performed to the music of one of the age's most distinguished composers, Henry Lawes, but remembered and adapted long after his death for the use of composers such as Arne and Handel. And it is to Milton that we should go for evidence of one aspect of the revolution in taste that took place in the relationship between those 'sphere-born harmonious sisters, voice and verse', as he himself put it.

The Stuart masque, to coin a phrase, 'had everything' for those involved, including exorbitant costs. It had spectacle, music, drama of a kind, lyric interludes, dancing and audience participation. It was, in fact, a kind of *Gesamtkunstwerk* with audience participation; and the composers of the Jacobean masques were often well paid for their contributions: Thomas Campion, for example, received at least £60 for one of his masques. True, this was a fleabite compared with the expenditure of thousands on the spectacle and scenery, but £60 was none the less a considerable sum in the early seventeenth century.

The masque was a *Gesamtkunstwerk* in another sense, too. At its most ambitious, like a Mahler symphony, it encompassed an entire universe. The farce and slapstick of the anti-masque, the symbolic and allegorical solemnity of the masque itself, the make-believe glory of the spectacular elements and the manner in which the guests of honour were involved: all these elements reflected both the baser aspects of society as it was and an idealised image of society as it ought to be.

But the most important element relevant to our theme was the kind of music that composers were expected to provide. It was theatre music. But it was not operatic music, sustaining the development of the dramatic plot, declaimed in enhanced speech- and dance-rhythms and intonations, and it was certainly not intended to re-create in modern terms the dramatic impact of ancient Greek tragedy. The music of the masques was not part of a tightly-organised dramatic action. It was there to underline unobtrusively the mood of the moment in the text rather than to project and develop it hand in hand with the verse. This was to have a significant – and in many respects ruinous – influence on the development of opera in English when it eventually reached the stage.

But English musicians did not ignore the innovations brought over from Italy. Interestingly enough, it is Milton again who provides the clue in his sonnet to Henry Lawes:

> Harry, whose tunefull and well measur'd song
> First taught our English Music how to span
> Words with just note and accent, not to scan
> With Midas' ears, committing short and long:
> Thy worth and skill exempts thee from the throng,
> With praise enough for Envy to look wan;
> To after age thou shalt be writ the man
> That with smooth air couldst honour best our tongue.
> Thou honour'st Verse, and Verse must lend her wing
> To honour thee, the priest of Phoebus' quire,
> That tun'st their happy lives in hymn or story.
> Dante shall give Fame leave to set thee higher
> Than his Casella, whom he wooed to sing
> Met in the milder shades of Purgatory.

It is surely more than a little unfair of Milton to dismiss Henry Lawes's predecessors as scanning English 'with Midas' ears'. What is fair in his eulogy of his friend was the fact that Lawes consciously tried to match his music to the natural verbal music – the speech-rhythms and intonations – of the texts that he set. And as he set some of the finest poets of his day, his attempts to do so merit our attention before we go on to consider Henry Purcell.

Lawes was the older and possibly the less imaginative of two gifted brothers. His younger brother William was killed at the siege of Chester in 1645; Henry survived into the reign of Charles II. Henry's more serious songs are assessed by Ian Spink as follows[18]:

---

[18] *The English Lute Song from Dowland to Purcell*

His sensitivity to nuances of diction and feeling in a poem result in a richness compared with which the style of the others [of his period] seems arid. It is he, really, who defines the declamatory ayre and against whom the rest are measured.

The Lawes brothers were the first English composers to write genuine continuo songs. Henry wrote over 400 of them; and while they are not all of first quality, many of them set some of the best lyrics of the age with an assurance and a sensitivity that matches that of the poems themselves. He was, if you like, a kind of Caroline Hugo Wolf who needed good verse to inspire him, rather than a Schubert who could turn the dross of near-doggerel verse into sheer gold by his musical gift. Good verse he certainly got: Charles I's court possessed a number of fine poets, such as Herrick, Lovelace, Waller, Suckling and Carewe. Lawes set poems by all of these and even tried his hand at setting verses by the metaphysical Francis Quarles (who was virtually ignored by composers after Lawes's time until Benjamin Britten chose one of his texts for his First Canticle a good three hundred years later). It is also worth noting, I think, that poets such as George Herbert, probably the greatest Caroline lyric poet of all after John Donne[19], were less frequently set to music, yet their verse betokened a solemn wit, a depth and quality of expression that reflected the essential seriousness of King Charles I's court.

William was perhaps more adventurous than Henry: he knew and absorbed what was going on on the continent in the development of new instrumental forms and skilfully blended them with the old traditional ones. His 'sets', as he called them, are virtually embryonic *sonate da camera*, comprising one or two of the old-style contrapuntal fantasias, a more lyrical air and a dance movement, nearly always a pavane. The sombre C minor Sett for six viols dates from about 1640 and its first fantasy is based on Lawes's setting of the penitential psalm 'I am weary of my groaning'. It also includes an *In nomine*, a fine example of a

---

[19] The text of Henry Lawes's *Loath to depart* is attributed to Donne. Purcell set at least two of Herbert's lyrics in the 1680s. Robert Wilson set Donne's *Wherefor peep'st thous, envious day.*

compositional form based on a point taken from a Mass by John Taverner that was and always remained peculiar to England alone for a good century and three quai ters. William also included violins in certain of his chamber works: the dancing-master's tavern fiddle, held under the chin rather than between the knees, was rapidly becoming respectable.

It is often claimed that the Puritan Commonwealth caused an irremediable break in the continuum of English musical life. This is simply not true. The reason why the idea gained so much ground is that one very important source of musical training – the choir schools for the great Anglican church establishments, such as the cathedrals and the Chapel Royal – was dispersed when the Anglican church was proscribed. Its professional musicians had to seek employment elsewhere in the country or abroad, its musical libraries were scattered and its organs dismantled. In many cases, these were undoubtedly acts of wanton and bigoted vandalism. But there was another side to the story. Complex church music for the Anglican rite may have been proscribed for public devotional use and the church as a patron of music and musical education may have been eliminated. But that does not mean that the Puritans were unresponsive or inimical to music. Milton was by no means alone in his love of the art. What they seem to have been was frightened of the powerful effect it might have in the wrong context. Their attitude seems to have been similar to that adopted by many philosophers from the time of Plato onwards (and to prevail among the empiricist and utilitarian philosophers who have dominated English philosophy from the 17th century to the present day). Some kinds of music were ear-tickling; some were even morally debilitating. But to some of the Puritans, at any rate, some kinds of music were uplifting, inducing an ecstasy that might even foreshadow that of the Life to Come, 'bringing all Heaven before my eyes', as Milton memorably put it; such music was to be encouraged.

Anglican church music, then, may have languished under the Commonwealth. Secular music flourished. The Lord Protector himself was very responsive to music (strangely enough, his taste in church music centred round the exiled Catholic composers Dering and Philips), had the former organ of Magdalen College, Oxford, dismantled, rebuilt and installed in his own residence and engaged Charles I's organist to perform on it for him. But quite apart from this, it was during the Commonwealth that the publication of English printed music really 'took off', that foreign virtuoso instrumentalists such as Thomas Baltzar came to this country and that the first operas in English were staged. The titles are significant: *The Siege of Rhodes, The Cruelty of the Spaniards in Peru* and *The History of Sir Francis Drake*. Not the classical myths that formed the basis of the majority of Italian and French opera, it will be noted, but near-contemporary historical events: patriotic political propaganda for the Protestant cause, in fact, of which the Puritans felt that they were God's chosen protagonists. Patriotism and religious fervour now went hand in hand. Throughout its short existence, the Commonwealth was beset with foreign enemies; and while opera was a convenient way of circumventing the Puritan ban on the 'straight' theatre, the subject matter chosen was such that no serious-minded patriotic parliamentarian could possible object to it. It is also significant that not a note of the music to these operas survived the restoration. It wasn't just the Puritan zealots, apparently, who destroyed or suppressed works of art that were anathema to them.

The Stuart monarchy was restored in 1660. There can be little doubt that much of the country heaved a collective sigh of relief. Eleven years of the austerity of the Puritan Commonwealth, with its stern, semi-military rule and its almost continuous state of war in defence of the new political order, of English status and overseas trade, were over. The Church of England was re-instated as the state church; choir schools for the cathedrals and the Chapel Royal were re-established. Theatres were re-opened. Britain could relax. The King, it was believed, had come into his own again. So, in a sense, he had. But there was no going back on the results of the twenty years of civil strife and Puritan Commonwealth: 'his own' was much restricted compared with the position of other monarchs and princes, both great and small, who ruled elsewhere in Europe, or, for that matter, in Asia and Africa. He knew that he occupied his throne on sufferance; and in his own words, the new king, Charles II, the easy-going and quick-witted son of the stubborn and devious Charles I, was determined not to 'go on his travels' – into exile abroad – again, as he had had to after the execution of his father in 1649. Even if he wanted to, which is questionable, Charles II could not afford to support the arts in the same lavish way as his father had.

Charles was a charming if somewhat feckless patron of music. He established a chair of music at Cambridge without allotting the professor the funds needed to do his job properly – and this in a university that had been the very first in Europe to grant degrees in music. He also sent his most promising young musicians abroad to absorb the latest styles, financing them out of the secret service funds. The almost direct antithesis of his cold, sober, puritanical father in every way save his political deviousness, he had little time for the solemn and elaborate music that Charles I, a highly competent viol-player, and even Cromwell, for that matter, seem to have enjoyed.

His musical tastes had been largely formed during his exile. They were dance-orientated, light-hearted and, above all, French. He liked music with catchy rhythms to which he could tap his feet, and he was easily bored with solemn counterpoint. This did not go down well with those who remembered and reacted to the older type of church music: they considered the new style redolent more of the theatre or the tavern than of the church. But there was another problem. Parliament would not allow Charles to finance the grandiose musical spectacles so beloved of his father or of Louis XIV, at whose court he had been an exile. So the musical establishment of the Chapel Royal was refurbished on French lines, but on a much more modest scale than that enjoyed by the absolute monarch Louis XIV. Louis had his 'Vingt-quatre violons du roi'; Charles likewise established a band of twenty-four musicians and a choir to sing the offices. But those offices were those of the Anglican liturgy, centring round the anthem, not of the Roman Catholic one, centring round the Mass. A new type of anthem developed. Phoenix-like, the verse anthem of the earlier part of the century arose from its own ashes; but the structure was now much more Frenchified.

Even so, there were important aspects in which patronage of the arts in England from the taste and manners adopted in France and to some considerable extent copied elsewhere on the continent. Among these are a number of features that influenced the way in which the arts developed, and particularly those associated with the theatre, such as opera.

The first of these was the establishment in France of an Academy to regulate taste and style in the language of poetry and drama. The Académie Française had been established in 1635 to perfect the French language and, in effect, to exercise a kind of aesthetic censorship on the literary French of novels, poetry and verse drama. It set up rules and models and began work on a dictionary that was limited only to the language used by 'polite' society. One by-product of its work was to confine the French language and the way in which it was used in literature almost exclusively to words derived from Latin and, to a much lesser degree, Greek. Words of low or vulgar origin were excluded. It has been estimated that the vocabulary used by the great French classical tragedian Jean Racine, for example, was limited to less than a quarter of that used by Shakespeare. The imagery and recommended metres permitted to poets of all kinds were likewise straitjacketed. Plays were subjected to the three unities recommended by Aristotle and to what were called 'les bienséances'. These were accepted conventions of taste that decreed what kind of action was suitable to high art and the kind of language in which that action was to be couched and forbade violent action onstage, or the mixing of genres such as comedy and tragedy in the same play. Good taste was restricted to that which was rational, balanced and technically well-finished. Ghosts and the supernatural were frowned upon, if not actually banned, at any rate in spoken drama. These conventions were known to and even respected by many Restoration dramatists but their observance in England was sporadic, so that even though they led indirectly to such things as the 'improvement' of Shakespeare to suit Restoration tastes, they were never allowed totally to prevail in Restoration drama. They later had a marked effect at absolutist courts on the continent, however, particularly in the 'reform' libretti of such poets as Metastasio (1698–1782) in the 18th century: hence the highly artificial nature of the literary style and action of many post-Handelian operas to Italian libretti, whatever the nationality of the composer.

Charles II's admiration of the procedures adopted at Versailles affected the most gifted of the younger Restoration composers, whose death at the age of 27 was possibly as great a loss to English music as that of Henry Purcell was at 35. This was Pelham Humfrey. Humfrey was sent to France in 1664 and remained there for some three years. During his leave of absence he was appointed a musician of the King's private chamber music, in March 1666, when he was about nineteen years of age. In January 1667 he became a Gentleman of the Chapel Royal; and in October of the same year he returned to England.

The famous diarist Samuel Pepys, who was almost as susceptible to the charms of music as he was to those of pretty women, knew Humfrey well. In his diary for 15 November 1667, he commented on young Humfrey in the following well-known scathing passage:

> Thence I away home (calling at my Mercer and tailor's) and there find, as I expected, Mr Caesar [Duffill] and little Pelham Humfrys, lately returned from France and is an absolute Monsieur, as full of form and confidence and vanity, and disparages everything and everybody's skill but his own. The truth is, everybody says he is very able; but to hear how he laughs at all the King's music here, as Blagrave and others, that they cannot keep time nor tune nor understand anything, and that Grebus the Frenchman, the King's Master of the Musique, how he understands nothing nor can play on any instrument and so cannot compose, and that he will give him a lift out of his place, and that he and the King are mighty great, and that he hath already spoke to the King of Grebus, would make a man piss.

Thomas Blagrave, a friend of Pepys, had been one of Cromwell's domestic musicians and was at this time Master of the Choristers at Westminster Abbey. Louis Grabus had succeeded Nicholas Lanier as Master of the King's Musick in 1666: Pepys commented favourably on the precision with which the King's band played under his direction. He also respected Humfrey as a composer, despite his adverse comments on his personal behaviour. None the less, it is clear from later developments that Humfrey's comments were not completely ill-founded; and his own music shows how well he had absorbed the mature baroque style that was brought to its peak in this country by his pupil Henry Purcell.

Purcell's other main teacher, Matthew Locke, was rather more conservative in his taste than Pelham Humfrey. Locke's approach to the harmonic revolution that had been taking place through the seventeenth century was interesting. His more ambitious anthems show that he was aware of the new practices; and he had a marked sense of the dramatic effect of the unexpected resolution of a chord progression, but he seems not to have been able to integrate such effects into a coherent design. The shifts of harmony, delightful and striking in themselves, often lead nowhere; their effect tends to be bizarre and momentary rather than to move towards a specific harmonic goal. The harmonic forces were being tapped, but they were not being properly harnessed. Purcell realised what could be done almost from the very first. He demonstrated this in 1680, when, at the age of twenty, he set about composing a set of fantasias for stringed instruments in the form of the old traditional fantasia.

These fantasias are in three, four, five, six and even seven parts; the six- and seven-part ones actually included two examples – the last ever known to have been composed – of the *In nomine.* In form and idiom, these pieces were to some degree conservative. They were in contrasting sections and they were not composed on the figured-bass pattern that had already swept the continent and was now sweeping England. But they were new in that they applied brilliantly and with a fine structural sense the very harmonic excursions with which Locke had experimented, but which he had not exploited to the full.

If eclecticism is one aspect of the English character, Purcell immediately demonstrated how eclectic he was. Having produced a set of instrumental masterworks in the traditional form, he immediately abandoned it for the new forms that were all the rage in Italy and elsewhere. Three years later he published his first set of trio sonatas after the modern Italian pattern. This was the first collection of trio sonatas published by an English composer; and even those who complained about the Frenchified taste of the King and his courtiers, such as Roger North, brother of Charles's Lord Chief Justice and an accomplished amateur musician, were impressed by the Italian style,

> for their measures were just and quick, set off with wonderful solemne Grave's, and full of variety.

The 'solemnity' of the Italian slow movements is presumably here being lauded at the expense of the pomposity of the French style. The Italian works, he seems to have thought, were nearer in spirit, in fact, to the varied moods and rhythms of the old fantasias and devoid of what they considered Gallic frivolity. Purcell himself takes a dig at the French in his preface, commending the 'seriousness' of the Italians and continuing:

> Tis time now, [that England] should begin to loath the levity, and balladry of our neighbours

– hardly, one would imagine, intended as an attack on the Dutch, the Irish or the Scots.

The sonatas are not merely attractive; they are learned as well, with some staggering yet remarkably unobtrusive feats of academic skill. Englishmen have generally had a horror of blatant displays of erudition – this must surely have been one of the reasons behind Pepys's distaste for Pelham Humfrey's manner and attitudes towards his contemporaries. Purcell, however, generally carries his learning lightly, for he had one of the most fertile gifts for a memorable tune that any of his countrymen ever possessed. In the eighteenth century the poet Smart praised him in these terms:

> But hark! The temple's hollow'd roof resounds
> And Purcell lives among the solemn sounds, –
> Mellifluous, yet manly too,
> He pours his strains along.
> As from the lion Samson slew,
> Comes sweetness from the strong.
> Not like the soft Italian swains,
> He trills the weak ennervate strains,
> Where sense and music are at strife;
> His vigorous notes with meaning teem,
> With fire, and force explain the theme,
> And sing the subject into life.

Roger North was quick to point out that Purcell's sonatas were also 'clog'd with somewhat of an English vein, for which they are unworthily despised' – 'the other fellow's country, right or wrong' is a fashion among English intellectuals that does not seem to have changed much, it seems – though what constituted the 'English vein' that North found in them, he does not say. From the context it seems to have been what he considered the weight and massive strength of some of the contrapuntal writing, as compared with, say, the swiftness and neatness of Corelli's contrapuntal movements that had come into fashion in the last years of the seventeenth century and the early eighteenth century, when North was writing.

Where Purcell's 'English' character shows at its most obvious, however, is in his setting of English texts and in the kind of texts that he chose to set. These varied from the pompous and ornate to the downright scatological. Purcell was quick to absorb and exploit the Frenchified rhythms that he knew appealed to Charles. He was also aware of what was happening in Italy; but he never lost sight of the inflections of his native language; and he was quick to exploit the more 'popular' aspects of native music when the character or the situation involved was appropriate – witness such movements as the sturdy sailors' chorus in *Dido and Aeneas*, the quotation of a Playford tune, *Hey boys, up go we,* in the bass line of 'Be lively and gay' from *Ye Tuneful Muses,* or his sly quotation of a Scottish air, 'Cold and raw', that Queen Mary is said to have preferred to one of his own in the bass line of 'May her blest example chase', part of a Birthday Ode for the Queen composed in 1692. Ian Spink[20] has pointed out how Italian innovations were incorporated in his vocal and instrumental music:

> . . . while the light, tuneful air patterned on the forms and rhythms of the dance was to retain its place to the end, at a deeper level, it was necessary to break through the formal and emotional restrictiveness of its small-scale symmetries. The influence of verse and dance forms had therefore to recede, and techniques of abstract musical construction – motivic repetition, development, sequence, imitation, tonal prolongation – take their place. In other words, the application of the Italian instrumental style to vocal music becomes an accomplished fact: the transformation of air into aria.

Purcell's alchemical ability to convert dross into gold is shown at its best in the numerous Welcome Songs that he composed for various royal birthdays and other similar anniversaries. The texts of these rarely rise above the level of a Restoration William McGonagall; yet in conveying the sentiments that they were intended to express, Purcell transcended their banality not merely with ease – that would hardly have been an achievement of any consequence – but with a skill that is often matched by sheer inspiration.

---

[20] Op. cit.

The Welcome Song is the English baroque equivalent of those equally impressive secular cantatas to often equally banal texts that J S Bach wrote for various German princelings. It was in fact the largest-scale ceremonial kind of composition of the age in England; and a glance at both the texts and the music gives a pretty fair idea of the sentiments deemed suitable for expression on such occasions. This kind of ceremonial music was one of the many areas in which Purcell excelled. He did not create it. What he did was to bring out the latent pomp and dignity in the style that was required, fuse it with a supreme ability to match text to music, invest it with a remarkable variety of musical devices expressing a wide range of emotions and thus lay the foundations of a truly English type of ceremonial music that has lasted from his day to our own. Without Purcell's welcome odes, Handel, Arne (*Rule, Britannia!*), even Arthur Sullivan ('When Britain really ruled the waves' in *Iolanthe*, for example), Hubert Parry, Elgar, Holst and Walton, to mention only a few, would have had to create the style afresh rather than build on the foundations he had laid.

That style derived in part from France (the processional preludes of Marc-Antoine Charpentier, for example, from which the dignified gait of a stirring tune like that of Queen Zempoalla's martial entry in *The Indian Queen* surely derives) and in part from 'the fam'd Italian masters', but it was Purcell's supreme ability to fuse English texts and attitudes with music from a range of sources that matters from our point of view. Its main qualities are a straightforward simplicity of melody and rhythm that is dignified without being brutally militaristic or pompous, a solid and firmly moving harmonic bass and a solemnity of gait. The dignity and solemnity possess none the less an underlying gentleness that reflects both an affectionate awareness of the majesty of the re-established monarchy as a symbol of national self-respect and a kind of sensitive scepticism not above slily poking fun at what is being venerated. It is as if the composer were in some way aware of the slight shabbiness of the pretensions to semi-divine dignity of a royal house that held its position on sufferance.

There is more, however, to Purcell's anthems and welcome songs than conventional ceremonial pomp. There is also pathos and mystery. Whilst he never forgot that the royal foot must be kept tapping, he was also alert to the emotive and illustrative potential of the texts that he set. When, for example, in the typical baroque exaggeration of 'From these Serene and Raptuorous Joys' his text-writer sanctimoniously and sycophantically likens the King's return to the court to the raising of Lazarus from the dead, Purcell sets it to what Bruce Wood rightly calls 'music of haunting eloquence'. And like his great admirer, Benjamin Britten, Purcell was well aware of the technical capacity of his intended performers, such as the voices in the Chapel Royal choir and the instrumentalists, especially the trumpeters, in the King's Musical Ensemble. If being aware of the practical rather than of the ideal is an English characteristic, then Purcell was certainly very English.

Just as there is more to the ceremonial pieces than pomp and circumstance, so also there is more to Purcell's sense of patriotism than the bellicose challenges of the Britons to the Saxon invaders in *King Arthur*. In addition to military pride, Dryden also celebrates in the same play the peaceful pastoral beauties of England. And here, too, Purcell rises to the occasion with one of his most celebrated tunes: 'Fairest Isle'. The temperate minuet-like lilt of this tune, with its syncopated nudges and restrained *fiorature,* fit alike the mood, metre, rhythms and speech-melody of Dryden's classicistic text. Englishmen had found a musician who could translate their feelings about their country into suitably clear and immediately appealing terms. These projections of English society – military (or naval) pride, sturdy independence and gentle pastoral calm – are woven into the musical texture of all our greatest and most 'national' musicians from Purcell's time onwards.

Yet scepticism was also in the air. Sometimes it took coarse and vulgar forms. I find this very 'restoration' and very English in its ability to combine respect with a tendency to take royal and human dignity with a grain of salt. One is reminded of the puritan Lord Protector's admonition to the man painting his portrait to ensure that it was done 'warts and all'. Purcell's melodic style and rhythms, particularly in movements such as the Sailors' Song, chorus and dance from *Dido and Aeneas,* not only far surpass that of any of his continental rivals, but also touch the roots of English popular music without ever degenerating into vulgarity or the commonplace.

This lusty earthiness and the ability to see the absurd in the pretentious crops up in the work of the first of our great native painters, William Hogarth, born two years after Purcell's death. The adjective 'Hogarthian' might well in fact be anachronistically applied to some of Purcell's catches. Even his most scatological catches are examples of immaculate – and often witty – musical craftsmanship. There is one, for example, that takes an apparently innocent text and so places the entries that what the listener hears is 'He gave her nine inches' – the innuendo of which it is hardly necessary to explain in any further detail. A man that could lavish his supreme technical skill on texts that the Victorian editors of the Purcell Society's scholarly edition felt it necessary to bowdlerise, pacing and placing the pauses in the text so that hidden innuendos were touched upon and underlined by the music, must surely have shared in the general nudge-nudge, wink-wink, know-what-I-mean attitude of those whose wit was expressed through words rather than music.

Restoration scepticism was not by any means confined to scatological trivia, however. It seems to turn up in somewhat unexpected contexts. One of the most interesting examples is the closing number of the Welcome Song for James II called *Why are all the Muses mute?* It was composed in 1685 to celebrate the King's return to London after the defeat of Monmouth's rebellion. Purcell sets the fulsome tributes to 'Caesar', as James II is referred to throughout the text, in a curiously muted, half-light tone: there are none of the ceremonial martial trumpets and drums that one would expect to exalt a monarch whose skill as an admiral, if not as a general, was well-known but simply strings to accompany the soloists. The Ode starts, not with a majestic symphony, but with a plaintive recitative: only when that has been delivered does the orchestra break in. Moreover, Purcell eschews all attempts to match the pomposity of the anonymous poet's fulsome epithets – even the alto solo 'Britain, thou now art great' is lyrical rather than pompous; and the extended finale, 'O how blest is the Isle to which Caesar is given', ends with a drooping chromatic farewell on which Robert King[21] appositely

---

[21] In his note to the Hyperion recording.

declares it to be worthy of Dido herself in *Dido and Aeneas,* adding that there is 'no more poignant ending in all Purcell's Odes'. Purcell was prompted no doubt by the curious ambiguity of the text:

> His name shall the Muses in triumph rehearse,
> As long as there's number in music and verse;
> His fame shall endure till all things decay,
> His fame and the world together shall die,
> Shall vanish together away.

Purcell's music emphasises not the reference to the King's enduring fame but the ephemeral nature of such renown, not the renown itself. Hardly what a self-willed and arrogant monarch (despite the references to his goodness and clemency earlier in the Ode) would have anticipated from a composer whose 'pomp and circumstance' music could easily match that produced by any of Louis XIV's musicians. Nor can it be claimed that Purcell's heart wasn't in the text: what he chose to emphasise, he emphasised with skill and touching pathos.

It is worth noting that it was during Purcell's lifetime that the foundations were developed of the English empirical school of philosophy, which started from the premise formulated by John Locke that 'No man's knowledge here can go beyond his experience', discounting all purely abstract speculation as untrustworthy and considering all revealed religion as either beyond the realm of earthly investigation or mere superstition. Before Locke, Thomas Hobbes had claimed that 'True and False [were] attributes of speech, not of things. And where speech is not, there is neither truth nor falsehood.' and that 'They that approve a private opinion, call it opinion; but they that mislike it, heresy: and yet heresy signifies no more than private opinion'. And as for the nature of human life itself, it was for the majority of men in the past and present, said Hobbes, '. . . solitary, poor, nasty, brutish and short.' (Hobbes himself prospered and died at the age of ninety-one. He was clearly not one of the majority).

Empirical scepticism and the move towards a relativistic morality did, however, lead to a re-appraisal of the place of music in the cosmos and the calling of the musician in society. Where a purely physical force, gravity, was now held to be that which underlay the harmony of the physical universe, there was no place for the Music of the Spheres. Music was reduced to being a mere pleasurable sensation; at best it engendered a mysterious thrill, at worst it provided a mere aural tickling. In his *Thoughts concerning Education* of 1693, that same John Locke also dismissed musicians (and therefore, by implication, their craft) in the following terms:

> I have among men of Parts and Business so seldom heard any one commended or esteemed for having an Excellency in Musick, that among those Things that ever come into the List of Accomplishments, I think I may give it the last place.

The urbanity of the eighteenth century and the all-too-prevalent philistinism even of educated Englishmen towards an art in which their countrymen had been held to excel is already foreshadowed in this disparaging throwaway line. It may well be a reflection on the age and the society in which he lived that the dignity and robust vigour of Purcell's music is utterly devoid of the ponderous, self-conscious posturing of such composers as Lully. He was too strongly aware of the delicacy and gaiety of the Italian tradition and the straightforwardness of our own to slip into such ways, even if one of his teachers had been the Frenchified Pelham Humfrey. This came about through a pleasing grafting of new Italianate techniques on to older English melodic declamation and French dance-rhythms.

Some of Purcell's solo songs, such as *The Blessed Virgin's Expostulation* and *I'll sail upon the Dog-star,* demonstrate a skill in depicting character and emotion through what were by now accepted operatic devices in such concentrated form that it is an immense pity that the commercial theatre to which Purcell – *pace* the dismissive Locke and his ilk – contributed much memorable music did not appear to be ready or willing to develop the new type of heroic opera that had been tentatively experimented with in the days of Cromwell. Instead, the fashion was for plays in which the music played a spectacular rather than a dramatic role. That he was capable, given the right kind of libretto, of producing music that would carry as well as underline the emotional charge of the action can be seen and heard in the miniature masterpiece *Dido and Aeneas.* Whatever may be said against the imagery of the libretto, which tin-eared English critics, all too often, one suspects, revelling in their ignorance of the function of the text in any music-drama, tend to criticise from a purely literary point of view, it does provide natural and dramatically apt situations for the music to develop the action and the characters' reactions to it – and thus, of course, to reveal varying aspects of their own characters.

This applied to established spoken drama as well; and it is here that Purcell also paid the penalty of being a child of the Restoration. The traditional masque became absorbed in the new all-purpose, raise-a-gasp theatrical spectacle, of which drama and music were but two constituents. In certain Shakespeare productions, for example, music was inserted on a lavish scale to accompany dances and lyrics that had no place in the original. While this certainly improved the quality and enhanced the impact of some of the fustian heroic tragedies perpetrated by contemporary authors, it is questionable whether it did much for Shakespeare. What it did do was provide Purcell with a chance to demonstrate his technical skill.

Purcell provided music for a tarted-up version of *The Tempest* – the music for Act V lasts as long as that for the other four acts put together, and the whole takes an hour to perform, while his splendid 'masque' inserted into Fletcher and Massinger's *History of Dioclesian* of 1622 (adapted, of course, to suit a contemporary audience) lasts a good hour and a half. The finest example of all is *The Fairy Queen*, a lavish and comprehensive masque inserted at various points into the action of *A Midsummer Night's Dream* (almost totally irrelevant to the plot, which of course had been suitably adulterated to suit Restoration taste). Quite rightly, it is now the custom to perform this strikingly expressive music in its own right, though the 'action' makes very little sense taken apart from the play. How much music there is – much of it brilliantly and imaginatively conceived – can be judged from the fact that a recent recording of it takes two hours.

Purcell was not afraid of experimenting. There is a well-substantiated story of Sir Edward Elgar being asked to orchestrate one of his anthems for performance at the Three Choirs Festival and being so surprised at the boldness of the harmonic progressions that he enquired whether the copy from which he had been working had been accurately transcribed. He was not questioning the quality of the writing: he was just astonished at the 'modern' effect of the music. Yet

Purcell always experimented within the framework of the traditions that he knew. This is perhaps one reason why so little of his vast output fell into the categories favoured by his major Italian, French or German contemporaries. His operatic works, for example, are mostly cast in a bastard form that, with one marvellous exception, renders them virtually unstageable today, despite the splendid music that lies buried within them. He composed no *concerti grossi* or solo concertos. His fine trio sonatas, whose formal scheme derives partly from the old English fantasias and partly from the forms developed by the mid-baroque Italian composers such as Draghi and Stradella, are quite different from those that we associate with other baroque masters such as Torelli and Corelli. (And in any case, his instrumental works constitute a very small fraction of his total output).

Purcell's stage music has to be wrenched from its context in the long-forgotten dramas for which it was originally composed and transferred to the concert-hall. We should not forget that even if music was not an integral component of 'straight' Restoration drama, it was at any rate a useful and almost obligatory embellishment of it, with overtures, 'act tunes', songs inserted into the spoken text, and so on. It is neither here nor there that the composer should in many cases have had not the remotest clue as to the action of the play for which he was writing. (Take, for example, Purcell's overtures to *Timon of Athens* or to *The Old Batchelor*, for example, which have no connection at all with the kind of play for which they were composed). In many cases, the musical items required an extensive range of moods, as for example those required for *Don Quixote*. The extended songs that Purcell composed can and do stand on their own merits as recital items, regardless of their original context in the theatre. They show an unparalleled appreciation of the expressive power and rhythmic force of the English language. The lessons that the pre-Commonwealth composers had absorbed and applied was now put to good use by backing it with a fully-developed baroque accompanimental style, but with one significant difference. The pre-Commonwealth composers delighted in setting lyrics which include some of the most charming in the English language. Purcell often had to, and managed to, invest a fustian verbal text with overwhelmingly vivid and effective musical imagery. But because the texts have dated, the music has until comparatively recently become neglected. The same is true of the odes and welcome-songs, which have been consigned to the lumber-room of dated forms and outmoded spectacles because they allude so skilfully to the occasions for which and the personalities for whom they were originally composed.

Similarly, the anthems that Purcell composed for the Chapel Royal, taken out of their context, have become part of the general heritage of Anglican church music, but in an emasculated form, with a voluptuous organ part supplanting the virile strings, oboes and sometimes recorders and trumpets of the original. Charles II may have tapped his feet and beaten time to Purcell's infectious rhythms; a modern congregation that followed his example in some great cathedral would be given very short shrift by the dean and vergers. Yet there are enough movements of moving pathos and majesty in them to embellish any service even today. The splendid 'Alleluia' from one of them, indeed, has been pressed into service as a hymn-tune in its own right, appropriately entitled 'Westminster Abbey'.

This is, I think, the penalty that Purcell paid for being a thorough child of his age, albeit one whose depth and imagination far transcended that of his contemporaries. He lived in an age and in a society whose attitude to music differed radically from that in most other countries in Europe. It was not just, nor even primarily, an embellishment of court ceremony. It was also a commercial commodity. We were among the first societies in the world to organise public concerts for fee-paying patrons. Our theatre was not just a vehicle for the *mores* and values of the court. It was also a commercial enterprise. Purcell's easy-going attitude to life made him the complete Restoration Man. Tolerant, eclectic, probably somewhat sceptical, marvellously inventive and musically witty, he served his patrons (and customers) right from the top to the bottom. He did not seem to mind whom he wrote for. His finest opera, for example, is thought to have been composed not for a sumptuous theatre but for a girls' school, though its has recently been suggested that it may have originated in a court masque. Whether he composed serious music for the Chapel Royal, ceremonial music for royal or courtly occasions, instrumental music for private performance, or scurrilous catches for drunken after-dinner carousals, his craftsmanship was so fluent and spontaneous that even his slightest pieces demonstrate his skill. His catches may be dismissed by priggish musical scholars as unworthy of him; they were none the less bound to appeal to the lascivious taste of the Restoration wits and blades who revelled in singing them (probably missing the point of many of Purcell's musical witticisms by wrong entries).

Purcell was a great composer in spite of rather than because of the musical environment in which he throve. Restoration man was quite prepared to accept music as the vehicle of spectacle and mystery; he was not prepared, however, to accept that it might convincingly underline and define the plot, action and character of a drama, whether sacred or secular, in his own language. Purcell was able and willing to provide even this kind of music if he had been called upon to do so, with his ability to create a genuinely English kind of recitative both in dramatic and rhetorical contexts that both carried emotional conviction and exploited the new way of using harmony that the Italians had steadily developed throughout the century. His awareness of the sounds, the rhythms and cadences of English pointed a way forward that was followed, alas, only in the lighter stage pieces performed in the century to come. And even then it was followed only fitfully, because those pieces tended to relegate the musical component to those moments when tension and emotion were heightened, leaving the dramatic action to be carried by the spoken word. For a new type of musical drama was about to be launched upon the English stage. Its texts were Italian and its main exponent a cosmopolitan Saxon of immense gifts. And this Saxon, Georg Friedrich Händel, was to find matters so much to his liking in Hanoverian England, where music was a component in an increasingly commerce-orientated society, that he actually assumed British nationality, left a fortune of some £20,000 (to say nothing of a judiciously-chosen collection of paintings) and applied his dramatic gifts with gusto, once the fashion for Italian opera had begun to fade, to setting his adopted language in the sublime field of oratorio. It is to him that we shall turn in our next chapter.

4 – An Honorary Englishman? Georg Friedrich Händel

Macnamara's famous band, you will recall, played at wakes and weddings; and when it played at funerals it played the March from *Saul*. The association is not purely fortuitous. For two-and-a- half centuries the dead march in *Saul* has been part of the panoply of English state funerals almost as a matter of course[22]. This is but one symptom of many that indicate how firmly the great Saxon composer has established himself as the great composer for state occasions in his adopted country. A German professor – claiming quite openly that he regarded Handel as an English, not a German, composer – once referred to *Messiah* in a letter to me as 'your national musical epic'.

Ever since his own lifetime, various qualities of Handel's style and aspects of his output have endeared him almost universally to different generations of English people (or perhaps I should say 'Britons'). Christmas was, and very largely still is, the traditional season for hundreds of performances of 'our national musical epic' to be performed all over the country, particularly in the Midlands and the North. 'See, the conquering hero comes!', from *Judas Maccabaeus*, has been taken to English hearts and pressed into service as an Anglican and Methodist hymn-tune for joyful occasions, just as the March in *Saul* has been hijacked for use at solemn ones. The glorious E-major melody from the Larghetto of the Opus 6 B minor Concerto Grosso was used by the BBC for years to introduce a meditational religious programme called 'Five to Ten'. The 'celebrated *Largo*' from his opera *Serse*, which thousands of British folk have surely mistaken for a devotional piece of some kind, can be more or less guaranteed to turn up at any English wedding as the

---

[22] Though Queen Victoria forbade it to be played at her funeral.

organist tries to create a suitably solemn mood among the congregation before the bride appears. If there is time, it is likely that an almost equally celebrated 'air from *Rinaldo'* or 'Minuet from *Berenice'* will turn up as well. Even in Handel's own time, a march from *Rinaldo* was pirated and used as the Rogues' March in *The Beggar's Opera.* Tunes like the 'alla hornpipe' from the *Water Music* not only appeal to a wide public but seem to have a peculiarly English ring to them; and of course at every coronation since 1727, since it first burst in all its majestic splendour (with 60 singers and an orchestra more than twice as large!), his anthem *Zadok the Priest* has been performed as an indispensable part of the service – alone, we might note, of the four that he composed for that occasion. When someone asked Sir Edward Elgar whence he derived his highly characteristic skill in writing for strings, he immediately replied: 'From old Handel, of course'.

So although at first blush it might be thought a bit of a cheat to include Handel as a major symbolic figure in English musical life, since he was born and basically trained in Germany and was technically at any rate in the service of the Elector of Hanover, he has certainly had a massive effect, mainly for good, on our national musical taste; and he certainly reflected at least as well as, if not better than, any native-born musician the spirit of the age in which he practised his craft in his adopted country[23].

You will notice that I advisedly used the word 'craft', not 'art'. Handel *was* a great artist; but his attitude to music was that of a craftsman. He is reputed to have said of the 'Hallelujah!' chorus: 'Methinks I did see the heavens open and the great God Himself'; and while this anecdote, like so many others about him, is almost certainly apocryphal, the heights attained by his music at its greatest are built on solid foundations of skilled craftsmanship, enviable facility, the ability to see further into the implications of other men's music than they did

---

[23] It is also mildly ironic that the two versions of his surname, with and without umlaut, translated into his adopted tongue as 'Strife' and 'Trade', as if he had exchanged the one for the other when taking his new nationality. He did, however, often sign his name as 'Hendel'.

themselves and a shrewd commercial sense of what his public would respond to.

Handel was one of music's great cosmopolitans. He was also one of music's great opportunists, one of its great 'characters' and one of its great survivors. Having left Germany as a young man, he spent several years with some considerable success in Italy before deciding to try his good fortune as a 25-year-old at the court of Queen Anne in 1710. He took a liking to the conditions of musical life in London, with its unrivalled opportunities for commercial success and financial independence (or conversely, of course, for failure and bankruptcy), instead of permanent contractual commitment in domestic servitude either to some secular potentate or to some prince of the church. He swiftly obtained leave of absence from his nominal employer, the Elector of Hanover, overstayed his leave, managed to make his peace with the Elector when the latter unexpectedly (and probably somewhat embarrassingly) appeared in London as the new King on Queen Anne's death in 1714 and settled permanently in England. In 1726 he took out British nationality. He must have been quite a charmer, too: having been granted a pension of £100 per annum by Queen Anne, he had it doubled by George I, despite having gone AWOL from his employer's service.

Yet Handel was never really a court servant in the same way as J S Bach was at Cöthen, Haydn at Esterháza or Mozart at Salzburg. We have already discussed how the control exercised by Parliament over royal expenditure precluded the disbursement by the crown of lavish sums on music in general and opera in particular. Louis XIV may have been able to declare that he *was* the state; but his English contemporaries could honestly do no more than claim that they were monarchs on sufferance. This was particularly true of the Hanoverians, the first of whom spoke no English at all and the second of whom never really mastered the language. (In any case, the international language of politics and diplomacy was French and that of science and scholarship, Latin.) Yet it was during the cosmopolitan eighteenth century that the seeds of the idea of the linguistic rather than the dynastic nation-state were sown. True, the harvest was not to be fully reaped until the Romantic movement generated a kind of nationalism that is still, unfortunately, all too prevalent. But the island kingdom with the

German ruling house was one of the first states in which patriotism developed into nationalism. The trend was already evident under Elizabeth and the Puritan Commonwealth. In Handel's time it became almost a national pestilence.

We like to think of Handel as one of our own; and I think we are right to do so. But until not so long ago, we tended to ignore the fact that his reputation in the earlier part of his own career in this country was built up mainly on his activities as a composer/impresario of opera in Italian, writing and marketing *opera seria* designed to show off the brilliant technique and musicianship of celebrated castrato and female sopranos. His total output of *opere serie* was no fewer than 42, nearly all of them composed for English audiences. One would hardly think that this was the stuff of musical Englishness. Yet there is more than one side to any equation, even a musical one. A 'polite and commercial people' whose standard of values owed more to the market-place than to military history were beginning to challenge the dominant land-owning classes who still commanded the loyalty of their hundreds of tenants, administered the law locally and sat in the legislature as by right. And in an age when Reason as well as Tradition was becoming the touchstone by which any institution was judged, the newly rich were able to buy their way into the landed classes, all too often impoverished by gambling and other debts, to become members of the House of Lords as well as the House of Commons and, above all, to invest in the arts and in artists. And although this phenomenon was not totally new, the gathering pace with which it occurred was. Handel was not content to simply watch it all happen; he became one of the new commercial classes, admired by the aristocracy as an artist and a character, on reasonable terms with the ruling house and capable of operating the market for his wares, sometimes with great success, sometimes disastrously, but on the whole managing to do much more than simply keep his financial head above water.

Handel's financial backers were all part of the new commercial set-up. They invested money in his opera companies and they expected a return on their investment. The shareholders came from the aristocracy, the royal house and the commercial world, but they were not subsidised out of the consolidated fund that administered the state's finances. Handel, for his part, composed the music and selected the singers.

Italian *opera seria* needed at least two important ingredients besides the music. It needed virtuoso singers with powerful, flexible voices; and it needed heroic, spectacular libretti. These did not have to be couched in great verse or projected as convincing drama; indeed, Dr Johnson's famous definition of opera as 'an exotick and irrational entertainment'- by which he meant *opera seria* in Italian, a fact that has often been overlooked – was pithy and accurate. This did not mean, however, that Handel's librettists were mediocre hacks. Paolo Antonio Rolli, for example, was a Fellow of the Royal Society, had translated *Paradise Lost* into Italian and must therefore have been pretty conversant with the tastes and the literature of his adopted country. Nicola Haym was not only a competent composer in his own right but also musical adviser and house musician to the Duke of Bedford. True, Rolli did not take libretto-writing too seriously. He cynically commented that he knocked up old dramas in a new style and tacked dedications on to them. If the directors of the opera house lost money on the ventures, the singers got blamed, not the librettist. As far as Rolli was concerned, his job was to plunder and adapt the works of the greater Italian poets to provide powerful and well-worn situations, singable verse and nicely contrasting emotions for his chosen composer to fill out with suitable music. He knew the cultural background and tastes of the English public of his day. They paid the piper; Rolli set up the plot; Handel called the tune.

Those tastes, as we have seen, had undergone a radical change. All over Europe, conceptions of the cosmos and its Creator – if indeed it had ever had a Creator, which some doubted – were undergoing radical change. Reason and moderation were gaining ground; untrammelled authority and extremes of view were being questioned. A comfortable deism supplanted religious fervour and fanaticism. Even Milton's *L'Allegro* and *Il Penseroso* had to be provided with a companion piece, *Il moderato*, when Handel came to set a carefully-pruned version of them to music. And although the Cosmos was no longer believed to be held together by the unheard Music of the Spheres, it was none the less a harmonious and well-lubricated machine; only the force that its Divine Creator had devised to set it in motion was different. A comfortable belief prevailed in a benevolent Divine Providence, together with a belief on a more mundane level that Britain's destiny lay in the expansion of trade (including one in negro slaves) with the world outside Europe and in claiming and settling by divine right of conquest what seemed to be vast uninhabited territories. Risks could be taken; enterprise was rewarded if not by a favoured place in the next world, at least by material prosperity in this one.

Such a society is hardly one to regard music as a mysterious force whose meaning none could penetrate. Music itself became more a matter of rational, systematised pattern-making, following agreed rules and procedures. Some theorists, indeed, actually attempted to codify not just the principles of harmony and part-writing but of melodic invention as well. And yet there still remained the undoubted and inexplicable power of music to arouse or assuage human moods and passions.

Handel himself was entirely suited to flourish in such an age. For a start, he was quite protean in his approach to musical styles. His sound training in Lutheran Germany and his exposure to Italian baroque theatre and church music ensured this. He knew both German and Italian well for all the stories about his accent, which seems to have varied, according to the source of the anecdote being told, from thick pseudo-Bavarian to burlesque all-purpose comic foreigner. (They rarely show anything remotely characteristic of the sounds of his native Saxony.) His English was both fluent and forceful. While he was at work on his Italian operas for the London stage, he was also involved in setting English texts, notably a series of noble anthems to texts from the Bible and John Gay's delightful pastoral *Acis and Galatea* that show that he was perfectly aware of the most effective way to set his adopted tongue, even though he made occasional mistakes in the stress[24]. He was a vigorous and enterprising man of business; and he so quickly

---

[24] Who doesn't occasionally? I have even heard a BBC television newscaster mispronounce the word 'Neanderthal', named after a valley in the Ruhr, as if the stress fell on the 'der' syllable instead of on the 'and' syllable, and the head-consonant of the last syllable were pronounced as if it were the English 'th' as in 'both' rather than the German 't' as in 'tennis', which is correct.

established himself as a 'character' that almost as many stories attached themselves to him as were later to do to Sir Thomas Beecham. (Incidentally, none have survived about any of his sexual exploits, unlike the scandalous anecdotes current about his near contemporary, Thomas Augustine Arne, for example). He absorbed not only the way of life of the prosperous eighteenth-century English middle-class worthy, but also the cadences and sonorities of the English language, and in particular of the Bible and – perhaps a little surprisingly – of John Milton. But until he had acquired English citizenship, he rarely, apart from the works already mentioned, chanced his arm with the setting of English words; and he never composed any full-scale operas in English. For them he stuck to Italian.

Handel is the only composer from the baroque era whose music[25] remained in favour from his day to our own. His music has gone through various changes in performance and interpretative styles, but much of it did not need to undergo re-discovery. Each generation seems to have taken from him what it needed. His star may have been temporarily eclipsed by that of others, but it never sank below the horizon in the way that those did of even the greatest of his contemporaries (to say nothing of lesser ones from whom he shamelessly lifted themes and even whole passages, making far more of them than the original composer had done). Even J S Bach's music fell out of fashion for more than half a century after his death.

Handel's claim to 'Englishness' rests mainly, though not exclusively, on his great oratorios. It is here that he differs from all his other distinguished and not so distinguished continental contemporaries who settled in the Land of Commercial Promise. If the English took Handel to their hearts (which not all of them did), he certainly took the majestic stories of the Old Testament to his. His last Italian opera flopped in 1742. From then onwards, all the texts that he set were in his adopted language. And in seizing the opportunity offered, he created a form of

---

[25] True, his operas began to fall into oblivion even during his lifetime and were not revived until the mid-20th century, but certain of his oratorios and certain of his instrumental works continued to be performed from his own day till ours.

oratorio that was as eclectic in musical style as it was original in conception. Here were uplifting, or at the very least admonitory stories, cast in a dramatic form that was basically that of *opera seria*, but in the vernacular and based on plots taken from the sacred book of the Christian religion, featuring not only colourful (and, it was believed, historical) figures, but also the people from which they sprang and the nations with which they were in conflict. Just as in *Gulliver's Travels* the Lilliputians represent England and the Blefuscudians France, so in Handel's oratorios can similar goodies and baddies be found. In *Judas Maccabaeus* the 'conquering hero' is surely the Duke of Cumberland; the defeated enemy, the (Papist) Highland Scots. In *Israel in Egypt* what matters is that the Lord is on the side of 'his people'; they have been freed from the bondage of subjection to a foreign yoke and the lilting triple-rhythm tune to which are set the words 'He led them forth like sheep' is not merely a pastoral convention raised to the power of sublimity (and cribbed from another composer into the bargain), it also conveys the calm and order of an emparked English landscape.

Such a God should not be confused with the *dei ex machinis* of classically-based music-drama or the allegorical figures such as Fortune, Mercury, Venus or Athena who might appear in the prologue of a baroque opera to explain the motivation and the forces at work behind the plot. This was an interventionist God who had strict moral standards from which His people, either as individuals or in the mass, backslid at their peril. He had chosen them to occupy His promised land, a land flowing with milk and honey such as Handelian Englishmen felt themselves to inhabit. And there was little doubt in the minds of many 18th-century Englishmen that they were the Israelites of their age. They were Christians, and therefore the heirs to God's Kingdom. They were Protestants and therefore defenders of the true Reformed faith against popish superstition and Islamic heresy. Not only was their land a land of freedom and justice, they had expelled the papist tyrant James II, had beaten the might of Louis XIV's armies under Marlborough, had driven out the Roman Catholic usurper (or rightful heir, depending on one's viewpoint) Bonnie Prince Charlie; and their navy as well as their army could take on and defeat all comers – especially the French. (Naval defeats were usually conveniently forgotten and at least one Admiral who failed to engage and defeat the enemy was court-martialled and shot 'pour encourager les autres', as Voltaire was informed).

It was not Handel but Thomas Augustine Arne that most explicitly expressed musically this military (or rather naval) pride in the final chorus of his masque *King Alfred,* also composed, like many of Handel's oratorios, in the early 1740s. But the imperative mood of the text indicates that British command of the seas was regarded as a divine mission:

> When Britain first at heav'ns command
> Arose from out the azure main,
> This was the charter of the land
> And guardian angels sang this strain:
> *Rule, Britannia! Britannia, rule the waves!*
> *Britons never will be slaves!*

We do not know which particular figures, if any, Handel and his librettists may have had in mind when projecting the moods and passions of characters such as Saul, Joshua, Samson and so on. But the situations against the background of which the action is played out are uncannily reminiscent of those obtaining in the England of the 1740s and 1750s. From 1738 onwards, she was constantly at war; and the main, though not the only, enemy was of course France. First, the War of Jenkins' Ear, then the War of the Austrian Succession (1740–1748) and finally the Seven Years' War (1756 – 63) occupied the country and its leaders. One of Handel's finest ceremonial works during this period was composed to celebrate the British victory in the Battle of Dettingen (the last time, incidentally, that a British sovereign led his troops personally into action). Another well-known work – the *Royal Fireworks Music* – was written to celebrate the Peace of Aix-la-Chappelle that ended the War of the Austrian Succession. Handel had been living in a country that had enjoyed twenty years of peace; now that war came, his music identified with the national cause.

Oddly enough, it was through French courtly classical drama that he found his way into oratorio in English. As is well known, his first two oratorios, *Esther* and *Athalia*, were based on biblical plots as adapted towards the end of his career by the great French tragic dramatist Jean Racine. The original version of *Esther* was composed at the time that

Handel was working for the Duke of Chandos. The work was revised and revived in 1732 and successfully performed in London. At this time, Handel was still writing Italian operas; and in July 1733, Handel composed a setting of a version of the second of Racine's biblical dramas for what was known as a 'Publick Act' at Oxford. While it was generally well received at both the performances, there were complaints about 'Handel and his lowsy Crew . . . a great number of foreign fidlers . . . the Theater was erected for other-guise Purposes, than to be prostituted to a Company of squeeking, bawling, out-landish Singsters', which seems to indicate that even though Handel was now English by naturalisation, and that the new work he had composed specially for the occasion was in English, there were some in Oxford that remained chauvinistically dissatisfied. The comment throws an ironic sidelight on the change in aesthetic values since the Restoration. The Puritans regarded the theatre as the haunt of prostitutes but would probably have accepted a musico-dramatic spectacle on a biblical subject. The Age of Reason seems to have regarded a Handelian oratorio as a prostitution of the Temple of Drama, especially if music and foreigners were involved.

There can be little doubt that Handel intended the main parts in *Athalia* to be performed by singers from his opera company and that therefore he saw little formal difference between a staged drama in Italian for the theatre and concert drama in English based on a biblical story. The advantage of oratorio, with its place for grand choruses, was, as Winton Dean has pointed out, that in opera, Handel could bring individuals to life but not nations, whereas in oratorio he could do both. It is this that singles him out as the great representative 'English' musician of his age. Whereas a choral interlude could be exploited by a lesser composer purely as a technical exercise, for Handel its naturally contrapuntal texture was a means to a dramatic end. That this is so can be indicated by the fact that so many of Handel's oratorios have been successfully mounted as stage pieces[26]. The Children of Israel figured

---

[26] It was once the custom for the Cambridge University Musical Society, for example, to stage a Handel oratorio operatically every three years; and Glyndebourne's gripping production of *Theodora,* set in a modern totalitarian state, is but one example of many that might be cited.

prominently in his oratorios; and it was with God's Chosen Race that the audiences were invited to identify.

This is not always the case: in *Athalia*, for example, the children of Israel are never presented as in direct conflict with any heathen race. But in *Deborah* and *Samson*, for example, they are. It was in fact not long before Handel embarked on the composition of *Deborah* in December 1732 that Aaron Hill wrote to him, with an appeal to:

> ... deliver us from our Italian bondage; and demonstrate, that English is soft enough for Opera, when composed by poets, who know how to distinguish the sweetness of our tongue from the strength of it, where the last is less necessary.

Time and again in the oratorios, the monumental choruses make the most immediate impact. The reasons for this are both musical and social. In his oratorios, Handel was able to introduce, illustrate and develop the 'great public moments' of the action, which had perforce to be merely hinted at in his operas. He was able to exploit massive choral effects and the command of English declamation that he had already mastered by the time he composed the Chandos anthems of 1715-17 and, of course, the great coronation anthems of 1727. The main reason why *Zadok the Priest* has featured at every coronation since is its sheer dignity, occasioned by its massive, slow-moving harmonies in the opening chorus and the rollicking 'Hallelujahs' in the closing one. It is dramatic, ceremonial and powerful. It is festive and sturdy. It involves 'the people' not only implicitly but explicitly as well. It is public and monumental. This formula recurs again and again in the oratorios. In the minds of his audiences, Handel's oratorios must have seemed as full-bloodedly English in their form, their sentiments and their ethos as Hogarth's paintings or Fielding's novels. They may not reflect quite so realistically the 'low-life' aspect of their subjects; but they do project a conflict between moral good and evil in terms of one between a virtuous people, or at any rate one striving to obey the will of God, and one that is avowedly (and sometimes voluptuously, even attractively) heathen. Their combination of rugged, yet fluent, counterpoint and sturdy block harmony is a kind of musical equivalent of roast beef and Yorkshire pudding: as wholesome, tasty and spiritually nourishing, especially for the 'involved' listener.

73

The mighty were free, if they wished, to admire and identify with or even despise or pity the individual characters, for even within the ranks of the virtuous, powerful and passionate backsliders such as Saul and Samson, fanatics, waverers and traitors to be found. Baroque opera is often stigmatised as a concert in costume; Handelian oratorio is opera without costume, with not just the individuals but the national background to them vividly portrayed in words and music. The result was that when English composers for nearly a century afterwards wished to strike what theorists called 'the Sublime' note, they could not possibly have found a better model than the giant Saxon. And not only Englishmen: what would the great opening chorus of Beethoven's Mass in D, to say nothing of far less exalted choruses, such as the Hallelujah from *Christ on the Mount of Olives,* be without Handel's example?

Are there, then, certain qualities of Handel's music that we may justifiably claim as specifically English rather than just splendidly baroque or purely Handelian? Or is it perhaps simpler to claim that 18th-century English life was itself Handelian in its robustness, its rational, matter-of-fact elegance, its sense of order, justice and freedom, its bold enterprise, its massive self-confidence, its basic seriousness, its dignity and underlying sensitivity?

Handel's last *opera seria* was a flop for various reasons, not all of them musical. The country was involved in its first war for two decades; public taste was reacting against this kind of opera, and up-and-coming young English composers like Arne and Boyce were attracting attention with their simpler, lighter stage pieces in English. Handel was still in his artistic prime, but having burned any boats that might transport him back into courtly servitude in his native country, he had to make a living in his adopted one. He did so by composing the series of great oratorios on which his fame rested with the generations that succeeded his own. It continued to do so almost unchallenged by any consideration of his other vocal works until the middle of our own century.

He was aware of what one section of his public would respond to. He advised the young Christoph Willibald Gluck when he came to England in 1746:

> What the English like is something they can beat time to, something that hits them straight on the ear.

This he himself continued to provide; yet he made no attempt to invade the lighter English musical theatre that flourished in his lifetime. He did not envisage his oratorios as to be performed as one-offs; he adopted a similar plan when putting them on to that which he had stuck to with his operas – a series run. This would ensure a considerable financial gain for him and his backers, for the same performers could be engaged for the run and, having rehearsed for the first performance, they would not need to rehearse for the others. By this means, *Esther,* for example, made Handel over £700 by the third performance alone.

Not so long ago, English music was said to have been 'crushed by the ponderous genius of Handel' for well over a century. This is nonsense; and the fact that Handel made no attempt to conquer the lighter stage is evidence of the fact. He left it well alone because he was able to make a living in a sphere where his prodigious melodic and technical gifts could find a more potent outlet.

It is also sometimes claimed that one of the landmarks of that theatre, *The Beggar's Opera*, killed Italian opera for the fashionable audiences that had supported it. This, too, is quite untrue. The audiences that flocked to Handel's operas went to hear the magnificent virtuoso singers that he engaged performing heroic, pathetic and amorous arias that he (and others, such as Bononcini) composed for them. Those who went to the lighter pieces (very often the same people) went for different reasons. The singers in these works were actors who could sing. They had to be native English speakers, as the action of the pieces was carried on in spoken dialogue, not sung recitative; and the whole mood and structure of the pieces themselves was less heroic, more 'realistic', less devoted to the action of kings and courtiers and more to that of pastoral or even recognisably contemporary figures. The characters were not symbols, in fact; they were flesh-and-blood individuals of the type so wonderfully brought to life by Mozart in his great da Ponte operas. *The Beggar's Opera* succeeded for the same reasons that the paintings of Hogarth succeeded – and it is not without significance that Hogarth painted pictures of scenes from the piece. Nor is it without significance that of all the musical forms devised in this country, it was the ballad opera that exported most successfully, particularly to the German-speaking world, where it evolved eventually into the *Singspiel* that found its finest exponent in Wolfgang Amadeus Mozart.

The Beggar's Opera held up a mirror not to idealised convention but to harsh reality. It was a thinly disguised satire not just on the squabbles of the self-important stars of the Italian opera, but on the corruption and intrigues of contemporary politicians. It was deliberately anti-heroic, showing up the pretensions to nobility and virtue of the high and mighty, so elegantly idealised in the plots of *opera seria*, for what they often were: posturing and hypocrisy. By invoking the overtones of the word 'opera' itself, the very title of the work underlined the cynicism of the text. In this 'Newgate Pastoral', as the author called it, highwaymen and prostitutes held the stage instead of kings and sorceresses, implying that there was little difference between them, whatever their pretensions to might and majesty. And once it had taken London by storm, the impresario who had made a huge profit from it went into partnership with none other than Handel himself.

Handel was more than a great composer; he was a shrewd impresario and that thing so beloved of Englishmen of all generations, a 'character'. He composed for his own seasons, his own singers and his own public. He assessed 'serious' English taste with such accuracy that he left a fortune comparable in present-day terms, if not to the vast sums earned by Andrew Lloyd Webber, at any rate to someone like Verdi or Rossini in the 19th century. Among his possessions were four paintings by Watteau and others by Andrea del Sarto, Canaletto, Caracci, de Momper, Ostade and Teniers. How many modern 'serious' composers can afford to own a Matisse, a Rouault, a Franz Marc or even a David Hockney, let alone, shall we say, four Corots? In an age of commerce and business expansion, he had an eye for good business and he knew his own value. Fortunately for his adopted countrymen, that value was very high indeed. Unfortunately for them, though there were many who wished to emulate him, there were very few with anything remotely approaching his talent. His music, and particularly his oratorios, stood for several generations as a symbol of all the grandest and most admired features that went to make up the self-image of the aspiring new Chosen Race of the burgeoning Age of Reason. Like the Elizabethans, like Purcell, like the English language itself, he was prepared to be eclectic and cosmopolitan, blending elements taken from a wide range of sources into his own strongly personal and highly expressive idiom. Those of his adopted countrymen who aspired to his sublimity of utterance often mistook, alas, dull ponderousness for genuine weight and empty academic complexity for inspired craftsmanship. But that was hardly Handel's fault.

5 – 'With Fitful Glimmer'

With fitful glimmer burnt my flame,
And I grew cold and coy
  – W S Gilbert: *Trial by Jury*

Throughout the post-Restoration period, as we have seen, the general status of music and the musician in English society was distinctly low. This was in keeping with a shift in values associated with first empiricist and then utilitarian philosophy. It was also part of a widespread suspicion in polite society of excess emotion – or excess anything, come to that.

Music appealed, in some cases very strongly, to the senses. Indeed, as those Puritans susceptible to its power such as John Milton and the Lord Protector himself would have been the first to admit, it could induce a mysterious quasi-sexual ecstasy in those receptive to it. It was this quality that made many Puritans ambivalent to music. It could inspire a congregation or an army and be the instrument of thanksgiving for victory after a battle, provided it was simple enough to be performed by a massed body. But the intricate polyphony of pre-Commonwealth church music was suspect on two counts. Firstly, it was too complex to be readily understood or performed by the untrained; and secondly, it was associated with Laudian ceremonial and tainted with 'popery'. Yet, as we have seen, the Lord Protector loved the polyphonic music of the English Catholic emigrés Deering and Shepherd and frequently had their anthems performed for him.

This was not a matter of hypocrisy. Many of the Puritans, like many of the cavalier courtiers, were undoubtedly philistines. So were many of their 18th-century successors. The Puritan philistines, however, revelled in the destruction of works of art and church and cathedral organs and other musicalia such as anthem parts. Cromwell himself was not a philistine – and neither were certain important members of his entourage. Again, we have seen how, under the Puritan regime, the first English operas were staged – and we have also noted that instead of allegorical, legendary or mythical figures, their plots concerned real-life events: *The Siege of Rhodes*, with its doughty Christian resistance to Muslim attack; *The Cruelty of the Spaniards in Peru*; and – most notably of all – *The History of Sir Francis Drake*, an English (and protestant) hero fighting against and defeating the Spanish (and Roman Catholic) hosts. A sense of national pride was being re-kindled and music was to be an important element in fanning the flames. Moreover, a definite ethos underlay these pieces: they were political propaganda – anti-Muslim and anti-catholic. That they were permitted to be staged at all indicates how they must have been viewed by a ruling clique that kept the theatres closed for the performance of 'straight' drama – not, one suspects, because the representation of actions on the stage before an audience was in itself immoral, but because the theatres were not only the setting for the plays but also for the activities of pickpockets and prostitutes. With the Restoration, the theatre again soon re-acquired more than a ghost of this reputation. Anyone connected with it ran the risk of being in its shadow, unless he was well in with the upper crust.

In 1711, in *The Spectator*, which did so much to influence taste and deportment in the Augustan age, we find Addison condescendingly claiming:

> Music is certainly a very agreeable Entertainment but if it would take the entire Possession of our Ears, it would make us incapable of hearing Sense, if it would exclude the Arts that have a much greater Tendency to the Refinement of Human nature; I must confess I would allow it no better Quarter than *Plato* has done, who banished it out of his Common-wealth.

But perhaps Addison was somewhat *parti pris* about the idea of music 'taking complete possession of our ears': his one attempt at writing an operatic libretto had been a complete flop, thanks to the incompetent composer, Thomas Clayton, who was chosen to set it. Then we have that censorious arbiter of 18th-century taste, Lord Chesterfield, in his *Letters to his Son* of 1749:

> [Music] puts a gentleman in a very frivolous contemptible light; brings him into a great deal of bad company; and takes up a great deal of time, which might be better employed.

The same might of course be said of gambling, prize-fighting and whoring, all recognised pursuits of the eighteenth-century upper classes.

The eighteenth century is also usually labelled the Age of Reason; and so, up to a point, it was. It was an age when the best minds of Europe were intent on reducing the principles of life as far as possible to a system and an order that was as far as possible logical and self-regulating. The scientific and physical laws of the universe had, it was thought, been given orderly and mathematical expression in the ideas of Newton. In 17th-century France, Descartes had evolved a philosophy that enthroned deductive human reason as the power that could account for everything, provided that the philosophical issues were reduced to clear, distinct and discrete ideas. In Germany, Leibnitz had capped that by developing a philosophical system that, based on mathematical reasoning, led to an argument that all was for the best in the best of possible worlds. He also gave a succinct definition of music as 'a subconscious act of counting by the mind'. This definition draws attention to the regular patterned beat of metre and rhythm – otherwise any act of counting would be impossible – but it does not account for the 'affective' nature of music: its impact on the emotions and the power of melody and harmony.

In the biological sciences, too, the Age of Order had dawned. Great systematisers such as the Swedish botanist Linnaeus built up the categories by which plants, insects, birds and mammals are classified to this day and cleared the ground for systematic foundations on which were developed the theory of evolution a hundred years later. In painting, sculpture, architecture and interior design, the massive ornate majesty of the baroque gave way first to the elegant frivolity of the rococo and then – perhaps even simultaneously, following a line established in the 17th-century Netherlands – to the earthy, ribald realism of Hogarth in England, the sober good sense of painters such as Chardin in France and the controlled elegance of Gainsborough and Reynolds, in whose work the iron fist of passion is safely contained within the velvet glove of well-modulated lines and colour patterns. Gainsborough, by the way, was an enthusiastic amateur musician and one of his most interesting portraits was of J S Bach's youngest son, Johann Christian, who settled in London in 1762 and died there twenty years later[27]. Even in horticulture, the contrived grandeur and grace of the Italian baroque garden was opposed by the relaxed and 'natural' open parkland of the English landscape garden designed by artists like Kent and Capability Brown. The more formal urban garden found its niche as the pleasure garden – with music providing one of its numerous amenities for recreation and dalliance.

Logical, geometrical order seemed to hold sway throughout the universe. Nature herself was orderly and could be tamed and brought under man's control. She was also in many senses predictable, so the key-words 'natural' and 'rational' came to be regarded as two sides of the same coin. The expression of strong emotion was to be controlled or allowed only moderate indulgence. In polite society, morality was essentially a matter of good form – sometimes equated with surface appearances and therefore suspect as hypocrisy – good manners and style. If the art of the age was at times cool, prosaic and rather superficial, this was the price it had to pay for being well-shaped, balanced and urbane. English literature of the period has little to offer in the way of genuinely heartfelt lyric poetry, though much in the way of elegant wit and well-turned pastoral charm. The essays of Steele and Addison, the tendentious moralising of Richardson, the boisterous realism of Fielding and the satires of Pope represent the main stream; the exuberant surrealism of Sterne and the sombre meditations of Gray and Young are tributaries that generated the powerful and passionate currents of a later age. There was also the newly established and sometimes exhilarating, though certainly less edifying and by no means uplifting, stock market. And in England, at any rate, there was the additional factor that the 18th century saw her transformation from a small and pugnacious trading nation into a major world power, with colonies in every continent and trade following – even in some cases preceding – the flag.

The claims of the passions and of the darker aspects of the human psyche were not of course to be totally denied. In a remarkable letter dated September 1739, Thomas Gray draws attention to the thrilling

---

[27] Having in the meantime become one of Gainsborough's favourite drinking companions.

'sublime' and untamed aspects of what he calls a 'romantic' landscape. The restraint and urbanity of the social norms of the age and the tolerant attitude of 'love and let live' permitted – encouraged, even – political corruption and gerrymandering and financial chicanery. Hogarth's famous series: *The Rake's Progress, The Election, The Harlot's Progress* and *Marriage à la Mode* reflect the grim realities of the time: gambling, whoring and bribery; and its calculated scepticism was upset in the 1740s by the stirring of the Methodist conscience, when a lackadaisical church was shaken by the zeal and fervour of a group of itinerant preachers both from within and from without the ranks of the established church. The growth of population led to urban slums, the prosperity engendered by increased maritime trade with markets outside Europe and by emergent industrialisation was also a prosperity based to a considerable measure on the slave-trade organised and conducted from such ports as Liverpool and Bristol. The self-satisfied intellectual torpor of the two major English universities was offset and challenged by the ferment of activity in the Scottish universities, especially Edinburgh, of the dissenting academies and by societies such as the Lunar Society in the Midlands that met to discuss and disseminate new ideas on scientific matters.

But even Nature was not quite as totally explicable as mankind would have wished. Disasters such as the great Lisbon earthquake of 1756 could hardly be explained away on a basis of 'Whatever is, is right' – an adage directly quoted in Handel's *Jephtha*, an echo indeed of Leibnizian optimism. Virtue, far from being its own Richardsonian reward, had to triumph over the uncertainties of human existence and the vice and frailty of the human character. The dark and selfish side of human nature was explained away as far as possible, though, as modern critics have pointed out, it is there if you look for it carefully enough in the art of the time. And the more man discovered about the power of nature and the scale of the universe, the more he tried to harness her power to drive the engines of his mines and factories, the more mysterious she became, though she was of course still rational.

As long, however, as an art-form could pay its way, the English leisured classes considered it an acceptable amenity. Johnson's definition of Italian opera accords well with the assessment of music given by Addison and quoted above. The noun – 'entertainment' – that Johnson chooses is at least as significant as the adjectives 'exotick and irrational'. For him, it would seem, opera was not a grand emotional experience: it was a diverting pastime. The public (by which we mean the leisured classes) paid to see and hear Handel's singers; which meant that they sat through his magnificent operas, sung, of course, in Italian; and they went expecting and prepared to pay for spectacular vocal displays. The thrill that these singers undoubtedly evoked in their audiences was not rational; and therefore it was either suspect or inferior to the urbane elegance of other aspects of the arts. The stricture matters. It was mainly as an opera composer that Handel made his reputation in England; between his arrival here in 1711 and 1742, when he composed his last opera, he wrote thirty-nine operas and only three oratorios. His only other major sacred compositions – and they were sporadic enough – were the four coronation anthems for George II, the eleven splendid anthems for the Duke of Chandos, and the *Utrecht Te Deum*.

After the failure of his last Italian opera in 1742, Handel, who, remember, was a business-man – an impresario – as well as one of the greatest composers of all time, had to seek another way of earning his living. He had to: although he had a useful pension from the monarch and became enough of a national figure to merit a memorial in Westminster Abbey, he was in no sense a court composer, part of the court musical establishment. He was accepted in the company of the intelligentsia and even patronised by the aristocracy, but he was also part of the world of commerce. He did not seek to emulate some of his English contemporaries by writing for the light commercial stage, however. He found something both to exploit his skill as a dramatic composer and to replenish his bank account through oratorio.

The nation state, with defined geographical, linguistic and demographic boundaries, was beginning to emerge as a viable political system in Europe. With the awareness of our national identity and a sense that Britain had a place in the world over and above occupying and exploiting her geographical position, there arose a definite linking of the arts to our national heritage and destiny. As we have already seen, the supreme examples of this in music were Handel's magnificent Old Testament oratorios, the plots of which enabled his audiences to identify with the Chosen People of God and their leaders: Joshua, Judas Maccabæus, Saul (the flawed king destined to be succeeded by David), Solomon, the grand but human monarch, the People Chosen by God first to win their own liberty and then to extend it (*Israel in Egypt*), and so on. Handel and his librettists also made a definite attempt to link up with the great literary heritage of the previous century, as in *L'Allegro* and *Samson*, the latter of course neatly combining Old Testament virtue with a doffing of the artistic cap towards Milton.

It was the deceptively simple majesty – what later 18th-century theorists were to define as sublimity – of Handel's awesomely magnificent and straightforward melodic style that immediately captivated his audiences; and it was that aspect of his style that seems to be most markedly reflected in the works of his lesser English contemporaries. Another of his stylistic modes – that of the graceful Italianate pastoral, also became common musical currency, while the sturdy and not too complex contrapuntal textures of his choruses became the stock-in-trade of any church composer wishing to write music on an elevated or sublime scale. In the last decade of his life there were a number of works on overtly patriotic themes, such as Arne's revised version of *King Alfred* and the same composer's *Eliza*. Boyce's *Heart of Oak*, still used as the ceremonial march-past of the Royal Navy, came from a stage work of 1759 (the year of victories). These composers did not need to use the stories of the Old Testament as allegories, enabling the audience to draw parallels between the chosen people of ancient Israel and the modern chosen race of protestant Britain. They provided overt examples of that national propaganda that sprouted in the age of Cromwell and emerged fitfully in the public theatres with works such as the Dryden/Purcell *King Arthur* during the Restoration period.

Strangely enough, the light stage pieces had their roots in the Commonwealth era, too. It was during the Commonwealth that the first printed publications of popular folk- and dance-tunes appeared. In 1651, John Playford published his first such collection. It was reprinted twice under Cromwell and continued to be popular under the Restoration and beyond, providing an arsenal of catchy tunes to be plundered by serious musicians such as Dr Pepusch for Gay's *The*

Beggar's Opera and other ballad operas, a practice that continued throughout the eighteenth century. Other, more scurrilous, publications, such as *Pills to Purge Melancholy,* were to follow; but the kind of music associated with them was emphatically different from the more solemn airs and graces of the mid-baroque style. None the less, Purcell was not above employing such tunes (suitably adapted and disguised) in his serious compositions; nor was he, as we have seen, above composing light-hearted catches and rounds to suitably scatological words, underlining *double-entendre* in the text by providing suitable places for apparently innocent words to appear in scurrilous juxtaposition. But, as with the use to which popular airs were put by Tudor and Jacobean composers, this did not constitute a basis for a new or native style.

The shape and cut of many a lighter tune by a 'serious' composer such as Arne or Boyce was surely influenced by the lilt and balance of these popular melodies. Arne's highly successful *Comus* of 1738 and *Thomas and Sally* (1761), for example, contain quite a number – in fact a surfeit – of catchy tunes in a dancing metre. Later on, in the 1770s, there came a veritable craze for the folk-melodies themselves – and even comic servants speaking regional dialects – in the lighter stage pieces. There was also at the same time (a parallel, incidentally, with the more or less contemporary *Sturm und Drang* movement in German literature), a vogue for 'outlaw' heroes – perhaps an echo of *The Beggar's Opera,* but no doubt also reflecting topical protests about contemporary political corruption or injustice. The outlaw-as-hero turns up, for example, in Arnold's *The Banditti* (1781) and Shield's *Robin Hood* (1784). Storace wrote an opera called *The Pirates* (1792), which Roger Fiske rates as his best work; and there is also a 'noble savage': ie, King Alfred in disguise – in *The Noble Peasant,* also by Shield and also dating from 1784.

The main composers to use this kind of material were William Shield (1748–1829) and Samuel Arnold (1740–1804). For example, in Arnold's *Castle of Andalusia,* there is a version of a tune that Cecil Sharp later collected as 'The Poacher'. Shield seems to have been particularly fond of 'Comin' thro' the Rye', variants of which are used in the overture to *The Nunnery* (1785) and *Rosina* 1782). The latter was the most popular opera at Covent Garden in the 1780s and was an instant money-spinner. The song 'Her mouth' may be described as a Shieldified folk-melody. Shield also used English traditional tunes in his pantomimes. A version of the folk-carol collected by Vaughan Williams in 1909 as 'The Truth Sent from Above' turns up in Arnold's *The Children in the Wood* (1793). And in Linley's *The Spanish Rivals* (1784) there is a comic Cumberland servant who speaks dialect and sings two folk-songs. The texts of both of these were almost certainly contributed by the librettist Mark Lonsdale, who came from Cumberland and published an anthology of dialect poems in 1839. There was thus much interest in folk-melodies, as there was in folk-poetry and ballads; but no attempt to integrate them into a 'national' musical style. That kind of treatment was to be an outcrop of Romanticism; and as one of the other components of Romanticism in this country (and elsewhere) was the cult of 'exotic' highland Scotland, it was the Scottish airs that were highlighted.

The music for these pieces remained comparatively unsophisticated, related more to the ballad opera than to the vocal pyrotechnics of *opera seria*. The singers required for their production were essentially native artistes whose main priorities were the ability to act and speak their native English clearly and convincingly. The ability to sing was a bonus; to sing difficult coloratura passages a blessing. Handel's Italian virtuosi were clearly ruled out of court on at least two of these counts. Besides, they would never have condescended to accept the fees offered by the companies staging the lighter pieces. But English singers were capable of managing his technically demanding parts, as the arias – and indeed the choruses – in his oratorios amply demonstrate.

Yet in 1762 Arne actually composed an *opera seria* in English. *Artaxerxes*, to a libretto of his own, was based on one written in Italian by the Viennese court poet Metastasio, one of the most prolific and gifted of operatic librettists of the century. It was a considerable success; when Haydn saw it some thirty years after its first performance, he was much impressed. Jane Austen, on the other hand, who saw a performance in 1814, found it boring. Tastes change, it is true, but the refined chronicler of upper-class matrimonial manoeuvrings among the country gentry and the subtleties of the characters involved in them would hardly have been much interested in the conspiracies of flamboyant, larger-than-life baroque political figures. Nor would she have been much taken by Arne's quite impressive musical heroics: the jigging rhythms of his lighter pieces would have been much more to her exquisite taste, as her own musical library indicates.

The revival of interest in the popular idiom had its beginnings in Scotland in the 1720s; and it was a mistake often made by romantic and post-romantic musicians (including our own) to believe that only the Celtic races of the United Kingdom had preserved native music of any value. Johann Christian Bach, for example, quotes a Scottish tune in the finale of one of his keyboard concertos composed for London; and James Hook does the same with what has become known as 'Scotland the Brave' in one of his. That the Celtic fringe was not the only source of good tunes is amply demonstrated by the appearance of tunes of undoubtedly English origin in light stage pieces in the latter part of the eighteenth century.

But the main use to which the 'popular' type of tune was put was undoubtedly the expression of idyllic pastoral innocence, whether of atmosphere or of mood. It was more 'natural' (ie, more easily memorable) than the roulades and motor-rhythms of the baroque display aria; it provided, in fact, a musical counterpart to emparked country-house garden landscapes designed by Kent and Capability Brown, immortalised on canvas by George Lambert and above all Gainsborough, and the somewhat artificial sighing after a simple country lifestyle of the sophisticated and essentially urban poets of the Hanoverian age.

There was at least some spark of ambition amongst English composers to cash in on the vogue for serious opera, which underwent something of a revival after Handel's death. It may well have been the combination of the removal of Handel and the interest of the upper-class public in the musically less elaborate 'galant' kind of serious opera of the kind purveyed by composers such as Johann Christian Bach, who arrived in London in 1762, prompted Arne to try his hand at an *opera seria* in English. As we have seen, *Artaxerxes* was an unprecedented success; but it was something of a flash in the pan; and Arne's attempt in 1765 to follow it up for the King's Theatre at the Haymarket with a suitable companion piece, *Olimpiade*, was a flop, possibly because this time he set a Metastasio libretto in the original Italian. The august Dr Burney (himself a pupil of Arne and possibly the composer of some of the airs attributed to his teacher) somewhat priggishly commented:

> The doctor had kept bad company: that is, had written for vulgar singers and hearers too long to be able to comport himself properly at the Opera-house, in the first circle of taste and fashion. . . . The common play-house and ballad passages, which occurred in almost every air in his opera, made the audience wonder how they got there.

This surely indicates what Burney must have considered the hierarchy of theatrical taste. Burney goes on to point out:

> . . . a different language, different singers, and a different audience, and style of Music, from his own, carried him out of his usual element, where he mangled the Italian poetry, energies, and accents, nearly as much as a native of Italy just arrived in London, would English, in a similar situation.

Burney mentions the 'different audience'. Italian opera required a strong financial commitment on the part of those who invested in its splendours. This meant in turn that it should attract a sufficiently enthusiastic and committed audience to offer them a viable return. Handel had managed this in the 1720s, but by the middle of the century, demand for this kind of opera was fading all over Europe; and though the advent of a new composer, such as Johann Christian Bach, or of a new style of music might give it a sporadic shot in the arm, no consistent tradition could be built up in London, where neither composers nor librettists were part of the established personnel at an absolutist court: salaried or stipendiary civil servants, in fact.

Arne also tinkered about with the work of earlier composers, notably Purcell, when the great actor-manager David Garrick revived *King Arthur* at Drury Lane in 1770. He described Purcell's songs as:

> infamously bad – so very bad, that they are privately the objects of sneer and ridicule to the Musicians; but I have not meddled with any, that are not come from the mouths of your principal Performers.

Like many another age before and since, the later eighteenth century knew where it stood in matters of taste both of its own age and of its predecessors! This sounds to us inadmissibly condescending and cavalier, to say the least, yet a contemporary composer of popular ballad operas to whom we shall come shortly, Thomas Dibdin, writing in 1788, maintained that Arne:

> . . . so far from mutilating Purcell, as a modern compiler would have done, with proper reverence for such great abilities, his whole study was to place his idolized predecessor in that conspicuous situation, the brilliancy of his reputation demanded.

In other words, to use an anachronistic term borrowed from another art, he bowdlerised him into the acceptable norms of 18th-century post-Handelian style.

Some of Arne's own contributions to Garrick's Shakespeare productions have deservedly survived. They may not be profound, but they are tuneful and reflect a simple, popular yet sophisticated musical idiom well abreast of the *galant* style that had superseded the baroque on the continent.

Perhaps the most remarkable contribution to musical settings of Shakespeare comes, however, not from London, nor even from Stratford-upon-Avon, but from Bath; and it comes from a composer whose career was tragically cut short by drowning in a sailing accident when he was only 22. In a letter dated 21 April 1770, Leopold Mozart wrote to his wife:

> In Florence we came across a young Englishman, who is a pupil of the famous violinist Nardini. This boy, who *plays most beautifully* and who is the same age as Wolfgang, came to the house of the learned poetess, Signora Corilla, where we happened to be on the introduction of M. De L'Augier. The two boys performed one after the other throughout the whole evening, constantly embracing each other. On the following day, the little Englishman, a most charming boy, had his violin brought to our rooms and played the whole afternoon, Wolfgang accompanying him on his own. On the next day we lunched with M. Gavard, the administrator of the grand ducal finances, and these two boys played in turn the whole afternoon, not like boys, but like men! Little Tommaso accompanied us home and wept bitter tears, because we were leaving on the following day.

Thomas Linley was born in 1756 – the same year as Mozart – and it is of some interest that both Mozart and he were teen-agers when they met. It is perhaps of equal interest that young Thomas's father was a composer himself and that his sister married the brilliant Anglo-Irish playwright Richard Brinsley Sheridan. Now anyone who has read Mozart's letters will know that he did not suffer fools gladly and he could be scathing about the talents – or lack of them – of other musicians. It would appear from the above that he and Linley got on very well together, playing one another's violin sonatas, each playing the fiddle and the keyboard parts in turn. Linley seems to have absorbed the elements of what may be called Viennese proto-classicism with ease; and by the time he was twenty, he was a composer of great promise and considerable achievement. Mozart himself said so. He told his first Don Basilio, the Irish singer Michael Kelly, that Linley was a true genius who, had he lived, would have been one of the greatest ornaments of the musical world. And the evidence is there in Linley's remarkable music to *The Tempest* and his short oratorio *The Song of Moses*. It is not so much the originality of this work that impresses the modern listener, with its interesting blend of massive Handelian choruses and *galant* arias, as its ability not merely to aim at the sublime but actually to achieve it. Here, if anywhere, is a composer who could marry the contrapuntal style and sublime block-choral effects of Handelian oratorio with the dramatic harmonic tensions and their graceful resolutions of the newly-developing *galant* idiom introduced to this country by Johann Christian Bach. This is particularly noticeable in such movements as the chorus 'The sea is before them' from *The Song of Moses*.

A further example of this potential to be found among Linley's compositions was a suite of incidental music to Shakespeare's *The Tempest*. This opens with a storm chorus of considerable imaginative power and originality. Had he lived, it is more than likely that he would have composed operas in English that would have rivalled those of his brilliant young Austrian friend in German and Italian. After all, by the time he was twenty-two, even Mozart's incomparable genius had still not developed to the full, though his technical skill was already equal to such demands as were made on it; and if Purcell had died at twenty-two, we should remember him only by his instrumental fantasias and trio sonatas – a mere fraction of his prodigious output. Linley, too, it seems, 'had what it takes'; but he was fated never to do more than demonstrate his immense promise rather than his mature achievement.

Linley was, like Mozart and Handel themselves, aware of what kind of idiom best suited what kind of emotional context; and he had the force of character to weld something of his own out of the disparate sources that he had mastered so early in his short life. But then again, musical conditions being what they were in late 18th-century England, he might simply have been tempted to take the line of least resistance. Even so, I would go so far as to say that his death was an even more grievous loss to English music than that of Purcell, for it was a musician of precisely his stature, imagination and technical achievement that the English musical stage needed to raise its standards from that of a mere adjunct to the straight theatre to that of an equal partner with it. Even as it was, English singers proved that they could match their continental colleagues: were not the Susanna, Nancy Storace, and the Don Basilio, Michael Kelly, in the first performance of Mozart's *Figaro* both British?

For all that, some of the music produced for the lighter stage repertoire was by no means to be sneered at. Perhaps the most successful composer of such pieces was Charles Dibdin (1745–1814). Dibdin was more or less self-taught as a composer and began his career as a singer in the chorus at the Covent Garden theatre. By 1770, he was much in demand as an actor-singer and as a composer, writing a series of successful comic operas for Drury Lane and Ranelagh Gardens, the second of London's three main pleasure gardens. Peter Holman says of him: ˙

> . . . he was capable of poor, hasty work, and he never had much interest in setting serious words or writing for instruments. Yet at his best he was unsurpassed in matching comic situations to vividly appropriate music which is often forward-looking and unconventional in melody, harmony and phrase-structure. And he was the first English composer to grasp the full implications of the *galant* style, with the matching of simple directional harmonies to charming melodies, often of a folk-like cast.

One, indeed, of Dibdin's more pathetic melodies, *Tom Bowling*, written as a tribute to a beloved brother who had died, has become almost a folk-song; and works like his black comedy *The Ephesian Matron*, described as a 'comic serenata' and composed for a 'Jubilee ridotto' at Ranelagh in May 1769, are worth revival on the modern stage. This delightful piece has a plot based to a considerable degree on that of Pergolesi's *La serva padrona*; and in it, Dibdin sends up to considerable effect some of the conventions of *opera seria*, such as distraught mad scenes, and introduces comic devices such as the patter aria and the dramatic ensemble.

In fact, one significant contributory factor to the development of a quasi-British musical dialect, if not quite a genuinely national style, was the rise of the pleasure garden. Here, music was an important component of the proceedings. Sometimes – as in Boyce's splendid serenata *Solomon* – it was intended to be listened to seriously. More frequently, it formed an agreeable background to dalliance of a less exalted kind, or at best an aid to polite or scurrilous conversation. The most famous of these gardens, at Vauxhall, had been opened to the public in 1732 with a *Ridotto al fresco*: an outdoor entertainment with music. The gardens themselves combined pseudo-gothic and pseudo-Chinese architecture with an expensive display of paintings in the various 'supper boxes'. There were also neatly-planted grottos and 'rural' walks and the whole site was dotted with statues and ornaments. Here, we may detect a style of music-making comparable with that of the outdoor serenades and divertimenti that feature among the lighter works of composers like Haydn and Mozart. The music could be listened to from close at hand, or it could simply impinge vaguely on the consciousness while other pleasures were enjoyed as it wafted across the evening air. A feature of the gardens was the organ; and keyboard concertos performed on the organ, whose sound carried much better in the open air than a harpsichord or fortepiano, were nearly always part of the musical proceedings. Some of the English practitioners of this style, such as James Hook, have a musical personality of their own. One of Hook's songs, indeed, *The Lass of Richmond Hill*, has often been taken for a folk-song.

The musical fare was varied and usually tasteful, though rarely profound: the same might be said of the divertimenti of Mozart and Haydn. Many of the songs performed at Vauxhall were published in anthologies, usually with a figured-bass line and an *ad lib* part for a wind instrument (normally a recorder). Gentlemen did not normally play keyboard instruments; that was left to their spouses or daughters. One such collection from the 1760s contains *I'll assure you, The Maid's*

Confession, Pretty Molly, The Yorkshireman's Resolution to Fight the French, The New Robin Hood and *John Barleycorn*. The liveliness of these themes stimulated the festive atmosphere, like others of the paintings which depicted *A shepherd playing on his pipe and decoying a shepherdess into a wood, Music and Singing, Players on bagpipes and hautboys* and *The kiss stolen*.

What was it that Shakespeare wrote in *Twelfth Night* about music being the food of love? But was this quite the kind of love that he had in mind?

Sometimes, the most promising musicians came from an unexpected source. Prominent among these were the two sons of the great Methodist hymn-writer Charles Wesley. Charles Wesley was younger brother of John Wesley, who founded the movement. Both of his sons early demonstrated considerable musical gifts. Certainly the more gifted of the two was the elder lad, Samuel. By his late teens he was composing fluently in the *galant* style that had developed during the century. At least one of the symphonies, that in D, which he composed and published at the age of 18 after the model of J C Bach, has a striking individuality of its own. The charm and suavity of this piece pays tribute to its model; but the more vital inner passages and open textures, eschewing the throbbing effects so loved of the Mannheim school and the *galant* composers in favour of more motoric rhythms, betray both Wesley's conservatism and his contrapuntal leanings. There is in fact a robust vigour about the two faster movements that lacks the polish of the *galant* composers in favour of a tougher, more sturdy rhythmic drive. There is also a certain squareness and shortness of breath about the secondary material that is more than made up for by Wesley's imaginative working-out section. It is a pity that there was not more of a demand to be met for English symphonies; after all, most of Mozart's and all of Haydn's symphonies composed up to and including their eighteenth year can be safely discounted: the same cannot be held totally true of Samuel Wesley's, though Charles's show less strength and originality.

The Wesley brothers also composed chamber music – Charles's string quartets in particular are attractive and are clearly aimed at a less technically skilled and musically sophisticated public than those of

Haydn and the young Mozart – but it was not unexpectedly in the field of church music that Samuel in particular excelled, as we shall shortly see.

Church music was in general at a low ebb. For one thing, there was little money in it. Cathedrals and colleges cut back on expenditure on music and good musicians either combined a cathedral post with some other activity, such as teaching or writing for the theatre, or sought employment at a large city church where the duties were lighter but where standards could be maintained. The style remained conservative to the point of being moribund. For another, the age was one in which the established church was content to leave things as they were. The cosy deism of so many eighteenth-century intellectuals was such that the Anglican church was accepted because it was the state church and didn't make too many demands on its adherents. Those places in its liturgy where music was inserted to embellish the service were exploited more as a matter of custom than as one of devotion. Anthems were composed, but on nowhere approaching the scale of Purcell's fine Chapel Royal pieces, let alone Handel's *Chandos Anthems*. Yet within the constraints of the Anglican anthem, some attractive pieces were composed. Most full anthems, however, seem to follow a conventional pattern of alternating contrapuntal passages with sections in block chords, and verse anthems seem to have done little that Purcell had not already done better.

Boyce, who straddled the gap between light theatre and serious church compositions, also compiled an impressive anthology of English cathedral music from various sources from the Tudor period to his own time and it is to his endeavours that we owe quite a number of pieces that had been preserved previously only in manuscript form. It was published in three volumes, in 1760, 1768 and 1773, a revised and enlarged edition being published with Samuel Arnold as editor in 1790, the same year as an abortive complete edition of Purcell's anthems was launched. Boyce's own church compositions are worthy rather than great; and his best efforts in this field are to be found in his ceremonial odes and anthems composed for special occasions.

Yet all was not smug complacency, either in the Anglican church or in its music. The church was shaken out of its torpor from the 1740s onward by the movement known as Methodism. Methodism, with its emphasis on individual conversion and repentance, appealed primarily not to the cool intellect but to the emotions; and from the very start of their movement, Methodists encouraged hearty congregational singing as the spontaneous expression of joy in religious conversion and guilt and repentance for sin. Many Methodist hymns were intended to be sung in four or more parts and others were, like so many reformist hymn-tunes from earlier eras, adapted from popular airs. Methodist congregations became used to singing not in block chords but in interweaving parts, with rolling, quite elaborate counterpoints to the main tune; and it was from the Methodist choirs that the great Victorian amateur choral societies were to draw many of their members in the industrial north and Midlands in the 19th century. The older of the two Wesley brothers, Samuel, was in fact one of the most gifted composers of church music since the days of Purcell. One problem was that he composed it, not for his father's branch of the protestant church, but for the Anglican and Roman Catholic rites. Moreover, he was a somewhat bizarre character, deserting his wife for a mistress to whom he remained constant for the rest of his life and converting to Roman Catholicism. His younger brother Charles seems to have fizzled out completely as a composer after his early promise.

Domestic and amateur music-making and concert life remained lively, however. There is evidence of this in the considerable body of chamber music that came out during the century. None of it is great, but much of it is good, solid, middle-of-the-road late baroque stuff, based on the forms established by Corelli and developed by Handel rather than on the more regular three- and four- movement works familiar from the output of Vivaldi and Bach. The concerti grossi of the Newcastle composer Thomas Avison and Boyce's splendid Trio Sonatas are among the most distinguished of these compositions. Avison in particular, a pupil and great admirer of the Italian composer Geminiani, had a decided gift for graceful and attractive melody and sturdy counterpoint.

But the tradition for domestic convivial vocal music-making continued. The quality may sometimes have been questionable, but there can be no doubt as to the quantity. Some of the gifted amateurs who enjoyed taking part in performances (often organised to raise money for charities) even composed works to be performed at them. One such musician, the solicitor John Marsh (1752–1828), disregarded the strictures laid by fashionable arbiters of public taste on 'gentleman-fiddlers' and not only performed but also composed, and kept a detailed diary of his activities. He even played in the orchestra at Drury Lane; and in 1784, the orchestra at Ranelagh Gardens played some of his overtures. His diary has many comments on the music-making in which he was involved. Here he is, for example, describing the church music at Bishop's Waltham, near Southampton, where he had moved in 1766:

> ... besides the Psalms, which were well sung in 4 parts, we had almost always a verse Anthem of an Afternoon & sometimes a Solo for Counter Tenor of which kind there was then a very good Singer. They also used generally to practise after Evening Service, which I (with a few of the Congregation & particularly old Mr Horner) used generally to stay & hear and was much pleased; the effect of singing in 4 parts accompanied by a soft Organ, being quite new to me.

Very often, and until quite late into the 19th century, the singing in country churches was accompanied not on the organ but by a small village band of half a dozen or so players. Not until the 1760s were there organs in all the City of London's churches and as late as 1790 only one of the twenty-eight parishes in York had a church organ.

Societies abounded both in the capital and elsewhere, where men of fashion would gather for an evening's music interspersed with drinking – or perhaps an evening's drinking interspersed with music-making. The pieces performed were usually composed in galant block harmonies; and one society perhaps deserves special mention for what would nowadays be called its 'theme-music'. This was the Anacreontic Society, founded in 1766, which prefaced all its meetings with a performance of a part-song by John Stafford Smith called *Anacreon, rise!* The words do not matter all that much today; what is of interest is the fact that Frances Scott Key took the tune and set new words to it. It has long since been familiar in the USA as *The Star-spangled banner*.

Concert life was dominated by the series of concerts run on a subscription basis by Johann Christian Bach and his friend Carl Friedrich Abel – another pothouse crony of the painter Gainsborough.

The Wesley brothers emulated them with a series of their own in the 1780s. The other interesting series of concerts was that of the Academy of Ancient Music, which had a rule that no composition could be performed at them that was not at least twenty years old. It is an interesting commentary on London's enterprising musical life in the later 18th century that any concert-giving body that gave music so up-to-date nowadays would probably go bankrupt within one season. These concerts brought before London audiences many of the latest compositions of continental masters, notably the two organisers themselves, but also of course exponents of the new style such as Joseph Haydn. And it was to Haydn that London turned in 1790 when looking for music of the highest calibre for a knowledgeable and appreciative audience. He did not, as we shall see, write down to his audience; in fact, the twelve symphonies he wrote for London were the wittiest and most sophisticated of his entire output. That in itself speaks volumes for the genuine music-lovers who flocked to hear his music.

6 – Paying for it

'The Italians and the Germans compose music; the English pay for it'
— Heinrich Heine

The London that welcomed Joseph Haydn in 1790 was the largest commercial centre in Europe. It was also the capital of a country that was rapidly developing into the first major industrial power and the centre of what was eventually to be the largest empire that the world had ever seen. Moreover, it was the place where every transaction was carried on in the language native to Shakespeare, Milton and the translators of the Authorised Version of the Bible, a language destined to become not just a literary instrument but a world medium of communication. And although Haydn did not as yet speak a word of it, as his friend Mozart pointed out, it did not matter: 'The language my music speaks,' Haydn said, 'is understood everywhere.'

He was certainly right as far as London was concerned. He came to a country that was to provide him not just commercial success and consolidate his widespread fame, but one where the music-loving public genuinely understood his music better than any other that he had served. His works had been familiar to the London musical public since at least 1772, when several of them went on sale in Britain. In 1781, Johann Christian Bach had introduced his symphony No 53 at one of his subscription concerts; and as the incomparable Haydn scholar H C Robbins Landon observes, 'it turned into the hit of the year and was played in piano arrangements[28] by every cultivated young lady throughout the kingdom.' This was so much the case that a definite

---

[28] One suspects he means 'keyboard' arrangements; even in London the harpsichord had not been replaced by the piano, though the square piano was beginning to become fashionable in middle-class drawing-rooms and harpsichords tended to be owned only by professional musicians.

attempt was made to attract Haydn himself to London the following year (1782); and three of his symphonies, Nos 76-78, were composed for the projected visit. His employer, Prince Nicholas of Esterhazy, however, vetoed the trip; and London did not make his personal acquaintance until nearly a decade later. This caused some consternation in the city, to the extent of a paragraph in the *Gazetteer & New Daily Advertiser* in January 1785 which ran as follows:

> There is something very distressing to a liberal mind in the history of Haydn. This wonderful man, who is the Shakespeare of music, and the triumph of the age in which we live, is doomed to reside in the court of a miserable German Prince, who is at once incapable of rewarding him, and unworthy of the honour. Haydn, the simplest as well as the greatest of men, is resigned to his condition, and is devoting his life to the rites and ceremonies of the Roman Catholic Church, which he carries even to superstition, is content to live a life immured in a place little better than a dungeon, subject to the domineering spirit of a petty Lord, and the clamorous temper of a scolding wife. Would it not be an achievement equal to a pilgrimage, for some aspiring youths to rescue him from his fortune and transplant him to Great Britain, the country for which his music seems to be made?

Now there are a number of ideas in the sub-text of this paragraph that are worth attending to. First of all, the reference to Haydn as the 'Shakespeare of music' is of great interest. The writer may well have admired Handel (he doesn't say), but at that time, thanks to Garrick and others, the phenomenon we know as bardolatry was taking root, not only here but in the German-speaking world as well. Shakespeare was becoming the poet of poets, the dramatist of dramatists – save of course in France – and to call Haydn 'the Shakespeare of music' was to elevate him to a pinnacle of repute above all other composers. Secondly, the 'miserable German Prince' was far from incapable of rewarding him, should he have chosen to do so. Nicholas respected his Director of Music; but he also treated him as one of his retinue of servants – England was not the only country where there were class distinctions. But the point being made is a sound one: just as Handel had made his fortune as a business-man and free citizen, so, the implication is, should Haydn be offered the chance to. Thirdly, the gross exaggeration of 'little better than a dungeon' serves to remind the reader that in England, Haydn would be a free agent, not the prisoner of a social system, subject to the dictates and whims of his secular and spiritual lords. Fourthly, a certain amount must have been known about Haydn's unhappy marriage, even in England, which gave him some gossip value, one imagines. Fifthly, if English composers were regarded as being 'in trade', Haydn seems not to have been: he was a genius, 'the Shakespeare of music', and therefore to be accorded the respect due to genius. Now the whole concept of genius and of the creative imagination was undergoing a fundamental change all over Europe during the last years of the eighteenth century. We shall come on to this subject and its implications later. And finally, the claim that Britain was 'the country for which his music seems to be made' is of particular interest. The urbanity, the wit, the passion always kept under firm control and the rhythmic dynamism, tempered by a lyric impulse, of Haydn's music were probably the features of which the writer was thinking.

Prince Nicholas died in 1790; and his successor cut his musical establishment back very considerably. Haydn was now free to travel if he wished; and Johann Peter Salomon, one of the scores of foreign musicians who had migrated to England and established themselves firmly in the country's musical life, immediately set out for Vienna on receiving the news and brought him to London without delay.

In the years preceding Haydn's arrival, concert life in London had built up to such an intensity that it has been described as the richest and the most varied in the world. But though there was much variety, there was no real consistent concert-giving series that built up a repertoire of standing played by a consistently recruited orchestra. There were, however, scores of excellent performers in Britain, and concert managements vied with one another to engage them. There were series of subscription concerts and concerts in private houses: the Concerts of Ancient Music, for example, aiming at a repertoire at least twenty years old, had been founded in 1776 and gave twelve concerts a year. At Drury Lane, regular performances of Handel oratorios had been given since 1785, followed three years later by a rival series at Covent Garden. At these, as at Handel's own oratorio performances, keyboard concertos were played between the acts.

Salomon's own concerts had been set up in rivalry to the 'Professional' Concerts, established in 1784 and commissioning a well-known foreign composer each season to write works specially for the series. Certainly many people hoped – as the rival operatic organisations had done in Handel's day – to cash in on a prospective personal rivalry and even animosity between the composers engaged to produce works for the two series. Haydn refused to be drawn, going out of his way to treat his 'rival' Pleyel with respect, even though – or possibly because – he probably knew that he was by far the greater musician. There were, as yet, no properly designed concerts halls in London – and few anywhere else in Europe, for that matter, but places like the Pantheon, a huge theatre in Oxford Street that had housed Christian Bach's concerts, were also used for dancing and opera. The lavish entertainments at the Pantheon caused the *London Magazine* to comment with some asperity in 1773:

> The playhouses, the operas, the masquerades, the Pantheon, Vauxhall, Ranelagh, Mrs Cornelys, the London Tavern etc are all crowded . . . The money squandered at the last masquerade was computed to be £20,000, though tradesmen go unpaid, and the industrious poor are starving.

£20,000 was a lot of money in those days to spend on one function, but one wonders how much money was squandered elsewhere on gambling and other such entertainments: landed gentry, not to mention their consorts, were known to bet their estates on a throw of the dice or a turn of the cards. The colourful Mrs Cornelys referred to here was a lady whose morals were suspect but whose energy in organising concerts and soirees was legendary.

Other concert venues included the Hickford Room in Brewer Street, the Great Room in Spring Gardens and taverns such as the *Crown and Anchor* in the Strand, a haunt of Dr Johnson and James Boswell that had a meeting-room capable of holding upwards of a thousand people for political meetings, convivial evenings and concerts. As for the pleasure gardens at Vauxhall, Marylebone and Ranelagh, a Frenchman wrote in the *Gentleman's Magazine* as early as 1742 of being 'dumb with surprise and astonishment' on his first visit to Ranelagh, finding himself:

> . . . in the middle of a vast amphitheatre, for structure Roman, for decorations of paint and gilding as gay as the Asiatic: four grand portals in the manner of

the ancient triumphal arches, and four times twelve boxes in a double row, with suitable pilasters in between, form the whole interior of this wonderful construction – except for the magnificent orchestra[29] that rises to the roof in the middle, from which are suspended several great branch candelabras containing a great number of candles enclosed in crystal glasses, at once to light and adorn this spacious rotunda.

But London was expanding; and in 1776 the Marylebone Gardens were built over. Still, Ranelagh and Vauxhall continued to attract the crowds – and to stage light operas. (They were not allowed to stage drama, as the Lord Chamberlain had not licensed them to do so).

Haydn's – or rather Salomon's – subscription series was held at the Hanover Square Rooms, where an audience of 800 could easily be accommodated – a much greater number than he had been accustomed to at Esterhaza.

He responded to the London public's enthusiasm by composing twelve of the most sophisticated, witty and profound symphonies that the musical world had so far seen. Six were for his 18-month stay in 1790/1 and six for his shorter second visit, in 1794/5. We should perhaps add that the proceeds of his benefit concert in May 1795 came to the equivalent of four years' worth of the pension that he had been granted by Prince Nicholas Esterhazy in 1790, so he had a substantial financial incentive for his visits. The generous terms that he had been offered were capped by what one might call this splendid additional windfall. He certainly considered settling in England, but the outbreak of the French Revolutionary Wars prevented it.

How much Haydn was appreciated by – and in his turn respected – his English admirers is perhaps best illustrated by a story related by one William Gardiner in his *Music and Friends*:

> One morning, a neat little gentleman came into [the] shop [of a music-dealer named Howell] and asked to look at some pianoforte music, and he laid before him some sonatas by Haydn which had just been published. The stranger turned them over and said: 'No, I don't like these'. Howell replied: 'Do you see they are by Haydn, Sir?' 'Well, Sir, I do, but I wish for something

---

[29] Meaning, of course, the arena where the orchestra played, not the players themselves.

better.' 'Better,' cried Howell indignantly, 'I am not anxious to serve a gentleman of your taste,' and was turning away when the customer made it known that he was Haydn himself. Howell, in astonishment, embraced him and the composer was so flattered by the interview that a long and intimate friendship followed.

Music publishing was indeed a growing business in Haydn's London, though few English composers challenged the supremacy of foreign masters such as Mozart or Haydn himself in the field of the piano sonata. One composer in particular, however, needs mentioning here: he was Italian by birth, but brought to this country as a lad of sixteen and remained here till he died. His name was Muzio Clementi. He became a publisher as well as a composer – his edition of Beethoven's fifth piano concerto was the very first published one – and what has only become known about him in the past third of a century was that in the early decades of the 19th century he composed some remarkable symphonies that were never published and that show him to have been a far bolder experimenter in terms of form and harmony than had hitherto been realised. The works published during his lifetime retain the elegance of outline, the facility and technical glitter that caused Mozart to dismiss him as a mere keyboard mechanic without a ha'porth of taste or feeling.

Mozart did not dismiss all British-based musicians quite so scathingly. One who gained his approval was Thomas Attwood, born in 1757, who went to Vienna to study with the great Austrian composer. Mozart's comment on Attwood was:

Attwood is a young man for whom I have a sincere affection and esteem; he conducts himself with great propriety; and I feel much pleasure in telling you that he partakes more of my style than any pupil I have ever had; and I predict that he will prove a sound musician.

That was, perhaps, the trouble: Attwood respected his teacher too much to try to break away from his influence. Mozart's high opinion was not borne out by later developments. In 1787, Attwood became music-master to the royal family. He established himself as a church musician, and was appointed organist, first of St Paul's Cathedral in 1796, and then of the Chapel Royal in the same year. He was a friend of Haydn and, later on, of Mendelssohn, and a celebrated composer both of theatre and keyboard music and of glees. He also composed one of the coronation anthems for George IV in 1821, but his music lacks depth and any character of its own. 'Mozart and water, and more water than Mozart', as a later musician and scholar might have said.

Hand in hand with the market for keyboard music went a market for keyboard instruments. The Swiss harpsichord manufacturer Burkhard Tshudi had settled in London in the 1770s; and with the invention of the new square piano-forte, his supremacy in the market was challenged by John Broadwood, with whom he eventually went into partnership. The wars with revolutionary France meant that the manufacture of pianos was reduced considerably in France and Austria, and by the turn of the century Broadwood's factory was turning out pianos at the rate of 2,000 a year. They quickly became famous all over Europe, on account of their powerful tone. The disadvantage was that they required a heavier action than that of the lighter Viennese pianos of manufacturers such as Stein. This meant that the delicate filigree decorative passage-work so familiar from galant pieces was more difficult to produce, but a much greater sonority was available. This in turn both reflected and was reflected in the compositions of the time – including the latest of Haydn's own sonatas. When Broadwood's instruments were introduced on the continent, they quickly found a ready market – one of the first composers to appreciate what they could offer was none other than Beethoven. It may be of interest to know that practitioners of 'period' instruments generally prefer to use a Viennese piano for the first four of Beethoven's concertos but a Broadwood for the fifth – known in this country as the 'Emperor'. It is also perhaps worth noting that there were a number of fine English violin-makers at this time, such as Fendt and Banks, though none of them achieved the reputation of the best Italian or French masters.

Like Handel before him and like Mendelssohn and Verdi after him, Haydn was tremendously impressed by the bustle and energy of London. A German visitor had observed that

> . . . every shop and warehouse is open by eight o'clock in the morning in the city; all is in motion and every body at work; whereas at the west end of this immense place, the streets are still empty and the houses shut; all, without excepting the servants, are still locked in the arms of sleep.

The West End, of course, was where the aristocracy, then as now, had their town houses.

Although the refined English gentlemen of the later 18th century were rarely brilliant instrumentalists, and although there was still a definite odour of 'trade' about music as a profession, there was none the less a good deal of amateur music-making of all kinds. Most of it was concentrated in what was called 'the season': that time in the autumn and winter when the landed gentry had left their country estates for their houses in the capital. There were numerous private musical societies devoted to the performance mainly of vocal music, but also of chamber music, generally of trio sonatas in the baroque style, which continued to be composed in England when the fashion for them had long since declined elsewhere. But new-fangled types of music, such as the string quartet and what was to become the piano trio, also flourished. Almost as soon as Haydn's great symphonies had been performed, arrangements of them were published for such private ensembles.

Perhaps the most widespread form of convivial music-making remained, however, the unaccompanied vocal ensemble. At least one society maintained the tradition of madrigal singing, but the fashion was generally for a newer type of composition in block harmony and in the 'galant' style: the glee. This was a style of composition in which a melodic upper part was accompanied in block harmony by the lower voices, with occasional excursions into not too serious imitative passages. It was particularly cultivated by English composers; and some of their works, though on a small scale, are none the less effective and affecting. The urbane charm of the music matched the Augustan style of the words, the themes of the verse usually centring around the enjoyment of drinking in congenial company, a mild nostalgia for a contented rural existence, the pleasures of music and those of love, requited or otherwise. Many of the most fashionable glee composers were church musicians who supplemented their income as organists at the fashionable London churches by composing for these bodies. One of them, indeed, the Catch Club, founded in 1763, had instituted an annual prize for the two best glees, one 'serious' and one 'cheerful'.

Among the composers of successful glees, one perhaps merits special attention, not because he was outstandingly good, but because his career and that of his family illustrates well the social problems with which the talented aristocratic musician was beset. Garret Wesley, the first Earl of Mornington (1735–1781), was raised to the peerage in 1760 by George III because of his skill as a musician and appointed Professor of Music at Trinity College, Dublin, in 1764. Mornington's son, Arthur, was a gifted violinist, but an academic dunce. It was beneath the dignity of a peer's son to earn his living as a professional performing musician, so his father purchased a commission for him in the army. On the day that he was commissioned in 1785, he destroyed his fiddle, and although he continued to the end of his long life (he died in 1852) to take a keen interest in music, he never played another note. The French in general and Napoleon in particular have cause to regret that Arthur Wellesley did not embark on a career as a violinist rather than as a soldier: he became the first Duke of Wellington.

As had been the case for most of the century, it was the aristocracy and the gentry rather than the court who set the tone for the arts, so there was no hard core, as it were, of patronage. Instead, there was a shifting sequence of alliances of the rich enthusiasts who were prepared to support a series of concerts, a season of operas, or a theatrical venture of some kind, or to attend a performance of some sacred work or other, new or old, in aid of some worthy charity. In addition to their town houses and country seats, they used also to 'take the waters' at fashionable spas, such as Bath, Buxton and Scarborough. It was at Bath that music and the drama were particularly cultivated. We have already seen how active the Linley family were in that town; and in the present context it is worth recalling that young Thomas Linley's sister married Sheridan and that Sheridan's play *The Rivals* is set in Bath. But what is even more relevant here is that the sung epilogues produced as after-pieces to the comedies often attracted the audiences even more than the plays did themselves. It seems at least in part that it was the music they went for, not the plays.

Although executant musicians were thus far less sure of a position in a permanent establishment than those at the many German courts, or at a great continental centre like Vienna, they could, if lucky, make much more money and enjoy much more freedom – to become rich or to starve, as the case might be. The very least they might hope for was a post in one of the London theatre orchestras or a job teaching. Training itself seems to have been something of a hit-or-miss affair. There was nothing in Britain that really corresponded to the conservatoires that had existed for centuries in Italy, where orphan children were taught the skills of music-making to fit them for some kind of service. There was nothing that corresponded to the former apprenticeship system leading to a recognised membership of a professional guild, such as still existed in some other continental countries. Nor was there anything yet that resembled the Royal Conservatoire of Music set up in Paris in 1785 and taken over by the new revolutionary state. Performing musicians were either virtually self-taught, like Dibdin, or picked up their skills from older musicians through individual lessons. Or, of course, they came to England having already developed their skills in Germany, Italy or elsewhere. Needless to say, apart from the bachelors' and doctors' degrees awarded by the universities, there was no kind of universally accepted professional qualification. And of course, where executant musicians were held in low esteem in society, it could hardly be expected that the major public schools should train them within their walls.

In the provinces – and that includes of course the two main university towns[30] – many of the ensembles that played to fashionable audiences might well draw on some talented local amateur players from among the gentry as well as professionals from the local theatre or the local regiment. But if a professional's work caught on and he became a popular figure, he might set up as an impresario and not only produce but also finance his own works, engaging hand-picked performers and enjoying access to the homes of the great – something to which a mere instrumentalist might not aspire.

As in previous ages, native composers were usually attached either to a theatre or a church or cathedral – or, in some fortunate cases, to both. This restricted the demand for their compositions mainly to music on a small scale, for the music of the established church was still confined mainly to hymns, psalm chants and anthems; and theatre pieces were as before mainly light and intended only as entertainment. The librettist

---

[30] Cambridge did not become a city until the early 1950s.

was definitely the senior partner and the composer very much his subordinate. Many 'straight' comedies, however, had songs inserted into their action and nearly all plays in the major theatres required some form of music before the curtain rose and between the acts. But if the music was part of a solid whole, English musicians were rarely allowed the opportunity to build up extended concerted movements of the kind that composers like Mozart had developed in collaboration with da Ponté in his great Italian comic operas. The moods and passions that playwrights required composers to express were rarely as intense as those customary in serious opera and usually more trite and trivial than even those in the best continental comedy pieces. There were exceptions. Arnold, Shield and Storace, as we have already seen, wrote pieces of considerable merit, some of which might well be revived today. Shield, for example, was paid £1,050 for his opera *The Woodman* in 1791, and one of his songs, *The Ploughboy*, appealed so much to Benjamin Britten that he arranged it and included it in a collection of folk-song settings. Arnold and Shield did in fact use and adapt traditional English airs in some of their pieces, but without any thought of cultivating a specifically 'English' musical style. Storace even composed a serious opera in 1792 on the subject of Dido, Queen of Carthage, which had sung recitatives. The audience responded poorly to them.

The 'serious' theatre, then, still meant plays in English and opera in Italian. This was staged at the King's Theatre in the Haymarket. The Italian opera was performed twice a week: on Tuesdays and Saturdays; and it attracted the best instrumentalists and composers of the day. Both the King's Theatre and the Covent Garden Theatre were large: Covent Garden held over 2,000 people; and from about 1760 onwards the proportion of operas staged at the London theatres increased an incredible *tenfold* over the previous generations. This is reflected in the publication of vocal scores of operatic and stage pieces. In the twenty years between 1742 and 1762, eleven operatic full scores and two vocal scores were published. Between 1762 and 1782, only two full scores, but no fewer than 80 vocal scores, appeared on the market. Part of the reason for the drop in the number of full scores is the fact that the 'galant' orchestra of the sixties and seventies required more staves on the page than the 'baroque' orchestra of the previous generation, when many arias were accompanied only by violins and a continuo bass or even by continuo alone. All theatre performances had to be licensed by the Lord Chamberlain – this was the result of political pressure when it was found that some plays, including entertainments with music, were rather close to the knuckle, so our much vaunted freedom of the press was actually subject to pressure if not to actual censorship. And painters of the quality of Hayman and Philip de Loutherbourg designed and painted sets for the theatres: a close parallel to Serge Diaghilev's action in engaging artists like Matisse and Picasso to paint the scenery for the Russian ballet in the early twentieth century.

Haydn himself, as part of his original contract, composed an opera for the theatre based on the Orpheus and Eurydice legend. It was never performed. The King, via his Lord Chamberlain, would not grant the theatre manager a license to stage the piece. We don't know why. Nevertheless, Haydn completed the piece and received a handsome fee for it; handsome is as handsome does: the score has survived almost intact and it contains some splendid music.

But the English theatre itself was by no means moribund. The comedy of manners was going through a silver age with the work of writers such as Goldsmith and Sheridan. Right through the period we are considering, incidental music was composed for Shakespeare plays, for example. The prevalent style remained that of the Italianate post-galant idiom of the imitators of Haydn and Mozart. This was understandable. The musical taste of the age was for wit and subtlety of humour, with just a touch of satire. These were the qualities, satire perhaps apart, that the cultivated London audiences appreciated in Haydn's 'London' symphonies. It was an audience that delighted in being gently teased; and Haydn was the greatest master of all time of the musical tease. Haydn must also have been impressed by the ability of the London audiences to understand and appreciate the wittiest turns of his musical procedures, for there is hardly a movement in any of these twelve masterpieces in which there is not some kind of musical *tour de force* that would appeal not just to an ordinary audience but to a highly sophisticated one, able to appreciate sudden changes of harmony and tonality, orchestral hoaxes and unexpected melting cadences. What

Haydn had yet to encounter, and what he encountered in England, was the sublimity of the oratorios of Handel.

That same George III whose Lord Chamberlain refused to license Haydn's *Orfeo* had solemnly promised the great Handel as a boy that he would protect his music after he was dead. He kept his promise; and six years before Haydn's arrival there was the first monster Handel Festival in Westminster Abbey. During Haydn's first visit a second festival was mounted, involving over 1,000 performers. It set the pattern for a style of choral music-making that was to persist throughout the next century and certainly up to my own adolescence and beyond: huge choirs, massive choral effects and a solemn, weighty manner of performance that has only within the last generation been replaced with lighter, more agile ways of doing the music. But the other thing that impressed Haydn was that Handel's works were performed in the language to which they were composed: English; and it is worth noting that when he came to write his own great oratorio, *The Creation*, he found that the adaptation from the English Bible and from Milton's *Paradise Lost* out of which the text had been fashioned sounded just as well in English as it did in German.

This attitude to Handel's music meant that the performance of choral works on a large scale became a notable feature of music-making in Britain during the early years of the industrial revolution. With it, arose the amateur choral society. This was more than a convivial body of like-minded dilettante gentlemen meeting to sing and drink together. It was a more serious affair altogether. The music to be performed was at its best uplifting and edifying; at its worst, pretentious and sentimental. Its avowed aim was as much moral as musical; and it aimed at stirring up feelings of religious awe, not at presenting an elegant and balanced design.

A new movement in fact was beginning to spread throughout Europe in all the arts that was to extol powerful emotional expression at the expense of form and good taste, the unfathomable against the rational and the sublime rather than the beautiful. A foretaste of it may be discernible in some of Haydn's symphonies of the 1770s – those that are erroneously but not altogether inaptly dubbed by the title of a literary fashion of the time in Germany: *Sturm und Drang*.

The movement was to be called Romanticism; and in keeping with the status that the Romantics bestowed on art, its practitioners took their work very seriously. But above all, the Romantics, and in particular the German Romantics, enthroned music as the supreme art, thereby enhancing the status of the creative musician if not of the performer. In Germany, above all, music, by its very nature, was enthroned as the supreme art, the supreme mystery, the short cut to divine revelation. Even the virtuoso performer, as exemplified by astonishingly gifted artists such as Paganini and, later, keyboard virtuosi of whom the greatest was Franz Liszt, also became salon lions. This was as yet not quite so evident in England in music as it was in painting, with the works of Turner and Constable, or in literature, with Wordsworth, Coleridge, Shelley, Keats and Byron.

In consequence, the creative artist became more and more regarded as a special type of human being: not just a skilled craftsman, but as someone with a unique vision of the world and insight into its mysteries. His imagination was to be used more and more to explore the sublime and thrill the audience with his vision of it, not simply to create elegant and harmonious patterns. The idea that the artist was in other matters a law unto himself because he had been granted this unique insight was certainly found in other ages: artists were tolerated as eccentrics because of the pleasure they provided. The quirky behaviour, for example, of a musician such as Sebastian Wesley, the 'crotchets and maggots' of Handel or the downright egocentricity of Arne, were accepted, though not outwardly condoned. But in the Romantic era, they were exalted to a status far above that of someone providing pleasure: they expected and were expected to uplift and thrill humanity with their productions. To the lady who said she had never seen anything in a sunset that resembled Turner's portrayal of one, the artist replied 'Don't you wish, madam, that you could?' a remark as revealing of the new attitude as it is trenchant as a rejoinder.

Things had not got this far with creative musicians in England, though in musical administration and training , as opposed to musical production, Romanticism began to make its presence felt in the period of the Napoleonic Wars and afterwards. In 1813 a society was established in London to sustain concerts of the highest quality offering the latest music to its subscribers. The performers were drawn from its members; its members were some of the most talented musicians in the capital; and they were expected to provide their services for the benefit of music itself, not for personal financial gain. For them, Art (with a capital 'A') was a vocation, not a profession or a hobby. It was called the Philharmonic Society[31]; and from the very start it made it part of its duty to cultivate the works of Beethoven, performing his symphonies within a few years of their composition, sending the dying composer a gift of £100 to ease his financial difficulties and commissioning the ninth and last of his completed symphonies from him. Had Beethoven not been handicapped by his deafness, the Society would certainly have lured him over to London to direct some of his works personally: the idea was actually mooted at one point. That the symphony when published bore a different dedication from the intended one to the Philharmonic Society was no fault of those who had commissioned it: and the first London performance advertised the work as 'composed expressly for this society'. All concerts of the Society to this day as presided over, as it were, by a bust of Beethoven on the concert platform.

At the universities, 'professional' music-making was still restricted to the provision of services in the college chapels, where an organist and a choir of varying musical standards of achievement was required to provide the music. In many cases, organistships were held in plurality; and it was not unknown for choristers to be involved in the singing at more than one college. At both Oxford and Cambridge there was a professor; but his duties were far less burdensome than they were to become later. He did not have to preside over a faculty board, to arrange for examinations or supervise research students. He did not have to lecture on the technique of composition or the theory of music save on a few chosen occasions. Nor was he paid for his troubles: the posts were purely honorary; and following the ancient medieval tradition, the undergraduates could only move on to the study of music once they had read for a degree in some other subject. One Oxford professor, indeed, William Crotch (1775–1847), who had been a child prodigy comparable

---

[31] Later, of course, the Royal Philharmonic Society.

to the young Mozart, and who also composed an impressive and successful oratorio, *Palestine,* transferred the main centre of his activities to London, where some of his professorial lectures were published in 1831, while retaining his post at Oxford. These lectures are highly readable and common-sensical. Yet even he shows which way the wind was blowing:

> Music can awaken the affections by her magic influence, producing at her will, and that instantly, serenity, complacency, pleasure, delight, ecstasy, melancholy, woe, pain, terror and distraction.

Crotch considered that the same principles, differently realised according to the medium employed, applied to all the arts; and he postulated three styles of music: the sublime, found in church music, which aimed to celebrate and express the glory of God, the beautiful, and the ornamental (which he seems to define as being akin to what the 18th century called the 'picturesque' in painting and landscape design). His own music is Haydnesque, craftsmanlike and unpretentious: aiming at what he would have called beauty rather than sublimity. The 'ornamental' in music corresponds, he claims, to:

> ... aged heads, old hovels, cottages, or mills, ruined temples or castles, rough animals, peasants at a fair, and the like, are picturesque. In music, eccentric and difficult melody; rapid, broken, and varied rhythm; wild and unexpected modulation, indicate this third style.

It is a pity that he did not provide any examples: one would imagine that if Crotch knew any of the music of the later Elizabethans, or the pre-Purcell baroque composers such as Locke, which he quite probably did, he may have had them in mind. Or was he thinking of some of his continental contemporaries? What is plain is that he felt that there was room in music for sublimity – as Beethoven was proving at the time when Crotch was formulating his theories.

In 1823, the first training college was established in this country expressly to educate professional musicians, both as executants and as teachers. It was called the Royal Academy of Music; and, like the [Royal] Philharmonic Society, it still exists. Crotch was one of the earliest teachers there; so, too was Cipriani Potter (1792–1871), a pupil for a short time of none other than Beethoven himself, who liked him and respected his musicianship. Potter even outdid his distinguished teacher in one respect: he completed no fewer than ten symphonies. But the impact of Beethoven, let alone of Romanticism, on English musical style was some way off yet. Yet the ground was being prepared; and a systematic training for musicians both creative and executant was built up.

Meanwhile, one particular aspect of Romanticism that was to appeal to musicians was manifesting itself. The impulse came from none other than Sir Walter Scott, whose novels of chivalry and adventure made a great impact on the reading public in England and abroad. I shall have more to say about this later; but it is worth while remembering the dates of Scott's novels. He started out as a translator from German, developed an interest in the oral ballad tradition of the Scottish border country where he lived, and in 1802 published a collection of imitation ballads called *Minstrelsy of the Scottish Border*. At one stroke, British Romanticism had its bedrock foundation that was to be built upon by poets and musicians from all over Europe. Or rather at two strokes, for in the 1790s, Robert Burns had established a claim to be the first great Scottish national lyric poet for three hundred and more years.

Scott's revelation of the allure of the Middle Ages (for example in *The Lay of the Last Minstrel*, in 1805, *Marmion*, in 1808, and *The Lady of the Lake*, in 1810) was crowned by the publication of *Waverley* in 1814. Here was a gothic revival of a more intense kind than the picturesque and sometimes overheated gothicisms of the later 18th century. It could be argued, by the way, that the rediscovery of the music of J S Bach, whose prime disciple in this country was Samuel Wesley, was an attempt to parallel the interest in the faith and integrity of the idealised age of chivalry by the cult of a musician whose service to the Lutheran church was manifest not only his choral works but in the intricate designs of his organ music. All this was part of the allure of an age less apparently prosaic and materialistic than the present, an age of Christian faith, mystery and chivalry, with stories often set in a country whose mists, lakes and mountains, to say nothing of its picturesque national costumes and the strange sounds of its essentially open-air musical tradition, made a strong appeal to sensitive and high-minded artists of all kinds. The cult of Scotland – intensified by the pageant following the coronation of George IV in 1820, when the new king wore full Highland dress on his coronation visit to Edinburgh – became of necessity a cult of Scott. *Waverley* was followed by a whole series of novels; and we shall see how many of these were adapted as operas not only in Britain but in France, Germany and Italy. Indeed, Rossini had already composed an operatic version of *The Lady of the Lake* as early as 1817. Scott became to the Romantics what Ariosto and Tasso had been to the librettists of the baroque age: a source of strong, colourful and exaggeratedly heroic plots.

Through its reading, and also through the vogue for Romantic native painters such as Turner, London society kept pace with contemporary developments, even if our composers did not.One of the first exponents of the romantic style in music was yet another distinguished German musician who came to this country in search of fortune if not of fame, which he had already through one of the most Romantic of all operas, *Der Freischütz*. His name was Carl Maria von Weber. He came to London in 1826 virtually in the wake of a triumphant tour by Gioachino Rossini, whose comic operas, with their brilliant vocal writing, had conquered Europe. Weber himself was a quiet, shy figure, a devoted husband and father and a sincere, devout catholic. His own demeanour and deportment were anything but those of a self-centred, would-be prophet, though his firmness in dealing with authorities and in exerting his own authority as a conductor was very considerable. *Oberon*, the opera he composed for London, suffered from the insistence of the librettist, J R Planché, that the plot should revolve round the spectacular element – that the work should be in fact a very superior form of pantomime, a mish-mash of debased baroque spectacle, ballad-opera dialogue, a plot that was only tangentially related to the musical episodes – in fact a kind of Regency rather than Restoration masque, a German romantic version of a baroque semi-opera like *The Fairy Queen*. Weber, knowing little English and nothing at all about the state of the English theatre, bowed to Planché's requests rather more than perhaps he should have done. Yet he was not entirely dissatisfied with the result, as a letter he wrote to Planché shows, dating from January 1825:

The cut of an English opera is certainly very different from a German one. The English is more a drama with songs; but in the first act of *Oberon* there is nothing I could wish to see changed, except the finale. The chorus is conducted to its place, I think, rather forcibly, and cannot excite the interesse of the public which is linked to the sentiment of Reiza. I would wish, consequently, for some more verses full of the greatest joy and hope for Reiza, which I might unite with the chorus, and treat the latter as subordinate to Reiza's sentiments.

Planché himself commented in his memoirs:

Had I constructed [*Oberon*] in the form which would have been most agreeable to me and acceptable to Weber, it could not have been performed by the company at Covent Garden, and if attempted must have proved a complete fiasco. None of our actors could sing, and but one singer could act ... No vocalist could be found to equal the part of Sherasmin ... Braham, the greatest English tenor perhaps ever known, was about the worst actor ever seen, and the most unromantic person in appearance that can well be imagined. ... My great object was to land Weber safe amidst an unmusical public, and I therefore wrote a melodrama with songs, instead of an opera.

Which may be a bit of special pleading, but is at any rate frank. And for the time being, at any rate, *Oberon* was frequently revived at Covent Garden well into the 1830s and 1840s; and it laid the foundations, as we shall see, for a peculiarly romantic kind of opera that had something of a boom during the mid-Victorian period.

All the same, he was well received in London, composed some of his most attractive music for the piece and died during its initial run at least believing that he had a financial success on his hands. Unfortunately, this 'English opera', as both he and Planché called it, was misconceived from the start, even though Weber showed himself remarkably well-attuned to the niceties of English intonation, stress and rhythms. But at least it was 'different'; and Weber's fairy world was also at this very time being brilliantly exploited by his younger and perhaps greater contemporary Felix Mendelssohn, who first visited Britain at the age of 20, some four years after Weber.

Mendelssohn liked it here; and his British friends, from the royal family downwards, liked him as well as his music. He was to return nine times, always to the acclamation of the public; and both his personality and his musicianship were to be much appreciated. He, too, was excited by the landscape of the Scottish highlands and the seascape of the islands, the bustle of London and the quaintness of Wales. He was not so appreciative of the native music that he heard, as we shall discover in due course. And he was essentially a serious person, a romantic, for all his clear-eyed, hard-headed realism, his wit, his charm and his high spirits, a composer determined to contribute to what Crotch would have classified as 'sublime' music as well as to music of the picturesque kind: *viz*, his highly successful forays into the depiction of a given landscape or national atmosphere.

Unfortunately, the high-minded Victorians saw and latched on to other aspects of Mendelssohn's art than the delicate traceries of his 'fairy' romanticism, the vivid pictorialism of *Fingal's Cave* or the picturesque exuberance of works like his *Italian Symphony*, without possessing the fire and genius of the original. And the tension was to become more and more evident between the demands of a utilitarian philosophy subscribed to by the majority of those who could afford to pay for the kind of music that he composed and the high-minded and idealistic attitude adopted by the composer himself and many of those who admired and imitated him. Was music there to uplift and to thrill, or merely to entertain? This was the unanswered (and possibly unacknowledged) question that faced Victorian patrons of music. And if it had a deeper role than mere entertainment, could native composers be relied on to compete with the foreign giants who came to England not only to display their gifts, but in search of financial gain? That is material for another chapter.

7 – The Victorian Dilemma: Sublimity or Utility?

It is tempting to entitle this chapter 'The Age of Mendelssohn' because the period to be covered coincides largely with the many visits that the great German composer paid to this country between 1829 and his death in 1847. He had a tremendous impact on English musical life; and he died at an almost unforgivably early age: he was only thirty-eight. But even so, he had enjoyed a career of over twenty years as a fully mature composer. In his case, more than any other perhaps, the predictable sequence becomes all too discernible: a craze or an enthusiasm becomes a fashion, the fashion becomes a habit, habit develops into style, style becomes convention and convention becomes cliché, with the inevitable and often exaggerated reaction. But it is unfair to blame Mendelssohn for the degeneration of his own style and lofty aspirations in other and inferior hands into a set of comfortable clichés acceptable to his posthumous audiences.

Many people have pointed out that it was Mendelssohn's personality as well as his music that endeared him to the early Victorians. This is true: he was well-bred, charming and tactful, impeccably behaved, witty and hard-working, an accomplished horseman and athlete who spoke fluent English, well-versed in arts other than music, a political liberal (with a small 'l') able to move in the most aristocratic as well as the most artistic circles with ease. He had all the gifts that opened the gates of society to him and was possessed of private means – his father was a successful banker – and a thoroughly professional training. He also had a mercurial temperament and a more than slightly mischievous sense of fun.

But though these gifts certainly were no handicap to him in his social life, they would have counted for nothing had he not also been a prodigiously gifted musician. Even more than Mozart, he was a prodigy.

Mozart produced nothing at the age of sixteen to compare in originality and personal technique to the wonderful octet for strings or the even more amazing overture to *A Midsummer Night's Dream*. What Mendelssohn gave to English musical life was a sense that a composer could be a gentleman as well as a genius; and a practical man of affairs as well as a romantic artist; unfortunately later Victorians seem often to have taken it to mean that you couldn't be a genius without being a gentleman as well. For the 'respectable' side of Mendelssohn, through no fault of the composer's own, cast something of a blight on the social position of the creative artist, as we shall see,

Mendelssohn's ten visits to England and the welcome he received on every one of them co-incided in time with a number of startling and rapid developments in our life as a nation. At the time of his first visit and more so as he got older, Great Britain was the richest and most powerful industrial nation in the world. She was also in the forefront of technical advance. In 1829, the transport system of the country relied mainly on horses and coaches, as it had done for centuries. The building of canals over the previous eighty years or so had enabled more goods to be transported safely in bulk, but at no greater speed. But when Mendelssohn made his journey from London to Birmingham in 1846 to direct the first performance of his oratorio *Elijah*, he travelled by train; and by the time he died a year later, the main network of our present railway system had been firmly established: all in less than twenty years. This was one of the most important aspects of the Industrial Revolution. Another was the gradual awakening of the Victorian moral conscience about the employment of female and child labour in mines and factories. The conditions described by Dickens in his novels of the 1840s and 1850s were gradually – all too gradually – improving as a result of changes in the law and the taxation system. A year after Mendelssohn's death, public unrest and the pressure for social and political reform led, not only in Britain but all over Europe, to what was called 'The Year of Revolutions'. This led to a radical shake-up of political life in many parts of Europe; and though reaction set in, things were gradually changing in the direction of a more open and democratic society. Consequently, Romanticism, which had contained a generous political element in its original form, changed character in a number of ways; we shall examine them in a minute, but they all affected the position and attitude of the artist.

Mendelssohn was a Romantic, though he preferred to express his Romanticism through traditional musical forms. Yet even he modified and adapted those forms to the kind of ideas that he was trying to express in his music. But such was his influence that all too many British composers who admired his works took *his* forms as the norm. It wasn't his fault that they had no new ideas with which to fill them; nor was it his fault that the public on whom they depended for a livelihood mistook the shadow for the substance.

The England that Mendelssohn visited for the first time in 1829 was still dominated by a ruling class whose attitudes were leisured, measured and rational. In a sense, the difference between the old order and the new Romantic era can be summed up by comparing the marching style of their armies. The old professional armies of the 18th-century absolute monarchs marched about the battlefield at 80 paces to the minute. Give or take a few paces, that's the tempo set by Beethoven ($\downarrow$ = 84) in the 'Alla marcia' section of the finale of the Ninth Symphony that so many modern conductors completely misread. But the undisciplined citizen armies of the French Revolution marched at 120 paces to the minute. This gave them a considerable advantage when manouevring and this was the tempo adopted by the armies of the 19th century.

Things were moving faster; controlled reason and a leisurely approach were giving place to excitement, restlessness and bustle. Romanticism at its most unbridled reflected the bustle and energy of the new machine age, however much the Romantics may have inveighed against the materialism and philistinism of the new middle classes. One of Turner's greatest paintings, *Rain, Steam and Speed,* is a reflection of this: here, the Romantic artist revels in the opportunity to express the dynamism of the new era and the awe inspired both by the train and by the stormy elements in terms of his own new, half-expressionist, half-impressionist technique. This kind of Romanticism itself was often hectic, irrational, glorying in the intensity and power of emotional appeal – including a glorification of the 'chivalrous' side of warfare – emphasising in its art the merits of powerful content above the constraints of balanced form, finding new, exciting and sometimes awesome depths in religion (especially in Roman Catholicism) and the art and architecture that Catholic Christianity developed in what the Romantics regarded as its heyday: the Middle Ages that preceded the Reformation. When it was reflective, it tended to be lyrical rather than coolly philosophical. This aspect of Romanticism can be summed up by Goethe's comment on Byron, the greatness and originality of whose work he certainly admired: 'Lord Byron ist nur groß, wenn er dichtet, sobald er reflektiert, ist er ein Kind': ('Byron is only great when he's writing poetry; the moment he starts contemplating, he's like a child'). It is worth noting, incidentally, that certain of the Romantics, such as Robert Schumann, disregarded any purely temporal parameters to the Romantic ages of the past and counted musicians such as Bach and Palestrina among their number.

Yet in an age in which Hector Berlioz, Fréderic Chopin, Mendelssohn himself, Robert Schumann, Giuseppe Verdi and Richard Wagner were all born within a decade of one another, Britain did not produce a single creative musician of any consequence. It was not as if she was lacking in artistic talent: some of our greatest poets and novelists and at least two of our greatest painters, both of whom were to leave their mark on the development of European painting, were active during this period. There was an impressive revival of neo-classical and of neo-gothic architecture during the first forty years of the 19th century. Why, then, was it in music alone that we seem to have fallen dismally short of the standards of the rest of Western Europe?

This question is of particular interest in that a new attitude towards the writing of music as a vocation rather than as a craft was developing with the rise of Romanticism. Berlioz, Schumann Verdi, Wagner and Mendelssohn himself, for example, did not come, as Mozart, Bach and Beethoven had come, from families where there was a tradition of professional musicianship. Berlioz was intended for medicine, Schumann for the law and Mendelssohn could have become a banker, like his father. What was it that prevented English musicians from following suit?

One reason was surely the lack of facilities for the enthusiastic newcomer to the music profession to study the technique of his art. A second contributory factor was the dearth of posts available outside of the popular theatre and the cathedral organ loft for the professional musician once he had trained. A third was the continuing suspicion of musicians as a class. And a fourth was the distinction between gentlemen and players, so to speak, that remained endemic in English attitudes to the music profession certainly well into my own lifetime. What did happen, however, as we shall see, was that amateur music-making, particularly in public and communally, began to thrive on a scale such as it had never experienced before.

When the teen-age Benjamin Britten was asked what he intended to be on reaching adulthood and replied 'A composer' the immediate response of his questioner was 'and what else?' In a society where the commercial laws of supply and demand counted for so much, the demand was for particular kinds of music; and the kinds of music in demand were not those in which composers like Wagner, Schumann, Verdi or Berlioz excelled. The one British composer, John Field, whose skill as a composer did in fact influence a major continental master sought his livelihood outside his own country – Ireland – in Tsarist Russia.

Field was a case of one of those musicians whose originality and talent were undeniable but limited. They were limited first by the fact that he seems to have had little interest in writing for any instrument save the piano; and by the fact that he was by nature easy-going and quite prepared to accept the second-best rather than polish his work until it became first-rate. The lack of self-criticism, the failure to realise that fluency of invention and skill in applying technique were only the composer's starting-block, not his finishing-tape, was a fatal flaw in the work of a number of gifted British composers of the Victorian era. To take three examples who all happened to be Irish, it affected Field at the beginning of the century, Sullivan in the middle and Stanford at the end of it. But what applied to them was equally applicable to a number of less gifted English composers, too.

The worlds of art music and commercial music were bound to overlap in a society such as that of early Victorian Britain; and no attempts to elevate the morality of the one above the other could eradicate this fact. Unless and until composers and their performers were provided with some kind of regular support independently of the market, whether from rich patrons or from the state, this was inevitable. It is interesting, by the way, that in the equally commerce-conscious society of the USA, the presence of a high proportion of immigrants who came from countries such as Germany, where there was a long tradition of consistent support of the arts both by the state and by private patrons, as a matter of duty, the situation did not arise in quite such an acute form as it did in Britain.

Nor was there any need felt by those with power and money in Britain for any form of national self-expression through art. If we look at the various 'folk-based' nationalisms that emerged during the 19th century, we shall find that there was a strong political element in many of them, such as those in what is now the Czech republic, in Italy, with the *risorgimento* operas of Verdi, in Russia and in Scandinavia. We have already seen that the great politico/musical epics of British history were the oratorios of Handel. It was in the 18th century, not the 19th, that Britain became powerfully aware of her national identity and what was conceived of as her national destiny. It was celebrated in actions, not in aspirations. We had no need to remind ourselves of our glorious national heritage, nor to use the arts as a vehicle to awaken an urge to throw off some alien yoke. It had already been done. Within the confines of our island, we were free from foreign rule.

There was, it must have seemed, no need to dig down into our national musical roots to discover what was truly English and what traditional qualities needed to be highlighted in a struggle to overthrow foreign oppressors. We were aware that the menace of foreign invasion and possible conquest was always present; but in order to invade us, the foreigner would have to cross the Channel, not simply march across a land frontier. It was the difference between defending what we already possessed and snatching for ourselves what others had usurped. And in this, English Romanticism differed politically from that of Germany, Italy and Bohemia. Where English Romantics were political radicals, as many of them were, it was in the name of defending freedoms already part of our heritage, not in wresting them from the hands of foreign rulers.

One aspect of Romanticism, then, that neither Mendelssohn nor most music-lovers in this country happened to share, however, was an interest in folk-music as a vessel to sustain national traditions and a national identity. He was exposed during his first visit to Britain not only to the music of the Scottish bagpipes, on which he seems not to have commented in any detail, though it seems from an aside in one of his letters that he was probably not unduly impressed. He certainly noted with some enthusiasm the colourful dress of the Scots on their way to the kirk on a Sunday. We do have his somewhat deprecatory reactions to the folk-music of Wales, however:

> Ten thousand devils take all national music! Here I am in Wales, and heaven help us! A harper sits in the hall of every reputable tavern, incessantly churning out so-called folk-melodies – i.e. dreadful, vulgar, out-of-tune rubbish with a hurdy-gurdy going *at the same time!* It has already given me tooth-ache. Scottish bag-pipes, Swiss cow-horns, Welsh harps: all playing the Huntsmen's Chorus with hideously improvised variations. . . . It's unspeakable. Anyone who, like myself, cannot stand Beethoven's national songs ought to come to Wales and hear them bellowed out by hoarse nasal voices to the crudest accompaniment – and then try to keep his temper. . . . It's making me so angry I can't continue.

Note the interesting phrase 'all playing the Huntsmen's Chorus with hideously improvised variations'. The chorus in question came from Weber's opera *Der Freischütz* and was regarded by all right-thinking Germans as a truly 'German' piece of music, sprung from the roots of the German character and a symbol of German love of the open air, of moral rectitude and clean living. Mendelssohn was much more cosmopolitan than many of his more nationalist contemporaries. His entire upbringing and social background made him so.

By the time that Mendelssohn died, however, a tiny minority of English scholars, many of them members of the Anglican clergy, were devoting some time to the language, the poetry and even the music of the people. Among them was the Rev John Broadwood, the Rector of Lyne, in Sussex. Many years later, his niece Lucy wrote of him:

> He was before his time in sympathising with the dialect, music and customs of the country-folk. Family tradition describes the polite boredom with which his traditional songs, sung exactly as the smocked labourers sang, were received by friends and relations. His accuracy of mind, his excellent ear and real love for old things combined to make him a valuable pioneer. When

Mr Dusart, the Worthing organist, was asked to harmonize Mr Broadwood's collection, he made great outcries over intervals which shocked his musical standards. A flat seventh never *was*, and never *could* be! And so forth. To which it is recorded that Mr Broadwood, confirming his intervals by vehement blasts on his flute, replied '*Musically* it may be wrong, but I *will* have it exactly as my singers sang it.'

The title-page of Broadwood's published collection, dating from 1843, is worth quoting *in extenso*. It runs:

Old English Songs,
as now sung by the Peasantry of the
Weald of Surrey and Sussex
and collected by one who has learnt them
by hearing them sung every Christmas since early Childhood
by
The Country People,
who go about to the Neighbouring Houses, Singing.
'Wassailing' as it is called, at that Season.
The Airs are set to Music exactly as they are now Sung,
to rescue them from oblivion, and to afford a specimen
of genuine Old English Melody:
The words are given in their original rough state,
with an occasional alteration to render the sense intelligible.

This is surely the attitude of a genuine antiquarian enthusiast, not of an academic, and certainly not of a trained musician trying to capture at least in part for political purposes the elements of a national style. Broadwood published sixteen songs only; the full harvest was not to be gathered in until a good half-century after his volume appeared, to the astonishment of those who thought that alone among the unlettered classes of Europe, the English possessed no traditional music of their own. It is doubtful whether Mendelssohn ever saw the work, or whether it aroused any interest if he did. Certainly, it remained isolated as a publication for a good few years before other tentative attempts were made to publish genuine folk-songs in their original form.

One of the first things that Mendelssohn had to do as a visitor on his first trip to Britain was to travel to Scotland: this in itself shows how Romanticism had taken hold: Haydn and Handel had never been any farther than sixty or so miles from London, to Oxford or Cambridge.

Mendelssohn and his friend Klingemann 'did' Scotland in style: they went to Edinburgh, where, on 30 July 1829 he wrote to his family:

> . . . in the deep twilight we visited the palace where Queen Mary lived and loved. A little room can be seen there with a spiral staircase to the door. They climbed up it and found Rizzio in the little room, dragged him out; and three rooms away is a dark corner where they murdered him. The chapel close by is now roofless: much grass and ivy grows in it and Mary was crowned Queen of Scotland at the crumbling altar. Everything is crumbling to pieces, dried up and the serene sky shines into it. I think I found the opening of my Scottish symphony there today.

He may have found the beginning there; but it was another thirteen years and several visits later that the *Scottish Symphony* – dedicated, of course, to Queen Victoria – was actually completed and performed. Of course he went to see Sir Walter Scott: he was

> . . . on the point of leaving Abbotsford; we gawped at him, having covered eighty miles and wasted a day for a half hour of trivial conversation.

Scott may not have had much time to spare for the eager young German musician, but he could not have been unaware that his novels and poems were attracting attention both in England and abroad as themes for operas. Henry Bishop (1786–1855), for example, composed music for dramatic adaptations of *Guy Mannering* (1816), *The Heart of Midlothian* (1819) and *The Antiquary* (1819).

In 1820, Walter Hazlitt, the famous essayist, commented:

> [contemporary English dramatists are] . . . periodical pensioners on the bounty of the Scottish press. Mr Walter Scott no sooner conjured up the Muse of old romance, and brings us acquainted with her in ancient hall, cavern, or mossy dell, than [the managers of our theatres] with all their tribe, instantly set their tailors to work to take the pattern of the dresses, their artists to paint the wildwood scenery or some proud dungeon-keep, their musicians to compose the fragments of bewildered ditties, and their penmen to correct the author's scattered narrative and broken dialogue into a sort of theatrical join-hand.

This was even more so on the continent of Europe. In Germany, Heinrich Marschner composed an Ivanhoe opera: *Der Templer und die Jüdin*. In France, Boïeldieu's *La Dame Blanche* was taken from Scott.

126

Italy, of course, could not escape the craze: Donizetti's *Lucia di Lammermoor* and Rossini's *La Donna del Lago* are still performed today.

The stories were popular, so they had to be exploited in the theatre as well as in the drawing room and the library. This led to some curious situations, for the theatres for 'straight' drama had to be licensed by the Lord Chamberlain. Licenses were not easy to obtain; and it seems that theatrical managements were unwilling to commission full-scale operas by British composers based on Scott's novels. The historian Eric Walter White points out:

> Music played some part in most of these stage adaptations, because of the fact that the patent theatres of Drury Lane and Covent Garden still held a virtual monopoly of legitimate drama, taken in conjunction with the accelerated increase in population caused by the industrial revolution, meant that the non-patent theatres that were beginning to spring up in such profusion used any device they could find to circumvent the law[32] and disguise the plays they wished to present. A favourite trick was to add sufficient incidental music to a play for it to be described as a burletta or some kind of musical entertainment. Any three-act play with not less than five interpolated songs was legally a burletta and could not be performed at one of the non-patent theatres.

Bishop, by the way, composed much music for the theatre: for over 100 stage pieces, in fact. He also edited and added bits to Arne's *Artaxerxes* and *Comus*, adapted operas by Mozart, Auber, Weber and Meyerbeer to contemporary English taste. He also became professor of music, first at Edinburgh and then at Oxford, and was knighted by Queen Victoria: the first musician ever to be so honoured.

Mendelssohn then went on to the Scottish Highlands, and especially to the western coast, where he was lost in awe at the sight of the distant islands:

> ... in order to show you how much the place impressed me, the following idea came to me there ...

---

[32]Just as had happened in Puritan times, in fact, with the first English operas.

and he there and then wrote out the first twenty bars or so of the overture that has since become known as *Fingal's Cave*, although it was not until the day after the letter was written that he visited the island of Staffa on which the cave is situated.

Three years later, in May 1832, he returned, and immediately felt he was among friends:

On Saturday morning, there was a rehearsal of the Philharmonic, but nothing of mine could be done, as my overture hadn't yet been fully copied out. After Beethoven's *Pastoral* symphony, during which I sat in a box, I wanted to go down into the hall, to greet some old friends. But hardly had I got down there than someone from the orchestra shouted: 'There is Mendelssohn!' and they all immediately began to clap, so that for some time I didn't know what to do. And when they had finished, someone else shouted 'Welcome to him!' and then the uproar began again and I had to clamber up on to the platform and thank them.

Look: I shall never forget that, for it meant more to me than any distinction: it showed that the *musicians* liked me and I felt happier than I can say.

And on one of his later visits, in 1842, he played for the Queen and Prince Albert at Buckingham Palace, praising their musicianship in a letter to his family and giving what amounts to an almost blow-by-blow description of the proceedings. In 1844, he again laid stress on the friendliness with which his London friends received him; but the really sensational reception came in 1846 in Birmingham, with the first performance of *Elijah*:

Never has any piece of mine gone off so well at the first performance and been received so enthusiastically by the musicians and the audience as this oratorio. I could see at the first rehearsal in London that they liked it and enjoyed singing and playing it; but that it would be received with such zest and enthusiasm, I must confess I had myself not expected. If only you [his brother Paul] had been there!

The performance lasted three and a half hours, apparently; the audience listened with reverent attention and the singers gave of their best. There wasn't, he said, a single mistake in the first part and only very few in the second. Four choruses and four arias had to be encored and:

... a young English tenor sang the final aria so beautifully that I had to pull myself together so as not to show my emotion and give a clear beat.

The relationship between Mendelssohn and his English audiences may without exaggeration be described as a mutual love affair. His music appealed directly and without problems to the British public. The great choral societies in the industrial north and Midlands, in Birmingham, Leeds, Huddersfield, and the Potteries, sang *Elijah, The Hymn of Praise* and *St Paul* alongside the works of Handel to which they were already accustomed; countless thousands of Victorian maidens strummed his *Songs without Words*; church choirs adapted choruses from his lesser choral works as anthems like *O for the wings of a dove* and orchestral societies took up *Fingal's Cave,* his other overtures and the *Scottish* symphony with alacrity.

The balance of political power was now gradually shifting so as to accommodate the economic power of the industrial middle classes. They, too, like the fashionable society hostesses of the gentry, were beginning to invite musicians to perform at private functions. They, too, were beginning to enjoy a more leisured approach to life; and their equivalent of the pleasure gardens at Vauxhall and Ranelagh were institutions like the promenade concerts that became all the vogue during the 1840s. The pleasure gardens had been declining in popularity for some time, and by the middle of the nineteenth century had been abandoned to the developers. At the promenade concerts, it was suggested, the music was only a secondary concern. The *Musical World* put it thus:

> The chief interest lies in the elegant perambulators themselves, who wander in pairs, finished by Stultz and the St James's Street milliners, and arranged to orchestral accompaniments by Strauss[33] and Musard.

Musard and Louis Antoine Juillien were the main organisers of these concerts. The programmes varied the music cleverly so that items that required concentrated listening, such as movements from symphonies, operatic arias and selections from works like *Elijah,* were mixed with

---

[33] Johann Strauss the elder, whose waltzes and marches were the talk of all Europe; not his more famous son.

popular dances, quadrilles and ballads. There were also spectacular displays of artificial fire and other crowd-pullers. The standard of performance was remarkably high, for Jullien and his rival conductors were efficient orchestral drill-masters in an age when the virtuoso conductor was virtually unknown. Showmanship and musicianship went hand in hand; as a contemporary critic J W Davison of *The Musical World* put it in 1860:

> Jullien was essentially and before all a man of the people; he loved to instruct the people; and the people were just as fond of being taught as of being amused by Jullien.

Promenade concerts of one kind or another have continued to this day; and we shall discuss them in greater detail later.

Middle-class tastes and aptitudes in music also found expression in the choral and charitable music societies of the great towns in the north and the Midlands where they lived. The first performance of *Elijah* was a case in point: the chorus was not a small professional body but a massed choir of several hundred mainly amateur performers. And an interest in widespread amateur music-making was beginning to spread all over the country, thanks to new ways of transcribing notes and rhythms so that even those unable to read music might be able to pitch a melody and hold a part in a chorus.

This process was greatly encouraged by the development of ways of setting music down on paper that circumvented the need to learn to read music. It was during the period that we are now considering that these techniques developed. The first of them was John Hullah (1812–1884), who was an exponent of the 'fixed-doh' method of teaching sight-singing; but it was the 'tonic sol-fa' system devised by John Curwen (1816–1880) that finally won the day. Curwen was a congregationalist minister who wished to improve the standard of music-making in his church. He was much influenced by the liberal ideas of the Swiss educational reformer Heinrich Pestalozzi. He also set up a successful music publishing firm, which lasted until 1971. The tonic sol-fa system developed out of a system devised by a lady called Sarah Glover – Curwen was always careful to acknowledge his debt to her – and it soon had tens of thousands of adherents. It proved so successful that in 1870 it was adopted by the state educational system for the teaching of singing in elementary schools.

It could also be applied to performance on instruments; and here we have a musical reform that until recently played a very important part in music-making among British industrial workers: the brass band. The invention of the valve system to brass instruments meant that skills acquired to perform on any brass instrument might quite successfully be transferred to performance on another. Thus a band composed entirely of cornets, flügelhorns, euphoniums and tubas could readily be established in a factory or coal-mine, a department store or a railway line. We shall have more to say about this later.

One subject that did interest Mendelssohn intensely was education; and he was able to see at first hand both the drawbacks and the advantages of the various systems adopted both in England and in France. What he admired most about the Paris Conservatoire was the quality of the instrumentalists it turned out and the way in which the conservatoire organised well-rehearsed concerts with an enterprising, high-quality repertoire. The Philharmonic Society in London had no such rehearsal policy, good though its instrumentalists were. One of the purposes of the foundation in 1823 of the Royal Academy of Music was to ensure that native instrumentalists could be provided with a training the ensure that any young person of talent could develop it at home rather than concert organisers and theatres having to rely on imported artists from abroad. As usual, money was the problem.

The Royal Academy of Music was originally intended to provide free residential education and training for 40 male and 40 female students. This was too ambitious, apparently, for the appeal for funds was not met in full; and it started its operations on a much more modest scale with ten students of each sex, each paying ten guineas (£10.50) a year towards their board and lodging.

The sexes followed separate timetables, the boys beginning their day with prayers at 6.30 am and the girls at 7. The days were divided up into instruction, practice and rehearsals, the curriculum including general education as well as music, and ended at 9 pm with more prayers. Clearly, what were to become 'Victorian values' were intended to be instilled at the RAM right from the start. The musical subjects taught included harmony and composition, singing and sight-reading, various instruments and – for girls only, it seems – dancing and piano-tuning.

As all instrumental instruction was conducted communally, the result must have been bedlam. One report mentions twenty pupils 'strumming on as many pianofortes' with students in the singing-room 'solfa-ing in every kind of voice' and similar noises (the sounds could hardly be defined as music) issuing from the violin room. The wind players might be anywhere from a small closet to the garret or the sky-loft (this was allotted, as might be guessed, to the trumpets). The percussion and heavy brass were banished to a small out-office in the yard. Things were organised rather more methodically in the numerous private piano-playing academies organised by the German educationist Bernhard Logier, several of which were established in England. The distinguished composer Louis Spohr, who visited London to conduct the Philharmonic in 1820, was most impressed by the way in which the young pupils were able to harmonise a simple chorale tune that he wrote up on the board for them and by the way in which Logier's method of having simple tunes written over a limited harmonic bass could be performed by players with differing degrees of technical skill at the same time. Because the harmonic progressions for the tunes being practised were the same at every level, there could be no question of cacophony if all the students were playing different melodic structures over the same harmonic foundation. By Mendelssohn's death, however, Logier's establishments had largely folded: the 'individualist' teachers, whose livelihoods were threatened by his 'mass-production' methods, had won their battle against him.

At this time, music academies were being set up all over Europe; and it is interesting to note that Mendelssohn was asked to organise one in Berlin in the 1830s and actually did found one in Leipzig in 1843. It started out on a deliberately modest scale, but under his leadership it was soon to become perhaps the most famous of all the German academies; and it seems that he may well have taken some of the ideas for it from the RAM. After his death, a scholarship was endowed at the Royal Academy of Music in his name, to enable students of limited means to study at Leipzig.

A quotation from George Eliot's *Daniel Deronda* may not come amiss here, for though it was written many years later, in the 1870s, it refers to an earlier period, not much later, if at all, than the one with which we are dealing. The distinguished and dedicated Jewish musician Klesmer listens to a young aspiring singer, Mirah Lapidoth, '[a] fleeing figure escaping from the moral death . . . of being the Count's mistress', as Graham Handley puts it in his introduction to the Penguin edition, and after laconically commenting on the first part of her performance by simply asking to hear more, Klesmer responds:

> . . . with a sudden unknitting of his brow and with beaming eyes, he put out his hand and said abruptly, 'Let us shake hands: you are a musician.'
>
> Mab felt herself beginning to cry, and all the three girls held Klesmer adorable. Mrs Meyrick took a long breath.
>
> But straightway the frown came again, the long hand, back uppermost, was stretched out in quite a different sense to touch with finger-tip the back of Mirah's and with protruded lip he said –
>
> 'Not for great tasks. No high roofs. We are no skylarks. We must be modest.' Klesmer paused here. And Mab ceased to think him adorable: 'as if Mirah had shown the least sign of conceit!'
>
> Mirah was silent, knowing that there was a specific opinion to be waited for, and Klesmer presently went on –
>
> 'I would not advise – I would not further your singing in any larger space than a private drawing-room. But you will do there. And here in London that is one of the best careers open . . .

Another of Eliot's characters, Catherine Arrowpoint, a more than competent musician herself, falls in love with the eccentric Klesmer. In fact, there is a good deal more about musical life in *Daniel Deronda* than there is in almost all other high-quality Victorian novels put together: perhaps that is one reason why it is usually dismissed by critics as something of a bore. But what is relevant to our purposes is the fierce dedication and integrity shown by the professional musician to his art and his refusal to compromise when expressing his opinion about Mirah's talents and prospects and the kind of audience at which she ought to aim: not the public at large but the appreciative audience of the private salon, such as Chopin played for when he came to London in the 1840s. And note: 'here in London that is one of the best careers open'. Or so it must have seemed to George Eliot.

But beyond the promenade concert, the salon, the brass band and the large choral society lay the world of the Victorian theatre. Here, during the 1840s, there was quite a ferment of activity; and not all the successful works were the product of foreign composers.

The most successful was the Irishman Michael Balfe (1808–1870). Balfe was born in Dublin and showed an early talent both for the violin and for singing, as well as for composition. At the age of 17 he came to London and was apprenticed to the German-born composer Charles Edward Horn, who wrote the popular tune *Cherry Ripe*. He was then taken by an Italian count to Italy, where he continued his studies in composition and appeared as a baritone singer on the professional stage. He settled in London in 1833 and from the start his operas were successful. His first success came in 1835 with *The Siege of Rochelle*, which ran for three months without a break; it was followed in 1836 by *The Maid of Artois*, which was equally successful. He was even commissioned to compose a Falstaff opera to an Italian text in 1838.

Balfe was a success not only in London but in France – he was one of the very few British composers to have works commissioned not only by the Opéra-comique in 1843 and 1844 but by the Opéra itself in 1845; and the opera by which he was best known, *The Bohemian Girl* (1843), was a smash hit in Paris and in Vienna as well as in London. Yet his operas are virtually unknown today. He had a gift for a good tune, but his sense of dramatic appropriateness and musical construction was far inferior to his melodic gift. He was easy-going and took the line of least resistance: he gave his audiences what they wanted and what he thought they deserved; and 'gems' from his operas proved to be singable and playable enough to enhance the appeal of private soirees for many years to come. When the first gramophone records were made many years after Balfe's death, some of the best sellers were from his operas.

Perhaps the most interesting of the British composers of this era was (Sir) George Macfarren (1813–1887), whose father had been a well-known dramatist. Macfarren took his point of departure not from Italian and French opera, as had Balfe, but from Mozart and even Beethoven. The best of his six operas was probably *Robin Hood*, first performed in 1860; and it is a feature of his work that he concentrated on subjects from British history and legend. One of his operas, in fact, is an adaptation of Goldsmith's comedy *She stoops to conquer.* No less a musician than Richard Wagner thought highly enough of his overture[34] to the melodrama *Chevy Chace,* composed in 1836, to include it in one of the concerts he conducted for the Philharmonic Society in 1855. He remarked on its 'peculiarly wild, passionate character'. It certainly has a good deal more fire, vitality and musical personality than much of the music composed by British musicians at this time. Macfarren eventually became principal of the Royal Academy of Music and, as so often happens, became set in his ways and unresponsive to new developments. *Chevy Chace,* by the way, was written by that same J R Planché who provided the libretto for Weber's *Oberon;* and ironically enough, Macfarren's overture was not eventually used in the theatre but performed as a concert overture in 1837. In the overture, Macfarren makes skilful use of one of the traditional tunes used for the ballad on which the story of the melodrama is based.

But the main influences on British composers of this time were essentially Mendelssohnian, filtered perhaps through the operatic style of Italian composers such as Rossini, Bellini and Donizetti. The features of Mendelssohn's music that influenced our own composers most were his mellifluous lyrical style, his fine harmonic sense and his sense of colour and atmosphere. Unfortunately, the harmonic devices that were fresh and arresting when he (and other distinguished German visitors such as Weber and Spohr) exploited them became tired and stale through over-use by inferior composers. Moreover, they often took devices effectively used by Mendelssohn in his smaller pieces, designed for private performance and enjoyment, and exploited them in large-scale works where they were inadequate to express the power and depth of the feelings involved.

That a similar musical language could be used much more effectively and powerfully was to be shown by the next great foreign musician to visit this country, which he did in 1847, the year of Mendelssohn's death.

---

[34] Though not of the composer: he referred to 'Mac Farrinc' (*sic*!) as a 'pompous, melancholy Scotsman' and referred to the overture by the title 'Steeple Chase', presumably because of its galloping rhythms. Despite his name, Macfarren was in fact English.

He was commissioned to compose an opera for Covent Garden. It was called *I Masnadieri* and it was based on a drama by the German playwright Friedrich Schiller. He was much interested in this country, and particularly in Shakespeare; and it is hardly surprising that he composed three operas on Shakespearean themes and considered a fourth, on the subject of King Lear. His name, of course, was Giuseppe Verdi.

8 – The Clown Who Would Be Hamlet: Arthur Sullivan

The arrival of Verdi alerted English opera musicians to a new and more powerful style of operatic composition. Verdi rather liked London. He detested the climate but was fascinated by the vitality and variety of what was at that time the largest metropolis in the world. He found the people sympathetic, though he did not like English customs and behaviour. The London press – with the exception of H F Chorley of the *Athenaeum*, whose adulation of Mendelssohn was to be surpassed only by Hanslick's idolisation of Brahms in Vienna – were impressed by *I Masnadieri,* the opera he composed for Her Majesty's Theatre in the Haymarket. The Queen herself attended and found the music 'inferior & commonplace'[35].

Opera – 'serious' opera, that is, was still expected to be performed in Italian; and it was still part of a commercial enterprise, with no assistance from state funds. The 'season' was restricted almost exclusively to the spring months, when Parliament was in session and there was a considerable concentration of 'class' and wealth in the capital. The Italian opera company performed only at Her Majesty's Theatre and paid very high prices for its star singers; and it was financed mainly by the sale of property boxes, as they were called, which were in effect a kind of extension of the owner's London house. He could sell it off to another if he lost interest, or he could of course attend performances whenever he felt like it. English opera, as it was called, was performed at Covent Garden and Drury Lane theatres, which continued

---

[35] Oddly enough, the Queen rather enjoyed Wagner's music if not Verdi's and specifically asked for the Good Friday Music from *Parsifal* to be included in the programme of a Royal Command Performance rather later in the century at Windsor.

137

to stage lighter works by native composers as well as pastiche works adapted from continental ones.

In the earlier part of the nineteenth century, things began to improve. In the 1830s, opera in German and French, properly staged and with the music more or less as the composer wrote it, was put on at the King's (later Her Majesty's) Theatre. And from 1836 the director of Her Majesty's, a young man named Benjamin Lumley, consolidated this process by gradually shifting the emphasis there on non-Italian opera. Not surprisingly, he incurred the wrath of the Italian singers and their supporters. In 1845, things came to such a pass that his Director of Music, Michael Costa, resigned and went to Covent Garden, where he greatly improved the standard of orchestral playing.

Within a decade, Verdi's visit was followed by London's first exposure to the music of Wagner, when he was invited over to conduct the Philharmonic Society in 1855. At this time, Wagner was in political exile, having run foul of the authorities in his native Saxony for his role in the 1848 uprisings. He had already sampled London life for a few days somewhat earlier in his career, on his way from Riga to Paris; but that was at a time when he was hardly known even in Germany itself; and it may well be imagined that he hardly found the highly commercialised organisation of the London theatre and London concert life much to his liking. On this occasion he stayed for four months; and although he liked neither the city, drawing attention to the misery in which he felt living in such a disgusting environment, nor the people (the philistine baddie in one of his prose tales is an Englishman), he had some interesting comments to make on the state of English orchestral playing. Of the Philharmonic, he wrote:

> A magnificent orchestra, as far as the principal members go. Superb tone – the leaders had the finest instruments I have ever listened to – strong *esprit de corps* – but no distinct style;

and again:

> [English musicians are] clever machines . . . artisanship and the spirit of the tradesman stifle everything.

Things could hardly be otherwise when the capital's principal concert-giving orchestra was drawn from the ranks of various other bodies and met together only for a limited number of concerts a year. And even then, the best players were not always available, however great the honour of playing for the Philharmonic:

> ... the Opera clashed with [the Philharmonic] concerts on Monday nights. Costa *would* have his men, and, on the part of the Society, Sir George Smart insisted that to change the date from the traditional Monday would be fatal! The result was a succession of deputy-players in the orchestra.

Wagner, in his usual completely self-absorbed and bigoted manner, attributed the comparative financial failure of his concerts to the cult of Mendelssohn – possibly true to some degree – and the fact that the London music critics were a gang of Jews hostile to his ideals – almost certainly grossly exaggerated, if not a downright lie. Yet he took care to include in his programmes not only the spritely *Chevy Chace* overture by Macfarren but a well-crafted symphony by Cipriani Potter, who had had lessons from Beethoven in the years following the Napoleonic Wars. This was not just politeness on Wagner's part; he had a good opinion of these works, whatever he might have thought of other composers in England or of the 'Mendelssohn tradition' of performance.

It is undoubtedly true that by the time of Wagner's visit, the Philharmonic had settled down into a comfortable routine that might have prejudiced his opinions; but it is also likely that Mendelssohn himself would have been rather vexed at the conservatism of its programmes and the lack of rehearsal time. However, a much-needed fillip to English concert life was about to come from two different sources, both of them as the result of the initiative of German immigrants.

In 1851 a great international exhibition celebrating the arts and industries was held in a gigantic specially built prefabricated glass and steel structure in Hyde Park; and with typically mid-Victorian enterprise and skill, the huge building was dismantled after the highly successful exhibition was over and re-erected in the fast-growing London suburb of Sydenham, within easy reach of the city itself by rail transport[36]. The

---

[36] The impressionist painter Sisley used this particular railway as the subject of one of his paintings.

building was called the Crystal Palace; it survived until 1936, when it succumbed to a huge fire; the site still bears its name, though it is now a national sports arena. Queen Victoria's energetic and highly musical consort, Prince Albert of Saxe-Coburg-Gotha, insisted that the re-sited building should be opened with a huge celebratory concert; and out of the band assembled for that occasion developed London's first fully permanent professional concert orchestra. Conscientiously rehearsed and ably directed for over forty years by August Manns, it quickly became celebrated for championing new music. Its regular Saturday evening concerts introduced a public that had hitherto not been exposed to concert music to a wide repertoire of established and less-established works, since many of those attending were precluded by religious or other scruples from spending their one regularly free evening of the week at the theatre (which they might not be able to afford anyway), the opera (which they certainly could not afford at all), the music-hall, or the pub. The Crystal Palace concerts became famous throughout the land; and the huge building also became the natural venue for other musical jamborees.

Principal among these were monster oratorio festivals, usually devoted to performances on a massive scale of the oratorios of Handel. More than 80,000 people were known to attend some of these concerts, at which a choir of some 4,000 amateur singers, backed by an orchestra of nearly 500 players, may not literally have raised the roof, but certainly produced a massive and exciting volume of sound. The sheer size of these undertakings, however, must surely have resulted in music-making of a somewhat ponderous nature; and the audiences were not treated to pure unadulterated Handel: the music had to be re-scored to fit the forces available.

Another feature of the Crystal Palace programmes was the competitive festival of music for brass bands, which, like the Crystal Palace Orchestra, was founded in the 1850s. This, like the choral festivals, was essentially a product of the increasing prosperity and democratisation of industrialised Victorian England. Emerging slowly – oh how slowly – from the grime and philistinism of Dickensian England, industrialists gradually began to realise that it was good for the morale of their workers and instilled pride in their membership of the workforce in a given cotton or woollen mill, coal-mine or shipyard if they were encouraged not only to engage in music-making in their spare time, but in competition against rival firms. The development of brass instruments equipped with piston-valves enabled these amateur musicians to move if needed from one instrument to another – hence that fact that music for all English brass-band instruments except the very deepest bass ones is still written in the treble clef – and to acquire an often enviable technical skill withal. The repertoire ranged from popular ballads and music-hall selections to arrangements of operatic favourites; later on, native composers of the front rank, such as Elgar, Holst, Vaughan Williams and, in our own day, Sir Harrison Birtwistle, were commissioned to write music either for individual bands or for the competitive festivals in which they participated. The intense local pride in a given band's prowess engendered by these festivals was often akin to that aroused by the exploits of a local football team[37].

The greatest centre of the burgeoning textile industry in North-west England, Manchester, was quick to develop a cultural life of its own. In 1858, Charles Hallé, brilliant pianist and friend and champion of the music of Hector Berlioz, inaugurated a concert season there, with an orchestra of hand-picked musicians. Having made a profit of 2/6d (12.5p) on his first season, Hallé was encouraged to create a permanent orchestra for Manchester. It still exists.

The earnestness of Victoria's court (with the notable exception of the behaviour of the heir to the throne) set the tone for English attitudes to 'serious' music. It was expected to produce uplift in the listener; and the emergence of large-scale choral societies among the middle classes led to a concentration on large-scale performances of uplifting choral works. Choral societies were amateur bodies dedicated to what became an adjunct to or a substitute for church-going, especially in the North, in Wales and the Midlands, where the congregational performance of music played an important part in non-conformist services. It should not be thought, however, that the Anglican church was left out of this: although we may now find repugnant the mawkish words, commonplace

---

[37] The moving film *Brassed Off* catches this aspect of banding superbly.

rhythms and over-sweet chromatic harmonies of many Victorian hymns, there was also a marked revival of the musical element in Victorian church-going. The trouble was that the hymn-writers composed in the only 'respectable' style available to them; and that was watered-down Mendelssohn or Spohr, applying their techniques without possessing their craftsmanship. Yet there are some fine examples of Victorian hymns; and there are a number of well-constructed Victorian anthems, notably by Samuel Sebastian Wesley, the natural son of Samuel Wesley and grandson of the great Methodist hymn-writer, Charles Wesley.

It is curiously typical of the Victorian age, however, that its most successful native composer really found his feet, not in oratorio, church anthem, symphonic music or 'grand' opera, but in a much lighter kind of stage piece that none the less gave him ample scope to display his excellent craftsmanship and flair for a good tune. Arthur Sullivan (1842–1900) had undergone a rigorous professional training as a boy at the Chapel Royal, at the Royal Academy of Music and, as the first holder of a scholarship established in memory of Mendelssohn, at the Leipzig Conservatoire. The son of an Irish clarinettist and a musical Italian mother, he was one of the most prodigiously gifted composers of the century, and not only in England[38]. But he also, as the late Eric Blom put it, had greatness thrust upon him in a form that he neither expected nor in fact relished.

Sullivan was already established as a promising white hope of English 'serious' music when he first met the struggling barrister and part-time humorous writer and playwright with whom he is inextricably associated in the minds of English-speaking people – William Schwenck Gilbert (1836–1911). At the age of eighteen he had composed some beautifully-crafted and tuneful incidental music to Shakespeare's *Tempest* and conducted it to great acclaim, both in Leipzig and in London. He was in some demand as a composer for provincial music festivals and had made a considerable reputation as a song and ballad writer. He was an accomplished organist and choirmaster and had

---

[38] One of his teachers had also taught Brahms, and maintained that Sullivan was by far the more naturally gifted composer of the two.

worked at the Royal Opera under the martinet Sir Michael Costa, who had revolutionised the standard of orchestral performance there. He had composed a symphony after a visit to Ireland and a cello concerto for the Italian virtuoso Piatti. In fact, all seemed set fair for him to become England's leading composer of concert music and oratorio.

Meeting Gilbert changed all that. Their first joint venture, in 1871, was a flop; and they parted company for some years. But in 1875 the impresario Richard D'Oyly Carte was looking for a short after-piece to fill the evening devoted mainly to Offenbach's *La Périchole* at his theatre, the Opéra-comique, in the West End of London. Gilbert had an unset one-act libretto available; Sullivan took an instant fancy to it; and within a fortnight the new work was ready. It quickly became the main attraction of the evening; and D'Oyly Carte realised that if he played his cards correctly he had a winning combination on his hands. So much so that at the beginning of the 1880s he had a new theatre built – the Savoy – to house his company and to put on the operettas.

What Gilbert provided for Sullivan was a quite new kind of operetta libretto. There are three aspects to each of his plots. The first is a paradoxical or absurd but none the less conceivable premise, developed with ruthless logic in terms of plot. The second is a virtuoso skill in conceiving and working out lively rhythms, enterprising verse-forms and audacious rhyme-schemes. And the third is a stimulating but gently sentimental kind of parody, often of cherished Victorian institutions. What Sullivan brought to Gilbert was a well-nigh incomparable gift for a catchy tune, a structural skill in handling a dramatic ensemble (heard especially in his first-act finales), a trained academic musical craftsman's capacity for musical parody and a deft flair for light-hearted musical characterisation. What Carte brought to them both was financial shrewdness and a talent for PR and publicity. And what differentiated the company that they assembled from similar bodies elsewhere was the almost puritanical moral discipline that Carte and Gilbert (not so much Sullivan) imposed on its members. The Savoy theatre was not only popular; it was respectable.

Year after year the Savoy operas, as they became known, followed one another; and nearly every one ran successfully for hundreds of consecutive performances until a new one replaced it[39]. Gilbert satirised the legal system (*Trial by Jury*), the political control of the Navy (*HMS Pinafore*), the army[40] and the police (*The Pirates of Penzance*), the aesthetic movement of Oscar Wilde and Swinburne (*Patience*), the House of Lords (*Iolanthe*), the idea of a women's university (*Princess Ida*), the fad for Japanese styles and tastes (*The Mikado*), theatrical melodrama (*Ruddigore*), the idea of universal egalitarian democracy (*The Gondoliers*) and the importation of British styles and attitudes in our far-flung empire (*Utopia Limited*). Only in one of the series, *The Yeomen of the Guard*, did he and Sullivan – at the latter's earnest request – attempt something more serious and less of a burlesque. Though musically and dramatically of interest, it fails. It is too solemn for an operetta, but not pointed enough for a genuine comic opera. Its sentimentality is not relieved by their normal tongue-in-cheek sauciness, nor do its characters all live happily ever after its ambivalent ending. Yet a measure of how seriously Sullivan took the work can be discerned in its remarkable overture: a finely-constructed symphonic first movement making astute use of quite a number of the main tunes from the operetta itself, scored with an unerring sense of instrumental sonority that deludes the listener into imagining that the modest forces employed are almost Wagnerian in scale.

And this was the trouble. The operettas were hugely successful. Gilbert sent up institutions without subverting them; Sullivan parodied musical styles – Handel, Donizetti, even – respectfully and decorously, of course – Mendelssohn (in the overture to *Iolanthe*) and possibly Berlioz (in the ghost song from *Ruddigore*[41]) and moved from the ranks

---

[39] The record was held by *The Mikado*, with an initial run of over 600 performances. *Princess Ida*, which managed a mere 243, was accounted a comparative failure.

[40] Gilbert was a militia officer.

[41] Gilbert disapproved. He wanted something lighter and less atmospheric in the way of a setting. 'It's like introducing fifty lines of *Paradise Lost* into a low farce,' he grumbled.

of the underpaid poor to the comfortably rich. He was not just a favourite of the aristocracy and the royal house; he was a regular guest at country house parties. And with financial success, he developed a taste for the high life, especially for the gaming tables at Monte Carlo and elsewhere. It was the income from the operettas that enabled him to lead this kind of life; and he knew it. Yet his heart was elsewhere. He wanted to make his mark in the world of 'serious' music. So did his earnest mentors, including the royal family and especially the Queen.

He never made it. His cantata *The Golden Legend* was rapturously acclaimed at the Leeds Festival in 1886 (at which he also conducted Bach's B minor mass[42] to the plaudits of the crowd), but it has failed to hold a place in the regular choral repertoire. It is, however, something of an indication of Victorian standards to read of Sullivan being hailed as 'the sinner that had repented' by one (C V Stanford) who considered himself one of the ninety-and-nine just persons that needed no repentance. Carte built a special new opera house for him so as to mount his lyrical, leisurely and surprisingly undramatic *Ivanhoe* (instigated by and dedicated to Queen Victoria). It ran for 160 nights – a remarkable achievement for an opera by an English composer – but ultimately it was a failure. Its idiom had been outdated by the innovations of Wagner and the later Verdi. As has often been pointed out, there was nothing really stageworthy to complement it in the repertoire once the initial run was over.

Sullivan himself knew this in his heart of hearts. 'A cobbler should stick to his last', he commented morosely. Yet he would have been surprised to learn that his operettas had lasted as well as they have. Part of the reason is that they can be encompassed by a competent cast of talented amateurs. This is not to say that professionals can dispense with them. Gilbert, Sullivan and Carte assembled a company and established a tradition that was guarded every bit as jealously by successive generations of performers as was that established by Wagner's widow at Bayreuth. What it does mean is that the challenges they offer are not such as to require large voices, deep acting technique, or sheer technical

---

[42] He said that he would have given everything he had ever composed just to have written the 'Sanctus' from Bach's masterpiece.

skill, either from the singers or the orchestra. But performed by professionals of companies such as the ENO, they reveal the charm and the craftsmanship at the composer's disposal better than any amount of amateur enthusiasm.

It is surprising how very few of the musical elements of the Savoy operettas are in fact purely and simply English. Like Purcell before him and Elgar after him, Sullivan was highly eclectic. And yet the whole is greater than the sum of the parts. From elements of French operetta, Schubertian lyricism, Mendelssohnian harmonic procedures, Italianate melodic turns and Handelian dignity, Sullivan forged an idiom that can be recognised in its own right. It is light without being too frivolous, saucy without being vulgar, dignified without being too earnest, vigorous without being hectic: in other words, it is English in its moderation and also, perhaps, in its gentility, even at times its debility and sentimentality. But the latter defects are far less common than Sullivan's detractors would have us believe. In the operettas, Sullivan was out to provide his audience with good, clean, tuneful fun, but he could not help showing the fact that he was a thoroughly professional composer with a technique that enabled him to harness his gift for a tune to a technique far in advance of that of any of his contemporaries either here or on the continent. These qualities can be heard in pieces like 'When I first put this uniform on' from *Patience*, 'When Britain really ruled the waves', from *Iolanthe*, or 'Rising early in the morning' from *The Gondoliers*.

Gilbert's versatility in providing a variety of rhythmic, metrical and stanzaic frameworks greatly assisted him here. Gilbert was, in fact, one of the most gifted and original librettists that ever worked for the light musical stage; and his skill in building up the tension in his Act I finales in particular enabled Sullivan to demonstrate his command of the ebb and flow of rhythmical tension and variety of tempo. This is particularly so in the first-act finales of *Patience, Iolanthe* (which I personally consider the finest piece of sustained musico-dramatic construction by any British composer before Britten), *The Mikado, Ruddigore*, and *The Gondoliers*. Even *The Yeomen of the Guard*, where Sullivan at one stage fails completely to match in imaginative power the dramatic tension of what is basically a serious situation, does build up eventually if not inexorably to the fine frenzy of confusion, as Gilbert requires it to.

It is in his martial-and-naval style that Sullivan is most obviously English, whether taking it seriously or sending it up. The entry of the Peers in *Iolanthe* may have its origins in Romantic Italian opera, but Sullivan's sturdy treatment of it adds a touch of Handelian Westminster-Abbey solemnity to it. Similarly, the closing martial section in his finale to the first act of the same operetta adds another touch of Handelian swagger to a very gallic tune. It is also noticeable when, following Gilbert's lead, he cocks a gentle snook at English patriotic pride, as in 'for he is an Englishman', he does so at Handel, as well as creating a tune that in its stylistic essentials bears a marked resemblance to the Norfolk folk-song *Ward the Pirate*. Perhaps both his tune and the folk-song can be traced back to a common eighteenth-century source.

Handel was, of course, fair game. The entry of the judge in *Trial by Jury* and the song of the three absurd warriors in *Princess Ida* are obvious enough examples; and though the little mock-baroque fugato that always introduces the Lord Chancellor in *Iolanthe* is more like Bach at his most genial than Handel, the same point is being made:

> The law is the true embodiment of everything that's excellent.
> It has no kind of fault or flaw; and I, my Lords, embody the Law.

If it's ceremonial majesty and obedience to the time-honoured rules of the musical Medes and Persians that you wish to symbolise – or to mock – , then you have to go back to the eighteenth century to do so.

But there is also in Sullivan's music a tender lyrical vein that is equally redolent of an older England than that in which Sullivan lived. You find it in 'The battle's roar is over, O my love'[43] from *Ruddigore*, in the charming pastoral music associated with Strephon and Phyllis in *Iolanthe* and in the elegant gavotte-like tread of 'I am a courtier, grave and serious' from *The Gondoliers* or of 'Prithee, pretty maiden' from *Patience*. This is music that harks back to the age of Arne and

---

[43] A tune, interestingly enough, which is virtually pentatonic save for its climactic phrase.

Gainsborough. The imitation is surely an act of homage, not a parody. When Sullivan engages in the more cloying lyricism of his own time, he can be tediously sentimental, especially when he is trying to soften some of Gilbert's more waspish jibes. The operettas are in fact the final and most distinguished descendants of the ballad opera. The more genteel and proper wit of Gilbert's libretti and his satire marks the change in taste from the robust age of Fielding to the more sentimental one of Dickens; the distinction of Sullivan's musical parodies and the more resourceful cut of his melodies, harmonies and rhythms adds a scholarly and artistic touch to a highly popular form of musical stage piece that had all too often been slapdash and vulgar.

By the time Sullivan and Gilbert were at the peak of their collaboration, in the 1880s, a general improvement was taking place in the whole status of music and musicians in Victorian society. After the Prince Consort's unexpected death in 1861, an extensive site was given over as a permanent memorial area to him in South Kensington. It was intended to commemorate his interest in the arts and sciences. As well as the numerous museums and the remarkable memorial to Albert, space was allocated on the site for a huge concert hall named after him. This originally catered for an audience of well over 5,000 and allowed space for a chorus of 1,000 and an orchestra of over 100. Plans were also laid for a building for the Royal College of Organists and one dedicated to the training of musicians, the National Training School, now known as the Royal College of Music. The NTS opened in 1883; and one of the principal directors was Sullivan himself. But the driving force behind the College was not a musician by profession. It was a gifted engineer and administrator, a friend of Sullivan's named George Grove.

Like Sullivan, Grove was a devotee of the music of Franz Schubert, at that time known to England only by some of his songs and a couple of his symphonies. Thanks to the efforts of Grove, Sullivan and August Manns (another Schubertomane), the taste of Victorian audiences was extended considerably. The Philharmonic Society and the provincial festivals, such as those in the north (notably Leeds) and the Three Choirs Festival in the West Midlands, invited musicians of the calibre of Gounod (who spent some years in this country), Saint-Saëns and Antonín Dvořák to compose for them. Handel and Mendelssohn were still popular, but a growing taste for newer music was evident; and English composers were able to keep pace with developments abroad. Wagner returned, this time to raise money for his festival theatre at Bayreuth[44]. Verdi returned, too, this time to conduct his *Requiem* at the Albert Hall; even the timid Anton Bruckner came. He was received with enthusiasm when he played on the Albert Hall organ and declared that his art was truly appreciated only in England. Johannes Brahms, however, refused all invitations to cross the North Sea, which was ironic, as his music was making remarkable headway amongst 'progressive' English musicians in the final quarter of the century. He became, in fact, what Handel was to 18th-century and Mendelssohn to early-Victorian audiences: the new idol of academic English musicians.

Victorian England was certainly not the 'Land without Music' that it was considered to be by continental musicians, who never bothered to investigate its musical life with a reasonably objective eye and ear. It was still, however, the land without permanent day-to-day musical institutions, such as civic and state-supported opera and orchestras. Concerts and operatic ventures abounded; and these included not only opera seasons at one or other of the larger London theatres but the remarkable chamber and recital concerts at the St James's Hall, built in the same decade as the Crystal Palace, that became known as the 'Monday Pops'. These, in fact, were celebrated enough to be jocularly referred to by Gilbert (and Sullivan, with an allusion to Bach's Great G minor organ fugue) in *The Mikado*. There were also numerous other concert-giving societies in addition to the Philharmonic; and in the provinces, the major industrial cities attracted attention not only nationally, but internationally with their large-scale choral festivals in aid of local charities. Yet musicians who visited Germany and Central Europe still cast envious eyes on the subsidised operatic institutions and permanent orchestras there; and when a British composer was foolhardy

---

[44] The dragon for the first performance of the *Ring* was designed and constructed in London, but thanks to the inveterate ignorance of English functionaries of foreign geography was despatched to Beirut in Lebanon, not Bayreuth in Bavaria. This error was hardly calculated to improve Wagner's image of Victorian England.

enough to write an opera without some commission from an opera company, there were cases where it had to be translated and performed in Germany before it reached the stage in its original form in England. Some improvement in the situation arrived with the foundation in 1875 by Carl Rosa (another German-born musician who settled in England) of an enterprising touring opera company that successfully brought opera in English to provincial audiences and even commissioned and performed operas by British composers. This may have palliated rather than solved the problem of reaching an opera-minded public, but it was at any rate a brave endeavour, and the company continued to operate until 1960.

But even in the haphazard and commercialised musical life of Victorian England, the unaccountability of genius meant that one could still emerge. Sullivan narrowly missed becoming an English Mozart, writing genuine comic opera rather than operetta simply because Victorian art had to be serious and 'chivalrous' for it to be taken seriously. Cultural as well as social snobbery was endemic in Victorian England: even Mozart's da Ponte operas were viewed with a certain condescension as frivolous and frothy; and *Cosi fan tutte* was dismissed (not only in England) as immoral and trivial. But one genius, self-taught, provincial in origins and coming from what was considered a tradesman's background, had already begun to compose who was to gain a considerable reputation in Germany as well as in his native country and whose music still commands respect because of its quintessentially English flavour. His name was Edward Elgar, and it is to him that we shall turn next.

9 – 'Knight, Gentleman and Soldier': Edward Elgar

The Order of Merit was instituted in 1902 by King Edward VII and is limited to 24 people chosen personally by the sovereign. It is generally regarded as the supreme accolade of personal distinction in the monarch's eyes rather than a mere formal acknowledgement of bland, nondescript rectitude awarded on the advice of the Prime Minister. Knighthoods and peerages are often conferred as political rewards to a particular premier or even, let it be gently whispered, as a reward for financial and other services to his or her party. In 1911, Edward's son George V awarded the OM in his coronation honours list to a self-taught composer who had been born in an undistinguished cottage in what was then the sleepy hamlet of Broadheath, three miles outside the cathedral city of Worcester. When he heard of the award, Sir Hubert Parry, Principal of the Royal College of Music, whose music Elgar greatly admired, commented: 'He's the right man for it. You see, he has reached the hearts of the people.'

Nobody who has witnessed the Last Night of the Proms can fail to recognise one way in which Elgar did this; and the story of the tune that has become almost our second national anthem is an interesting one. At the turn of our century, Elgar had just established himself as a composer to be reckoned with, thanks to his *Enigma Variations* and his *Dream of Gerontius*. The latter may have been a failure at its first performance but it was recognised both by perceptive musicians in this country and abroad as a masterpiece. He now composed two military marches of what were eventually to become a set of five, the idea being that if a funeral march could be treated symphonically, as was the case in Beethoven's 'Eroica' symphony or Wagner's funeral music for Siegfried in *Götterdämmerung,* the same thing might be done with the ordinary quick parade-ground march. The first of these had a tune in its central section that made an immediate impact on its first audience, so much so, indeed, that the conductor, Henry Wood, had to encore the piece not once but twice before the audience was satisfied.

The beautifully proportioned and stirring tune was clearly destined to have patriotic words to be set to it; and for the coronation of Edward VII in 1902, words were duly provided by A C Benson, who was to become Master of Madgalene College, Cambridge. The words he wrote for the tune in its new guise, as the finale of a substantial ode for the coronation, run as follows:

> Land of hope and glory,
> Mother of the free.
> How shall we extol thee,
> Who are born of thee?
> Truth and Right and Freedom,
> Each a holy gem,
> Stars of solemn brightness,
> Weave thy diadem.

The message is clear. Britain is indeed presented as a land of hope and glory, but the things that she stands for and that contribute both to the glory that she enjoys and the hope that is to come are humanitarian social and political virtues: Truth, Right and Freedom. Moreover, they are holy and solemn; and they constitute the moral crown jewels, so to speak, that the newly-crowned king's own material crown symbolises. These are the original words that were directly inspired by Elgar's simple and noble tune. There is nothing of the brash, chest-beating vulgarity of the swaggering, self-satisfied, imperialistic version that is sung on jingoistic occasions such as the close of the Tory Party conference nowadays. This was how Elgar reached the hearts of the people; and it is worth examining what qualities both in this tune and in other works of his are a projection of 'English-ness'.

But before we look at Elgar the artist, let us take a glance at Elgar the man. No musician could possibly have looked less like an artist. Throughout his mature life, Elgar strove to cultivate the image of a country gentleman. His marriage to the daughter of an Indian Army Major-General may have had something to do with this. Throughout his life he was aware of the sacrifice made by his wife on marrying him. She came from a background and a social class that ranked considerably higher than his own in the rigid and starchy hierarchy of late-Victorian society; and the fact that she married a lower-middle-class 'tradesman' in whose musical genius she fervently believed cost her a considerable inheritance. His military bearing and outlook became and remained such that towards the end of his life Sir Osbert Sitwell, an unsympathetic observer[45], was so taken in by it as to refer to him as 'with his grey moustache, grey hair, grey top hat and frock-coat [looking] every inch the personification of Colonel Bogey'. Sitwell clearly mistook the surface for the substance; there was much more to Elgar's complex personality than this. Elgar's self-projection of himself as a country gentleman was at least in part an elaborate role-play. He wasn't an army officer; he wasn't a country squire; he wasn't even a gentleman farmer. He was a touchy, moody, highly emotional, insecure creative artist and visionary; and throughout his life he bore a chip on his shoulder because his father had been a 'tradesman', a piano-tuner who kept a music-shop in a provincial county town. No composer has so strenuously dissociated himself in the public eye from his academically-trained contemporaries. The fact that he was virtually self-taught was almost certainly one factor contributing to this attitude; but for whatever reason, he delighted in representing himself as an 'ordinary' golf-playing, pipe-smoking, even philistine man-in-the-street from the English county gentry who followed horse-racing and kept dogs and frequented Brooks' Club as well as the Athenaeum.

In reality, he was nothing of the kind; and his letters to intimate friends criticising the philistine nature of English society prove this. No composer's music has been accepted as the epitome of all that is most English more than has Elgar's. Its appeal has been well summed up by his great successor Ralph Vaughan Williams, whose sincere admiration

---

[45] It is strange that Sitwell, admirer and patron of William Walton, could not recognise that his protégé was Elgar's obvious successor in the field of ceremonial music. He cannot have listened very carefully to parts of the *Sinfonia Concertante* for piano and orchestra dedicated to him and his siblings, to the parade of the heathen gods from *Belshazzar's Feast* or the close of the First Symphony, let alone to *Crown Imperial*.

for Elgar's music stopped well short of idolatry. His obituary tribute to Elgar in 1934 echoed the words of his own revered teacher Hubert Parry:

> ... There are certain pieces of music which are so much part of our national consciousness that we cease to criticize them. We know that they must be good, otherwise they would not occupy the position they do in our hearts. We do not consciously appraise them, but accept them without comment as definitely belonging to us. Such must be the attitude of mind of a German to his best-loved chorales, to the Wälsung theme in the *Ring*, to Schubert's *An die Musik*. Such is our feeling towards *Fairest Isle, Lazarus,* or *St. Anne,* and during the last thirty years certain pieces by Elgar have come to hold that position for many of us; such things as *Nimrod* and *W. N.,* or *Softly and Gently* have this peculiar quality. When hearing such music as this we are no longer critical or analytical, but passively receptive. It falls to the lot of very few composers, and to them not often, to achieve this bond of unity with their countrymen. Elgar has achieved this more often than most and, be it noted, not when he is being deliberately 'popular,' as in *Land of Hope and Glory* or *Cockaigne*, but at those moments when he seems to have retired into the solitude of his own sanctuary.

There are many aspects of Elgar, often found cheek by jowl in the same work. There is the state ceremonial bard. This was the aspect of him that chimed in with the brash and somewhat self-conscious imperialist ethos of the age in which he matured, when the might of the Royal Navy and the courage of the thin red line of English infantry kept foreigners at bay and protected the British dominions beyond the seas from submission to Russia, France, or the new imperial Germany. This is the Tory squire Elgar corresponding to his external appearance of a knight, gentleman and soldier. But to accept this as all there is of the real 'English' Elgar is merely to scratch the surface of a protean musical personality. As Vaughan Williams observed, there is also the withdrawn dreamer, the country lad who spent his leisure hours indulging in musical day-dreams down by the Rivers Teme and Severn[46]. There is

---

[46] There is a well-attested story of Elgar trying to stir a somewhat stolid London Symphony Orchestra into giving him the emotional expression he wanted at a certain passage in one of his symphonies by asking them to play it 'like something you hear down by the river'.

also the almost morbidly introverted mystic, evident in the opening pages and the passage depicting the Angel of the Agony in *Gerontius*, much influenced by Wagner's *Parsifal* and yet somehow gentler, less theatrical and more reserved. There is the worldly, full-blooded sybarite, highly moral yet wistfully gentle and certainly no puritan, as depicted in *Falstaff*. There is also the amiable, child-like fantasist and English eccentric, capable of setting the antics of a bulldog to music and of poking good-natured fun at a forceful friend who peremptorily told his guests at a country house party what the orders of the day would be. There is the other kind of visionary who felt the brutality that underlay the glories of Rome in that astonishing passage from *In the South* or the shivering guilt that underlay a certain kind of passion or longing (see, for example, parts of the first and third movements of the Second Symphony). And there is the world-weariness of the Cello Concerto[47] and the disillusion that makes the nihilistic Judas Iscariot of *The Apostles* one of Elgar's most fascinating creations.

That there is something that marks Elgar's music off from the various continental influences, notably those of Brahms and Wagner, to which he might have been subject, can be discerned from the following comment by the distinguished Viennese composer, conductor and musicologist, Dr Mosco Carner:

> Nationalism is not always a matter of literal quotation of folk-song motives, or the absorption, however complete and organic, of folksong elements into one's own personal style. It often expresses itself in a characteristic attitude of the musical mind, in a certain way of musical thinking and of tackling technical problems. This higher and more subtle kind of nationalism is the kind we meet in . . . Elgar. . . . It does not lie only in the shape and expression of Elgar's lyrical phrases. It is also felt in those quiet moments which Elgar is fond of introducing after his great emotional outbursts, moments in which the music reaches a maximum of beautifully poetic expression tinged with wistfulness. The foreign musician is perhaps better able than the Englishman

---

[47] And, if Anthony Payne's superb realisation of the sketches for the Third Symphony corresponds in any way to Elgar's intentions, of the bleak splendour of that work's slow movement.

to detect these national elements; they strike him as something new and different from the symphonic style of German music.

This is, I think, one of the shrewdest comments ever made on the 'national' element in Elgar; and it is hardly surprising that it should have come from a man who had studied and absorbed the music of Mahler, Schoenberg and Richard Strauss as a young man and who had come to know Elgar's music after emigrating from Hitler's Thousand-year Empire, with its 'blood-and-soil' racist doctrines. It may be this compatibility with the Germanic tradition that has made Elgar and Britten in particular easier for thoughtful and discerning expatriate musicians such as Dr Carner and Hans Keller to respond to than the music of such a 'towering figure' (Keller's phrase) as Vaughan Williams, who, as we shall see, was much more responsive to the techniques of impressionist composers like Debussy and Ravel than he was to the Austro-German tradition.

The main fruits of nationalism on the continent of Europe were in the field of opera and the epic symphonic poem. In the latter particularly, which could convey all sorts of overtones that could slip past the censor, we find pride in a national chivalric past particularly powerfully expressed. Yet there can be no doubt that opera, too, played a significant part in creating a sense of national pride and unity, notably in Italy, in Russia and in what is now the Czech republic. There is hardly an opera of Verdi's, for example, between *Nabucco* and *Il Trovatore* that does not allude at some point to the political situation of Italy, whether by direct reference or by symbolism. Even as late as *Don Carlos* there is the tremendous confrontation between established power and the desire for freedom, between family loyalty and patriotic duty and – most notably – between the repressive power of the Church and the natural inclination to at least a semblance of tolerance on the part of the Crown. Romantic musical nationalism was strongly political.

The economic and socio-political circumstances of independent, imperial and industrial England conditioned the type of 'serious' music that appealed most directly to Victorian audiences; and an output of large-scale illustrative orchestral and operatic compositions celebrating a now defunct heroic or legendary national past in order to stir up the desire to re-create a nation-state was quite unnecessary. The symbols of

Britain's industrial and political might were there for all to see[48]. Ordinary English-speaking people felt that, however miserable their lot, they were at least ruled by their own people, however incompetent; and they did enjoy a modicum of freedom and equality before the law, however limited. They had not suffered any genuine foreign rule for eight hundred years, for all that their Royal Family had been of German extraction since 1714. It was not only England's past that was glorious, but her present as well; and reminders of her past heroic valour, as for example Stanford projected in his setting of Tennyson's[49] *Revenge,* were essentially an idealised, even self-satisfied, celebration of present realities rather than the pious and fervent expression of future hopes. When Beecham referred to Elgar's A♭ Symphony as 'the musical equivalent of St Pancras station', the gibe was by no means the unmitigated insult that he probably intended it to be. The Victorian gothicists were building in a serious sense of chivalric historical achievement into their modern constructions. Similarly, Elgar's 'massive hope in the future' was based on pride in the present as well as the past.

One of Elgar's most sophisticated works, and one that appealed most strongly to the distinguished Scottish musician Donald Francis Tovey, is his rich and colourful 'symphonic study', as he called it, on the character of Shakespeare's *Falstaff.* Elgar was careful in his designation of this remarkable work. It is to a certain degree illustrative: incidents in the *Henry IV* plays are depicted in intimate detail; but it is mainly intended to be an exposition in musical terms of the moods and character of the central figure, that is to say his reactions to the various incidents referred to as well as a graphic account of them in musical

---

[48] They were even projected back into the remote past, as in the final chorus of Elgar's *Caractacus.* Elgar wanted something stirring patriotic and uplifting to bring the work to a triumphant conclusion; and he was somewhat put out when his librettist went overboard and wallowed in a jingoism that the composer found somewhat distasteful.

[49] It is interesting, by the way, that the poem Stanford chose to set, like *The Charge of the Light Brigade*, celebrates heroic defeat rather than glorious victory.

terms. It gives us, as Tovey points out in his masterly essay on the work, Falstaff from his own point of view. But what is perhaps most remarkable of all about it is the portrait that it gives the listener of Elgar himself.

To some extent most of Elgar's major works are subjective. The *Enigma Variations* are affectionate portrayals of friends as he saw them; the Violin Concerto certainly expresses his view of the relationship between himself and Alice Stewart-Wortley. The Second Symphony he referred to as 'the passionate pilgrimage of a soul', the soul being without question that of the composer himself. He described the Cello Concerto as summing up a man's attitude to life; and there can be little doubt that in *The Dream of Gerontius* he identified very closely with Newman's central figure. There is even a good case for claiming that the figure of Judas in *The Apostles* draws to a considerable degree on the doubts and nihilistic moods that overtook him from time to time. But in none of his works does he provide so well-rounded a picture of himself, if the image may be forgiven, as in *Falstaff.*

Elgar's portrait of Shakespeare's great anti-hero is highly individual. He took as his starting point an essay by the 18th-century commentator Maurice Morgann, who described Falstaff as

> ... a knave without malice, a lyar without deceit; and a knight, a gentleman and a soldier, without either dignity, decency, or honour.

Yet Elgar's approach to his subject immediately confronts us with a problem. How can such characteristics as those he quotes from Morgann be expressed in music? Music has been associated from time immemorial with pageantry and ceremony; and since its pageantry and ceremonial have been overwhelmingly associated with the court and the church, those outward trappings – a steady, majestic processional gait, dignity and rich splendour – should not be difficult to conjure up through slowly-moving harmonies, regular, stately rhythms and fullness of instrumentation. These characteristics were all readily recognisable in Elgar's highly personal musical idiom, at least from the time that he composed his first large-scale orchestral piece, the concert overture *Froissart.* They would obviously fit the character of Falstaff's complement, Prince Hal. But how could he project the character of Hal against what was for him the more fascinating character of his 'knight, gentleman and soldier' who was a knave and a liar, without either dignity, decency, or honour? What in *Gerontius* and the Second Symphony is the story of 'There, one day perhaps, go I' becomes more a matter of 'There, but for the grace of God, go I'.

To say that the work is to a large degree subjective is not to maintain that Elgar was a liar, or that he lacked dignity, decency, or honour. But he must have reasoned, for musical as well as personal reasons, that Shakespeare's Falstaff, at any rate in his own estimation, possessed other characteristics than those outlined by Morgann. And these other characteristics were part of Elgar's own make-up: nostalgia for a more innocent past, a boisterous sense of fun[50], ambition and the realisation that he was only partially a man of this world. Not for nothing does he point out that the reference to Henry V's 'military' theme as the penultimate gesture in the work indicates that 'the man of stern reality has triumphed'. As an artist, he felt himself not to be a 'man of stern reality' but one of those 'dreamers of dreams' who created great cities and empires of the imagination, as the O'Shaughnessy poem puts it that he set in his choral work *The Music-makers* that was virtually contemporary with *Falstaff*. Elgar the dreamer is just as prominent a figure in his music as the Elgar who commemorates[51] the 'pomp and circumstance', whether of 'glorious war' or of anything else.

Although a fictional character, Falstaff is, in a sense, in what was to become the tradition of great English eccentrics: people who were a law unto themselves, so confident in their own abilities that they felt able to

---

[50] One aspect of this is his partiality for what he called 'japes', such as spoof letters and high-spirited games with the schoolboy children of one of his friends pictured in the *Enigma* Variations, taking the role of the reprobate sea-captain Nanty Ewart from Scott's *Redgauntlet*.

[51] Elgar knew his *Othello* well enough, when choosing the generic title for his five marches, that the phrase came from a reflective and nostalgic speech in which Othello bids farewell to that same pomp and circumstance. Careful consideration of the less frequently played of the marches, especially Nos 2 and 3, shows military music from a markedly different viewpoint from that of the more popular Nos 1 and 4.

'do their own thing'. It is this Falstaff who is the monarch of the Boar's Head tavern in Eastcheap. It is this Falstaff who is the central figure of Elgar's study and the relaxed, sybaritic, amoral antipode to the young Prince Hal. Realisation of this fact enables the spectator (and, by extension, the listener) to appreciate his slyness, his laxity in bending the rules, even that evasiveness and unwillingness to offend that foreigners sometimes misconstrue as hypocrisy. In portraying Falstaff, Elgar was paying his tribute to someone typically English. Moreover, he seized, consciously or unconsciously, on certain aspects of his beloved West Midlands, the scene for the exquisite interlude set in Justice Shallow's orchard. The two interludes from the work are thus complementary to the main action in portraying not just the background to Falstaff and in rounding out his character, but in projecting Elgar himself and *his* background as a reflection of Shakespeare's magnificent buffoon.

Falstaff is almost the last and possibly the greatest of a long series of commemorations of Romantic chivalry and the gentleman ideal in his output. As well as *Froissart,* already mentioned, which bears the heading from Keats 'When chivalry lifted up her lance on high', there is the early cantata *The Black Knight;* there are also the later cantatas *The Banner of Saint George, Scenes from the Saga of King Olaf* and *Caractacus.* Their very titles tell their own story. During the First World War there was to follow the choral triptych *The Spirit of England,* especially the valedictory and poignant *For the Fallen,* one of Elgar's noblest and most moving short choral works[52]. In many of these works, Elgar cast a nostalgic glance back at an era when noble knights and warriors jousted for the favours of virtuous maidens, and bards inspired armies with a lusty battle-song. That this view of an heroic past totally ignored the dirt, disease, oppression, superstition and double-dealing that were just

---

[52] It is of more than incidental interest here that the curious, almost grotesque central march section of that work, depicting the armies going brave and smiling into battle, is based on a theme rather like a conflation of the march of Falstaff's scarecrow army and the demons' music from *Gerontius* while the chorus declaims the relevant section of Binyon's poem in a hushed monotone, as if to underline the grim pitilessness of modern mechanised warfare.

as closely woven into the fabric of the time is neither here nor there: the essential function of chivalry, according to the historian Maurice Keen, is to hold up an idealised image of armed conflict in defiance of the harsh realities of actual warfare. Yet in Elgar's case, there is a vein of sceptical realism running through the whole: Falstaff's army is anything but disciplined, valorous or chivalrous. Yet in one of the most magical acts of thematic transformation in the entire work, the theme that portrays its slouching gait gradually melts into a gentle lyrical version that leads into the old men's colloquy in Justice Shallow's orchard.

It seems to me that Elgar was well aware that the idealised picture of an age with a stern code of honour and obligation, of religious faith and sexual chastity (conveniently overlooking the fact that in those days royal and noble bastards were, if not ten a penny, at any rate common coinage) was fine stuff on which to base stirring and uplifting musical narratives: 'tales', as he and his remarkable mother called them. Britain had, he felt, a role to play in the world. She was still, and despite the growing industrial might of the United States and Germany, the workshop of the world. Her people were no longer just a 'polite and commercial people', she had a restless and energetic, thrustful middle class, looking not only to the Old Testament Hebrews as their political and religious role-models, but to the ancient Romans and the medieval knights. Moreover, there can be no doubt that, rightly or wrongly, this secular and paternalistic ethos was felt by many sensitive Englishman, including Elgar, to be one on which the benevolent features of British imperial rule were unshakably based. In this, they took their cue from Virgil, on whose works those of them who had enjoyed the privileged education of a Victorian public school[53] had been brought up:

> Tu regere imperio populos, Romane, memento
> (Hae tibi erunt artes), pacique imponere morem,
> Parcere subiectis et debellare superbos.

It was the role of the British, as the modern equivalent of the ancient Romans, to 'impose ordered ways upon a state of peace, to spare those

---

[53] Elgar was, of course, not one of these. His much admired colleague Hubert Parry, however, was.

who have submitted and to subdue the arrogant'. Perhaps those who claimed to subscribe to this code of conduct may have been mistaking the shadow for the substance, but many of them genuinely believed that they were carrying out Virgil's injunction.

Elgar genuinely accepted as ideals the values that they stood for; as a projection of reality, he knew there was more to the story of the Age of Chivalry than that. Elgar was not simply an idealist Romantic with glamorised view of human nature. The very qualities that could be aimed at as an ideal could be perverted into vice and degradation. The music for the demons in *Gerontius* tells us as much. It has been frequently criticised – in my view with an astonishing naivety and a complete misunderstanding of catholic moral theology – as being 'too gentlemanly'. This is, in fact, a back-handed compliment. As a Roman Catholic, Elgar would have been aware that Pride is the seventh and deadliest of the seven deadly sins. The music of the demons projects a kind of petulant pride in what is in fact a brilliant self-parody[54]. It is not marked to be played 'nobilmente'; but Elgar does employ the term 'grandioso', the same word that he applies to the brutal 'Roman' episode[55] of *In the South* and also, as we shall see, to an important passage in *Falstaff*.

The medieval and chivalric Victorian revival has been fascinatingly traced by Marc Girouard in *The Return to Camelot*. This study of 'chivalry and the English gentleman' relates the theme to various strands in English 19th-century life, including the cult of the self-deprecating gentleman amateur athlete, the ethos promulgated by the Victorian public school and the life and work of such national heroes as General Gordon, once considered but finally abandoned by Elgar as the subject of a large-scale symphonic work, Captain Scott and his ill-fated

---

[54] Benjamin Britten saw the point at once. When rehearsing the CUMS chorus for a memorable Aldeburgh Festival performance of *Gerontius*, he specifically warned them off the idea of investing the music with a kind of cloak-and-dagger melodramatic pantomime-demon posturing. He wanted it cold, arrogant and sulky.

[55] So much for Virgil's 'parcere subiectis'!

companions on their expedition to the South Pole. How then does Falstaff fit into the picture?

Falstaff tries to tell the whole story; it is what Aldous Huxley called 'whole-truth' art. From the outset, Elgar consciously envisages him as 'in a green old age, mellow, frank, gay, easy, corpulent, loose, unprincipled, and luxurious'. Elgar clearly had no intention of emasculating the old rogue into a decorous Victorian public-school gentleman. This Falstaff is by no means modest, playful, self-indulgent and wheedling. He is also tender-hearted, wistful and regretful of the contrast between what is and what might have been.

As a study in musical terms of human psychology, *Falstaff* thus centres basically round the tension between the central figure and the heir to the throne, Prince Hal. In moral terms, the tension expressed is that between the uninhibited and irresponsible, even anti-social, elements in human character and those of self-discipline, social restraint and responsibility. So much for the 'study' aspect of Elgar's title. What of the 'symphonic' one?

The 'symphonic' nature of the work is shown in a number of ways. First of all, as Tovey pointed out long ago, it is completely independent of the idea that all the themes in a tone-poem should derive from one basic cell. It does not grow out of a single germinal motif, but out of the interplay of two kinds of theme, each associated with a basic tonality. Elgar allots at least two main themes to Prince Hal and several to Falstaff himself. Falstaff is seen (or rather heard of) not just from the objective point of view but from his own. 'Tell Delius,' he wrote once, 'that I grow more like Falstaff every day'. There is a theme, for example, that portrays him as 'a goodly, portly man, of a cheerful look, a pleasing eye and a most noble carriage', that is eventually wittily combined in counterpoint with one indicating his boastfulness and colossal mendacity[56]. And since Falstaff is not only witty in himself, but the cause

---

[56] The 'boastful' theme is used in augmentation, through one of Elgar's cheekiest strokes of verbal and musical punning, when Falstaff declares that on the accession of the new king, he and his friends will all be 'augmented in the fount of honour'. It also becomes his reaction to the sentence of banishment: he thinks the King is just putting on a show.

that there is wit in others, other themes are generated by a kind of chain reaction by the main ones. Significant but incidental figures in Falstaff's environment, such as Mrs Quickly, Doll Tearsheet and her 'dozen or fourteen honest gentlewomen' and rogues like Pistol, Bardolph and Poins also play their part in the musical action.

The basic key of the work is C minor – a curious key for such a superficially jovial subject, associated as it is with such works as Beethoven's Fifth and Brahms's First Symphonies. Yet the essential seriousness and monumentality of Elgar's work (he claimed when at work on it that it would last twenty minutes; in fact it takes a good half hour to perform) are at least partially demonstrated by his choice of basic key. Falstaff also has an important theme in E minor; and the two meditative interludes: the tender passage in which Falstaff dreams of his youth and the episode in Shallow's orchard – are in and around A minor. The complementary key to C minor – E♭ major – clearly established with the entry of Prince Hal's 'courtly and genial' theme, as Elgar puts it, is used to project the aspect of the prince that would endear him to his subjects but would also demonstrate his fundamental nobility. Yet, again as Tovey pointed out long ago, Elgar never designates it with his favourite term 'nobilmente'[57]. Tovey's comment that the theme should none the less be played as if it were so marked is shrewd. Hal's first exit speech in *Henry IV* Part I is highly significant. Of Falstaff and his companions, he soliloquises thus:

> I know you all, and will a while uphold
> The unyoked humour of your idleness.
> Yet herein will I imitate the sun,
> Who doth permit the base contagious clouds
> To smother up his beauty from the world,
> That when he please again to be himself,
> Being wanted may be more wondered at

---

[57] I cannot see why this term should be considered 'self-conscious' and therefore reprehensible. It indicates how Elgar wants the theme to be played; it does *not* mean that he self-importantly considered the theme itself to be noble. And anyway, 'nobilmente' also means 'expansively, generously'.

By breaking through the foul and ugly mists
Of vapours that did seem to strangle him.

Elgar's appreciation of the irony of the situation is surely indicated, possibly unconsciously, by two touches. Firstly by his choice of the term 'grandioso' even when the new King appears in his coronation regalia towards the end of the work and the theme rings out in the full panoply of the Elgarian orchestra at its most sonorous and brilliant; and secondly by the fact that the full statement of this theme always incurs a brief excursion into the minor mode, as if to undermine, even if only momentarily, its confident self-assertion. Elgar, like Brahms, treats the third and sixth degrees of the scale as ambivalent: they may be either major or minor[58]. It is this theme that undergoes some of Elgar's most imaginative modifications during the course of the work, its rhythm transformed and broken into spritely repeated quavers with a triplet background when the Prince is in mischievous mood, or dispersed in an almost Webern-like pointillist manner when his presence in the background is merely hinted at.

Hal's geniality and recklessness lie all on the surface. He is chivalrous; but his chivalry is tempered by a steely firmness. Thus his theme appears in a skittish and playful variant in the passage portraying the Gadshill plot, to be projected in company with diminished variants both of Falstaff's own main theme and of the theme illustrating his boastfulness, treated as a vigorous fugato that graphically illustrates how the original two men in buckram become twenty in Falstaff's mendacious and colourful account of the episode. And when Falstaff's pretensions are deflated, the 'goodly, cheerful' theme returns and the company dissolves in ribald laughter at his discomfiture. And Falstaff

---

[58] Some commentators consider the ambivalent use of the major and minor degrees of the scale as one hallmark of a particularly English style; this should be taken with a fair-sized pinch of salt. Schubert, Brahms and Mahler were in no sense honorary Englishmen; and Brahms's Third Symphony, in which he exploits this ambivalence most poetically as a structural device, was one of Elgar's favourites. The sweep and power of the opening must surely have influenced that of his own Second Symphony.

drops off to sleep behind the arras, his principal theme gradually descends in augmentation through a splendid haze of impressionistic scoring that conveys graphically the onset of a drunken descent into unconsciousness.

The King invades Falstaff's tonal territory, too. He has another theme in C minor, Falstaff's own key, a loose and rhythmically distorted inversion of his 'noble' one. Where the 'noble' theme curves downwards and then rises upward as if in aspiration, this one arches upward only to drop abruptly downwards, gradually gaining in strength and menace as it does so. Where the 'noble' theme is fluent, expansive, processional and stately, this one is austere, terse and fragmentary. Where the tonality of the 'noble' theme is clear and diatonic, the harmonisation of the 'military' one is ambivalent, centring as it does round the chord of the diminished seventh. And unlike many a theme in Elgar, it is starkly devoid of those typically Elgarian chromatic inner counter-melodies that add such warmth and almost regretful wistfulness to so many of his themes.[59] Elgar uses it to represent the King's stark and stern military character; and it is this theme, as has already been pointed out, that has the last word. It is also the theme used to underline the new King's brutal rejection of Falstaff's offer of loyalty:

> I know thee not, old man. Fall to thy prayers
> How ill white hairs become a fool and jester!
> I have long dreamt of such a kind of man,
> So surfeit-swelled, so old and so profane,
> But being awake, I do despise my dream.
> Make less thy body hence and more thy grace.

Used in this manner, it not only casts a shadow across the moving final section of the work, an elegiac and romantic farewell as pathetic

---

[59] To give but three examples of many, the middle section of the march from the second *Wand of Youth* Suite, the exquisite viola counter-theme to the string tune in the Larghetto of the Second Symphony, or the meandering horn tune that is woven into the texture of the second main theme of the finale of the same work.

and moving in its way as that of the end of the Cello Concerto composed some five years later.

Elgar's attitude to 'the pomp and circumstance of glorious war' in *Falstaff* is in fact distinctly ambivalent. Both Hal and Falstaff are soldiers; and Elgar's unrivalled command of march rhythms and a martial bearing underlines the fact. But what is remarkable about the work is his equally secure command of the 'anti-chivalrous' aspects of warfare. This is most obviously seen in the witty and marvellously telling portrayal of the slouching march of Falstaff's scarecrow army, recruited on the cheap and ready to run at the first sign of the enemy. This music is developed with imagination and flexibility, combining with the themes associated with Falstaff's pot-house companions and the 'honest gentlewomen' as if to suggest that this army is distinguished more for its prowess in the tavern and the bawdy-house than on the battlefield.

J B Priestley once argued that Falstaff represented an older, more easy-going England than the tight-lipped, superficially well-behaved and self-controlled England of Victorian times. Elgar seems to conform to this view, consciously or otherwise, in his attitude to him. This is particularly notable in his sharply focused but none the less sympathetic portrayal of Doll Tearsheet and her dozen or fourteen honest gentlewomen: outwardly somewhat prim and coy, but harbouring a coquettish spriteliness that betrays their true and rather less respectable nature. The theme that represents what they mean to Falstaff is presented first in brusque and fragmentary form; only after the Gadshill episode are they raised symphonically to the status of a lyrical, scherzo-like episode, lasting 90 bars, if the repeat is observed, with scoring that is at one and the same time brash and delicate (and with some typical melting Elgarian inner parts). The 'gentlewomen' don't take the old rogue too seriously; nor he them, though his thoughts are at times with them during the battle sequence; and they are also in the background when he dies. (And why not? Mrs Quickly gives the account of his death in *Henry V*, where it is claimed that as well as babbling of green fields, he also babbled of women). Moreover, the theme of the 'dream' sequence is markedly similar in outline to what might be a romanticised version of their theme, a reminiscence, as it might be, of his feelings for a nurse, his mother, or a childhood or adolescent sweetheart rather than for the sharp and worldly ladies of his current mode of existence.

Coupled to this is Elgar's wonderful awareness of the calm and freshness of the English countryside and the gentleness that George Orwell found at the heart of our way of life. We have already touched on this. The association of countryside with childhood is most marked in Elgar; and a further association is with the concept of innocence. But Elgar's innocence is not merely thought of with regret for its loss. It is fresh and unblemished, touched with a sense of wonder and serenity, before the sophistication of adulthood blows away the 'clouds of glory' rather than with regret at is passing. This kind of innocence pervades, for example, the opening of Part II of *Gerontius*, where the soul of Gerontius (again in the semblance of a dream) is transported into the next world. It is also found in the Beatitude sequence in *The Apostles* and above all in certain episodes in the two Symphonies, in the *Enigma Variations*, particularly in WN and Dorabella, and the Violin Concerto.

This is not all, however. There is also a sense of menace, an almost prophetic menace, not far short of rage and violence, in certain passages in Elgar. Cases in point are the hushed, hectic opening of the third *Pomp and Circumstance* march, the similar mood of the opening of the scherzo of the First Symphony, bursting out as it does into a swaggering theme that would not be out of place in one of the marches, and above all in two remarkable passages, one from *In the South* and the other from the scherzo of the Second Symphony. These two passages show an aspect of Elgar, and of 'Englishness', that is unusual, yet that crops up in composers after him, notably Vaughan Williams and Britten.

The 'Roman army' passage from *In the South* was singled out by Tovey in his enthusiastic essay on the piece. It is reminiscent more of Strauss or Mahler in its almost brutal intensity; what seems to me to be English about it is the matter-of-fact manner in which it eventually subsides and fades away into the distance. This, surely, is one of those passages alluded to by Dr Carner as one of those great emotional outbursts followed by quiet moments in which the music reaches a maximum of beautifully poetic expression tinged with wistfulness 'that strike the foreign musician as something new and different from the

168

symphonic style of German music'[60]. Elgar is aware of the brutality. He does not wallow in it, nor does he hammer away at it *ad nauseam*; it is part of the fabric of things. He acknowledges its existence, but he seems unwilling to abandon himself to the examination of its implications. It is allowed to impinge upon, but not to disrupt, the normal pattern of life.

The passage from the Second Symphony, Elgar said, represents 'the *madness* that attends the excess or abuse of passion' – something akin to what Strauss portrayed with spectacular skill in works such as *Elektra, Salome* or Mahler in the Fifth and Sixth Symphonies. But again, the fascination is only momentary. It is not the norm, but a deviation from it; and it is not allowed to become obsessive. Elgar accepts the underlying violence – hysteria, if you will – as a fact of life, but he pushes it away from him, half in regret, half in fear of the consequences of the force that he has unleashed. In relation to both these amazing passages, it is worth remembering that Elgar quoted from Tennyson to point up his musical image. Regarding *In the South*, the passage (from *The Daisy*) runs:

> What Roman strength Turbia showed
> In ruin by the mountain road.

And in the Second Symphony, when a sinister chromatic theme 'a malign influence in the garden on a summer night', as Elgar himself described it, emerges half out of the shadows in the first movement recurs with shattering intensity in the third, the quotation is from *Maud*:

> Dead, long dead,
> Long dead!
> And my heart is a handful of dust,
> And the wheels go over my head,
> And my bones are shaken with pain,
> For into a shallow grave they are thrust,
> Only a yard beneath the street,
> And the hoofs of the horses beat, beat
> The hoofs of the horses beat,
> Beat into my scalp and brain.

---

[60] Or contemporary Italian opera: witness *Tosca* and *Turandot*.

Elgar seems to have associated both these passages in his music with death and ruin – 'that sense of ruin which is worse than pain', to quote *Gerontius*. Falstaff's death, too, has its brutal side. After the glowing coda, recalling all his human contacts and their main themes before his own disintegrates rather in the manner of the coda of the great funeral march in Beethoven's *Eroica* Symphony, there is the quiet moment of death itself and a curt and vivid reminiscence of 'the man of stern reality'. Death is a fact of life, whether it is faced in anguish, as in *Gerontius*, or in nihilistic fatalism, as with Judas in *The Apostles*, or conceived of as prelude to a nightmare. Elgar takes it seriously, whether in the awesome opening to *Gerontius*, the remarkable part-song *Death on the Hills*, or in the climax of the slow movement of the Second Symphony, which Antony Hopkins associates with St Paul's 'O Death, where is thy sting; O Grave, where is thy victory?'. Here is the sense of a life that may have ended with the grave, but still ended in triumph. Yet even here, at the very end of the movement, the consoling thought and the great triumphant gesture die away into the chill reality of the tomb, just as does the shadowy processional opening of *For the Fallen*, striking subdominant harmonies instead of the expected dominant ones and reminding the listener who knows the Second Symphony that the proud second theme of the finale has a more sombre reverse side to show.

Such music gives the sense of a supernatural that strikes chill, not comfort or self-fulfilment. For the moment, all sense of chivalry and triumph are banished; nor is there any sense of a nobler and better world to come. There is just a bleak sense of something transcending normal human emotion. Whereas on its first appearance the phantom and tonally ambiguous theme in the Second Symphony is simply eerie and disturbing – 'a malign influence on a summer evening', as Elgar described it in a letter to Alice Stewart-Wortley[61] – its consummation as it emerges from the half-light frolicking of the scherzo is menacing if not downright terrifying. But even that is not the whole story: the resolution of all this occurs in the coda of the finale after the 'noble action' has led

---

[61] Possibly relating to some guilty feeling of erotic arousal?

170

to the hero's apotheosis[62] in terms of 'Well done, thou good and faithful servant'. This is no look back in nostalgia, but a sober and measured summing up of the whole 'passionate pilgrimage' that was launched so impetuously in the first movement.

When Elgar really does wish to express regret for days long gone, few can match him in sheer intensity. The brief slow movement of the Cello Concerto and the poignant passage towards the end of the finale that eventually leads into an allusion to part of that movement are indications of this. For years after this, Elgar avoided any profound emotional expression, so much so that until recently it has always been assumed that after the death of his wife he lost all desire to compose on any scale, except for a few escapist fantasies into the realm of childhood, such as the *Nursery Suite* composed for the present Queen and her sister in 1930 and that interesting celebration of 'democratic' music-making, the *Severn Suite* for brass band of the same year. These seem to show 'the mixture as before'. Yet it would seem from Anthony Payne's realisation of the voluminous sketches for the Third Symphony on which Elgar was working until his last final illness that this was not so. There is enough genuine first-hand Elgar in this reconstruction of what the work might have been like to show that it would not have been just a re-hash of familiar Elgarian characteristics, but that it would have projected a new resoluteness and austerity, born not of impotence but as the logical outcome of that resignation that features so prominently in the Cello Concerto. Yet even there, as the great French cellist Paul Tortelier pointed out in a televised master-class, 'Elgar was an Englishman, a stoic. Life must go on.' The present may seem to be regretful; but it must be faced and accepted. There may have been moments of doubt and difficulty, but the whole venture of life is worth it, both in human and non-human terms.

This seems to me the message of so many of Elgar's great spacious codas, like those at the end of *Gerontius* and *The Apostles*, where the music reaches the haven of a calm yet glowing transcendental fulfilment. Maybe neither Falstaff nor Prince Hal quite measures up to this. The

---

[62] Elgar's own comment: see Canon W H Temple Gairdner's essay on the Second Symphony.

one is too lax and self-indulgent, the other too much of a prig. And though at times Elgar might appear to be a bit of both, at his greatest and most inspired he was neither. Eclectic and versatile, open to influences from abroad – he enjoyed the music of Bizet[63], Delibes, Massenet, Fauré and Verdi, as well as that of the great Austro-German masters, developed an interest in jazz late in his life and was himself a lifelong master of the elegant miniature – the white heat of his inspiration fused all that he loved into a highly personal and very English idiom.

---

[63] I have always thought that the trio section of the second *Pomp and Circumstance* march owes more than a little to the march in Bizet's *Jeux d'Enfants*.

10 – The Rebel Conformist: Ralph Vaughan Williams

English music-lovers sometimes take a kind of 'hands off our English music' attitude to foreigners. This may result from snobbery, chauvinism, or a stubborn, self-conscious determination to prove to the world that the Land Without Music is nothing of the kind and that therefore foreigners are bound to misunderstand English music. It may, on the other hand, simply be a matter of rueful and guilty surprise that foreign musicians can show us that there is sometimes more to our own music than we ourselves realise. I neither care nor wish to conjecture. But when Toscanini conducted the *Enigma Variations* and Casals played the Elgar Cello Concerto in the 1930s, they weren't exactly damned with faint praise[64]. They were, however, taken to task by English critics for certain 'un-English' aspects of their interpretations of these two great English masterpieces. Elgar himself had no qualms about foreigners performing his music. He commended the first German performance of *Gerontius* and was quite willing to write the solo part in his Violin Concerto for Fritz Kreisler, with whom he wanted to record the work in the last decade of his life[65]. At least four of the finest interpreters of the Cello Concerto have been French or of French extraction: Tortelier, Gendron, Fournier and Jacqueline du Pré. And although non-English

---

[64] Attitudes changed during the post-World War II period. Casals was hailed as a master interpreter of the work; and when Sir Adrian Boult, who conducted for him both before and after the War, was asked what differed in his post-war interpretation from his pre-war one, he replied tersely: 'Nothing'.

[65] Thereby hangs a tale. Instead of Kreisler, the Gramophone Company enlisted the teenage Yehudi Menuhin, who not only loved the work but struck up a warm friendship with the composer himself.

conductors have sometimes generated controversy about their interpretations of, for example, the *Enigma*[66], most of them have thrown new light on works, movements and passages that we thought we knew.

Similarly, there is a regrettable but understandable tendency to regard Ralph Vaughan Williams as so 'English' a composer that only Englishmen can be genuinely deeply affected by his music. The converse of this narrow view of his musical personality is either to claim that he led English music into a nationalistic cul-de-sac or, alternatively, that we are in duty bound to ignore the numerous foreign influences that he, like Purcell, Handel and Elgar before him, was able successfully to absorb. To draw attention to them, it seems, constitutes an act of musical treason, or at the very least of some kind of unspecified aesthetic sabotage.

To some extent this is understandable. After all, Vaughan Williams was a great musical patriot. He collected over 800 folk-songs in the field. He edited a hymn-book that became famous as *The English Hymnal*. He edited two volumes of Welcome Songs for the Purcell Society and was a notable figure in the revival of interest not only of Purcell's music but of that of the Elizabethans. He insisted throughout his career that Englishmen should cultivate and learn from their own national musical heritage rather than writing second-hand German music in the style approved by his own teachers. He was quick to defend that heritage from any inroads that might be made into it by immigrant musicians from whatever culture. In short, he was both consciously and subconsciously a truly English musician.

Yet I personally believe that Vaughan Williams, for all his undoubted awareness of his English heritage and his staunch musical patriotism, was one of the greatest and most gifted of the international generation of impressionist composers such as Debussy, the early Stravinsky, Falla, Albeniz and Ravel. In one sense this is hardly surprising, as Ravel was one of his teachers. But he was also exposed to, and to some extent absorbed, the expressionist ethos that developed out

---

[66] Notably Leonard Bernstein; but then Elgar was not the only composer to be subjected to idiosyncratic treatment by this enormously gifted but often wilful musician.

of the work of Strauss and Mahler (both composers whose music he cordially disliked) and led to the dodecaphonic music of Schoenberg and his followers[67]. His music is certainly English; but it is much more broadly-based than that – which, paradoxically, makes it more English still, if the ability to react to, assimilate and adapt foreign influences is as true of English music as it assuredly is of the English language.

If the avowed intention to create music deeply rooted in English life and culture is the supreme criterion of Englishness, one would surely consider Vaughan Williams as the most English composer of all. By birth and upbringing he was a sturdy product of the Victorian professional middle classes: descended from the famous pottery manufacturing family of the Wedgwoods and from the Darwins on his mother's side; and he was also the offspring of a family distinguished in the learned professions on his father's. His father himself was an Anglican clergyman, his grandfather a High Court judge. One of his uncles was the world-famous naturalist who had sent a colossal tremor through the bedrock of Victorian religious faith with *The Origin of Species*. Educated at Charterhouse School, Trinity College, Cambridge (where he took a good degree in History as well as graduating as a Bachelor of Music and where he was a contemporary, amongst others, of the philosopher Bertrand Russell), he bears all the hallmarks of a serious-minded Victorian intellectual. His circle of friends and acquaintances at Cambridge included the daughters of the Master of Downing College, with whom Peter Ilyitch Tchaikovsky stayed when he came to Cambridge to receive an honorary doctorate in 1893; and Vaughan Williams himself was one of the guests at the ceremonial dinner given in honour of Tchaikovsky and his fellow honorary graduands.

At the time of his graduation, Vaughan Williams claims he was 'the complete musical prig'. His seriousness was marked not only by his musical preferences but by his assiduous application to his intellectual development. Bach, Beethoven ('ex officio', as he put it: although he

---

[67] Vaughan Williams mistrusted what he felt to be the Teutonic academicism of the 12-note school, though as an old man he went to see both the dress-rehearsal and the opening night of *Wozzeck* at Covent Garden.

composed nine symphonies himself, he never really felt a great sympathy for the Beethoven idiom), Wagner and Brahms were his acknowledged musical idols[68]; and during his vacations, he and a group of like-minded friends would go on serious reading parties in outlying parts of Britain such as the Yorkshire Dales, the Lake District, the Scottish islands and Cornwall.

There was more to it, however, than high-minded seriousness. There was within him a strain, not only of the English individualist freethinker and pioneer but even perhaps of the English eccentric. For all his outward conformity with the code of his class and tribe, as it were, there was a strong sense of the questing, earnestly searching explorer and a highly-developed sense of fun. Such men and women were not uncommon in Victorian England; but by the time Vaughan Williams came to maturity in the 1890s, they were becoming increasingly rare.

Only in one aspect was Vaughan Williams was an explorer in the physical sense – that of actually collecting folk-songs from folk musicians – but he could still explore new intellectual and spiritual horizons, becoming, as it were, a kind of David Livingstone of the human spirit. All his life he was drawn to the kind of person that sought to meet a difficult challenge, whether physical or intellectual, and to discover what inner resources he possessed to meet such a challenge. When he was just over thirty years of age, he composed a song-cycle to poems by Robert Louis Stevenson called *Songs of Travel* in which he nails what were to become his characteristic artistic colours firmly to the mast: the idea of the traveller who is prepared to risk all in the quest for aesthetic and spiritual truth. One of his first large-scale published works was a setting of a poem by the American writer Walt Whitman that begins:

> Darest thou now, O soul,
> Walk out with me toward the unknown region
> Where neither ground is for the feet nor any path to follow?

---

[68] Officially, of course. He had also developed a clandestine taste for less 'approved' works, such as Verdi's Requiem and Bizet's *Carmen*.

This search for an unknown spiritual region occupied Vaughan Williams all his life; and the imagery in which it was expressed took various widely differing forms. Even the ninth and last of his symphonies, composed when he was considerably over eighty years of age, sought to break new ground in form and content. Yet like so many English artists, he was loth to throw out the baby with the bath-water. Musically, he refused to abandon the tonal heritage within which he had been brought up; spiritually, he sought to express his explorations through not just avowedly 'New-style' writers such as Whitman, but through the imagery of Shakespeare, the Authorised Version of the Bible, Bunyan's *Pilgrim's Progress* and poets such as George Herbert. His stylistic search for an idiom that fully expressed what he felt he had to say took in many elements, some of them deliberately archaic, simply because he felt that they would have a 'resonance' with most of his fellow-countrymen. He was for much of his life an atheist, but he responded to the imagery, the cadences and the underlying ethos of the Bible and the Book of Common Prayer, which is why he so frequently chose biblical or liturgical texts to set to music, nearly always handling them in an unexpected or unconventional manner. Without ever pandering to his public, he bore in mind what, in an almost mystical way, would reach them through the traditions that they had absorbed almost by right of birth.

It took Vaughan Williams some time to find his feet as a composer. He began by adopting the prevalent Germanic, almost Brahmsian, idiom of his teachers Parry and Stanford; and certain features of even his earliest style remained with him all his life. He discarded very little; he wasted nothing. For him, each new work set problems that had to be solved on its own terms, not forced to fit a pre-ordained formula. His style did not ossify; he absorbed new elements that he found useful into his very personal idiom, but each in its way modified a style that was already well-marked by the time he reached full artistic maturity in the years just before the outbreak of World War I. As well as mapping out in detail new lands that other composers had stumbled on, he was forever re-exploring familiar territory and drawing attention to new landmarks in it.

As a young man, his tastes in poetry centred on the later Romantics and the pre-Raphaelite poets such as the Rossettis; and his individual voice can be heard fitfully in early works such as the song-cycle *The House of Life* and particularly his first published work – which remained one of his most popular – the setting of the Dorset poet William Barnes's *Linden Lea*. Whitman became one liberating influence; the discovery of the great Russian nationalist composers, notably Mussorgsky, another. But there were two influences above all that were to stamp his musical style indelibly. One was the discovery of English folk-song; the other that of Impressionism.

Much, often too much, has been made of the influence of folk-song on Vaughan Williams's musical personality. The study and assimilation of national folk-song and ballads had been a marked characteristic of late 19th-century musical Romanticism in Bohemia and Slovakia and Russia, as it was becoming in Vaughan Williams's own time in Hungary, Scandinavia and Spain. Romanticism is often dismissed as an airy-fairy, cloud-cuckoo structure of idealistic aesthetic sentimentality. It was not. Right from the start of the Romantic movement, the idea of a nation-state based on a unity of those who spoke the same language was a strong influence in the development of the arts and in particular of opera. There was a strong, idealistic, but none the less hard-headed socio-political component. Weber's consciously German songs of the period of the Wars of Liberation against Napoleon were symptoms of a developing German national political consciousness. Wagner's mature music-dramas consciously sought to recreate from Germanic myths and legends a cultural synthesis that, free from any foreign contamination, would have the same effect on the Germans as Attic tragedy was held to have had on the ancient Greeks. Verdi's middle-period operas were often consciously based on stories from medieval and ancient history in which a united Italy was the protagonist of a moral and Christian culture against heathen invaders, or where an oppressed people under alien rule were quickly identified, like the Hebrew slaves in *Nabucco*, with the Italians held under Habsburg or other foreign domination. Smetana's ambitious pageant-operas and tone poems were inspired to a large degree by patriotic plots, such as Czech resistance to the 13th-century Germanic invasion of Bohemia, the foundation of the Bohemian kingdom itself, or the perceived glories of Czech history, legend or landscape. Mussorgsky's great epic operas *Boris Godunov* and *Khovanschina* were appeals to the Russian people to get their act together through a glimpse at stirring episodes in their past.

Vaughan Williams was indeed passionately interested in and affected by the music of the people; but he approached it from a rather different angle from continental nationalist composers such as the Russians, the Czechs and Bela Bartók. For them, there was an intensely political element in their musical nationalism. He, on the other hand, had been born into the privileged classes and grew up in an age and an England that was proud, powerful and independent. It was governed by a parliament whose members were elected by more or less universal manhood suffrage. Social discontent and patriotic feeling undoubtedly existed; but except in Ireland, social resentment was at least directed against a native rather than an alien ruling class. Political patriotism generally took the form of a sense of present national superiority. It was not a nostalgic look back to the past or forward into the future.

For Vaughan Williams the political element was necessarily much more limited. He was no ivory-tower musician. His political opinions were generous, liberal and humanitarian[69], not narrow and chauvinistic. As a trained historian, he was aware that England had already been for centuries a nation-state of the kind towards the achievement of which the continental Romantic nationalists were striving. The nearest musical equivalent in Britain to the *Risorgimento* operas of Verdi, the *Leier und Schwert* songs of Weber at the time of the Napoleonic Wars, the reticent Germanic idealism of Schumann, the deliberate cultivation of Polish dance-forms by Chopin, the epic saga-operas of Mussorgsky and Smetana, not forgetting the latter's cycle of tone-poems *Ma Vlast*, or the grandiose manipulation of primitive Teutonic myths of Wagner lies much further back in the past – in the Old Testament oratorios of Handel. Hubert Parry's 'English' aspirations were in a sense a case of charging at an already open door; it is Parry's blend of elements from Brahms, Wagner, 18th-century musicians like Boyce and Arne and

---

[69] Save for one occasion, he always voted either Liberal (or 'radical', as he put it) or Labour all his life.

Handel in a very personal idiom that gives some of his music an 'English' flavour that appealed amongst others to Elgar. Stanford's Irish nationalism generally failed to achieve more than pretty-pretty local colouring superimposed on a thoroughly Brahmsian idiom, simply because it was basically the genteel and purely cultural rebellion of a musician born into the protestant Anglicised professional middle classes. (It is significant that one of the few 'Irish' works where he allowed his political views to come to the surface – the *Fourth Irish Rhapsody* – is also one of his most deeply felt, most individual and most moving[70]).

What Vaughan Williams sought to do, and to persuade other creative musicians to do, was to look to our own musical heritage as well as to that of other countries. He wanted budding English composers to avoid 'off-scourings of the classics', as he put it; and he was convinced that one of the ways of doing this was to study, assimilate and emulate (*not* copy) the music of our great past, notably the Elizabethans and Purcell. Another was to study and assimilate the music of the English people, a rich harvest of which had been gathered in during his early adulthood by collectors like Frank Kidson, Cecil Sharp and Vaughan Williams himself. But throwing off what he regarded as the Germanic musical yoke needed more than just this; it needed the study of other, non-Germanic musical cultures, notably those of the Slavs, particularly Russia, and above all of the acquisition of what he called 'a little French polish'.

The Victorian Age was noted for its high-minded seriousness. This was hardly surprising. The example was set from the throne, not so much by the Queen herself as by her consort, Prince Albert. It was an age of unprecedented scientific, industrial and commercial progress, in which the traditional religious attitudes were steadily undermined by more and more discoveries that seemed to disprove what had traditionally been

---

[70] The *Fourth Rhapsody* ('The Fisherman of Lough Neagh and what he saw') is a hymn in praise of the loyalty, the aspirations and the toughness of the people of Ulster, who, at the time of its composition, had declared their steadfast opposition, even to the point of armed resistance, to any kind of Irish home rule.

accepted as revealed religious truth. The Bible itself was subjected to intense critical analysis. Text previously considered as the inspired Word of God, and therefore valid for all time, were compared and worked over, inconsistencies pointed out, apparent interpolations checked against the style of the document of which they were part and often found to be traceable to other documents and even other civilisations.

Yet high-minded men and women who rejected the codes and sanctions of orthodox religion still tended to believe in some kind of moral order; and moral fervour, at any rate in public matters, often led to undoubted hypocrisy when the need to keep up public appearances conflicted with actual private practice and prejudices. It sometimes led to appalling displays of prurient moral cruelty, as in the shameful persecution of Oscar Wilde, who, until he challenged the accepted canons of public sexual morality, had been the darling of the West End theatre. It embraced a sense of mission, whether religious, commercial, political, or a combination of them, that is best summed up in Kipling's adjuration to the United States to 'take up the white man's burden', the Victorian equivalent of the medieval/chivalric 'noblesse oblige' in that what a misapplied Darwinism regarded as the superior races had a duty to teach the inferior ones the blessings of civilisation, whether Christian or simply commercial.

This, too, led to a tension between high moral principles and the pursuit of expedient financial gain and the exercise of sheer naked power. It embraced, as we have seen, the renewal and updating of what was conceived as being the spirit of chivalry. This was taken up with enthusiasm by idealistic masters at public schools and led in turn to the cult of 'the game for the sake of the game' and the belief that 'character' – which implied a kind of smug secular stoicism, a stiff-upper-lip self-control, a sense that 'British was best' and a narrow conformity with a prescribed code of conduct based on 'good form' – playing the game according to the rules – was regarded as preferable to the process of thinking problems through by the application of inductive or deductive reasoning. It embraced a utilitarian outlook that distrusted abstract reasoning in favour of a pragmatism that claimed that if a thing worked, it should be left alone rather than improved; and that if it wasn't working too well, it should still be left alone in case 'tinkering about' with it made it worse. That which was not immediately useful, such as music, might be entertaining, a pleasant icing on life's rich plum cake. Rich if you were a member of the leisured classes, that is. If it aimed to be anything more ambitious, it was mistrusted (unless, of course, like many of the large-scale choral works commissioned for music festivals, it projected the ethos accepted by social conformity and could be harnessed to the cause of making money for some worthy cause).

Vaughan Williams may have had the outward appearance of a conventional post-Victorian intellectual in that he was an ostensible conformist in moral and other behavioural matters. But he took nothing for granted, at least in music. He respected authority, but was always prepared to go his own way while allowing others the right to go theirs. Not for nothing was a volume of the letters that passed between him and his lifelong friend Gustav Holst entitled *Heirs and Rebels* by its editors, his widow Ursula and Holst's daughter Imogen. They were heirs of a tradition and rebels against it. He even advised his pupils, therefore, to submit to their teachers' pedagogical whims while maintaining a silent 'eppur si muove' as they did so. Tolerance, solidity, a quite unconceited sense of his own worth and a patriotism that never sought to belittle the qualities or achievements of other nations or cultures were ingrained in his character. These are also aspects of his English heritage that are most apparent to many of his fellow-countrymen who love his music.

By the time that he matured as a young musician in the late 1890s and first decade of the 20th century, he felt restless and dissatisfied both with his own music and with the musical training that he had enjoyed. He found it constricting and academic; and though he was thrilled by the achievements of the great Austro-German Romantics and post-Romantics whose work was held up in universities and academies as a model to emulate, both in spirit and in form, he came to feel that they offered him personally nothing but a blind alley as a composer. He felt that the plant of his style as a composer should either spring from or be grafted onto other stock that did not have its roots in Bayreuth (he was a devotee of Wagner), Leipzig or Vienna. He recognised Elgar as a liberating force in English music, though his own background and training gave him greater sympathy with the music of Hubert Parry[71], but he didn't wish to compose second-hand Elgar any more than second-hand Brahms or Wagner. 'The mantle of *Elijah*,' he once wrote, 'like most second-hand clothing, is usually a misfit'. He was, however, excited and stimulated by the new and very English voice that he discerned in Elgar's music, particularly in *The Dream of Gerontius* and the *Enigma Variations*. He looked for new musical stimuli.

He had begun as a young man in a shadowy way to discover where they were to be found before he had settled down to the academic study of his craft. The untrained and apparently spontaneous art of English folk-song as performed by traditional singers had already been explored to a limited degree by some 19th-century scholars; and their work had already aroused his curiosity. Under the influence of the greatest of English folk-song collectors, Cecil Sharp, Vaughan Williams set out to become one of the collectors himself. His interest in doing so was threefold. First of all, he wanted to play his part in saving what he felt must be a rich heritage of buried musical treasure. Secondly, he wanted to discover whether the riches of English folk-song would play a part in helping him find his own individual voice as a composer. And thirdly, he wished to demonstrate to his countrymen that the heritage was there for them to enjoy as well as for him to profit from. What English folk-song could not be was a component in any form of political protest in the name of national self-determination against foreign rule. Apart from Nelson, few English military or naval heroes are celebrated in folk-song, though there are plenty of references to the hardships of war and of life at sea. Convict and transportation songs also abound. Moreover, any social or political protest Vaughan Williams found in folk-song – and there was plenty in the songs that he collected – was to be found in the words, not the tunes; and all too often he dismissed the words of the songs he collected as either unimportant or available from some other source. 'The tune's the thing,' he commented when reviewing Britten's first published folk-song arrangements; and the same was true of his own

---

[71] He maintained throughout his life that Parry's spacious and proto-Elgarian setting of Milton's *Ode at a Solemn Music* was the finest piece of music ever composed by an Englishman.

work. Out of the 810 folk-songs that he collected, he took down the words of some 237 – about a quarter of the total.

Folk-song might not, then, be part of a political protest for him. It could, however, be an aesthetic one; and it was as a component in his self-realisation as a composer that English folk-song counts most in its value to RVW. Even though he composed modal waltzes for Stanford as a student and though even his earliest published works (such as 'Whither must I wander' from the *Songs of Travel* and *Linden Lea* itself) breathe the atmosphere and betray the melodic outline of genuine English folk-song, it is only with his own personal discovery of orally transmitted folk-song that he began to break loose from the shackles of his academic training. His encounter with Tudor church music, further stimulated by his work in editing *The English Hymnal* and with Purcell, through editing two volumes of *Welcome Songs,* further broadened his musical horizons and strengthened and deepened his English roots. Yet even then two further encounters had to be experienced, though he was not yet aware of them: the encounter with Impressionism, through his studies with Ravel; and the encounter with violent death, in the First World War. These two experiences between them, the one aesthetic and the other psychological, were the catalyst from which emerged his true style as a composer in works such as *On Wenlock Edge,* the *Fantasia on a Theme by Thomas Tallis,* the symphonies from the *London Symphony* onwards, *Sancta Civitas, Flos Campi, Job,* the Piano Concerto and his operas.

The period spent with Ravel opened new doors form him in two fields: the exploitation of harmony in a manner totally alien to that practised by traditional academic methods and brought to its highest pitch by the great Viennese classical composers and their successors, mainly in Germany; and in the scintillating use of points rather than blends or lines of orchestral colour. Studying in France was in itself unusual for an English musician. For generations, since the time of Mendelssohn, the English musical establishment – unconsciously perhaps following the Victorian path of moral rectitude even in matters aesthetic – had over-valued the earnest Germanic approach to musical form and content, emphasising the value of counterpoint and the intrinsic worth of academic compositional devices. There seems to have been in academic circles an unspoken contempt for what were regarded as the theatrical, village-band, oom-pah, rum-ti-tum rhythms and ostentatiously vulgar self-contained march or dance-tunes and blatantly emotional arias of the Italians or of the trivial balletic frivolities and salon sentimentalities of the French. That composers such as Verdi, Bizet or Fauré, to name only three, were capable of expressing not merely powerful but profound and elegant sentiments and moods within the constraints of these devices was overlooked. Vaughan Williams loved the music of Verdi, Puccini and Bizet when it was considered almost improper to do so, yet even he rejected Stanford's advice that he should go in 1897 to study Italian opera at Milan, choosing instead to go to Berlin[72].

Vaughan Williams and Ravel became personal friends; and RVW acknowledged his debt to his teacher in the following words[73]:

> ... I learnt much from him. For example, that the heavy Teutonic manner was not necessary; 'complexe, mais pas compliqué', was his motto. He showed me how to orchestrate in points of colour rather than in lines. It was an invigorating experience to find all artistic problems looked at from what was to me an entirely new angle. ... He was against development for its own sake – one should only develop for the sake of arriving at something better. He used to say that there was an implied melodic outline in all vital music and instanced the opening of the C minor Symphony as an example of a tune which was not stated but was implicit.

Ravel also introduced Vaughan Williams to 'bits of Rimsky and Borodin, to whom he introduced me for the first time'. This was all something quite different from the emphasis on the primacy of harmony and counterpoint as structural elements and the significance given to the theme or the motif instead of the balanced melody. Such an approach had its drawbacks. If a theme is dull and colourless the right way up, it

---

[72] 'The only town at that time where they performed the *Ring* without cuts' was the reason he gave for his choice of Berlin and Bruch rather than Milan and Italian opera.

[73] *A Musical Autobiography,* in *National Music and Other Essays* (Oxford 1986, p 191).

doesn't necessarily sound any better upside down[74] or in notes half its length, though the ability to generate new harmonic sequences as a result of inverting or diminishing the theme clearly counts for more in academic ears than the ability to create an immediately appealing tune. Vaughan Williams was clearly on the side of the melodic angels rather than the academic apes here, rating the 'reed shaken by the wind' Dvořák above his more technically sophisticated contemporaries because of his vastly superior melodic gifts. Yet sobriety of expression and its concomitant, dullness of scoring, counted for more with Vaughan Williams's teachers than brilliance, lightness, or colour; and his own scoring is sometimes dismissed as chunky and clumsy by critics who have never bothered to examine in detail such subtleties as are thrown up even by a cursory glance at the first ten bars of a work like the *Pastoral* Symphony. Yet those subtleties flow past unnoticed, simply because the changes of orchestral colour and texture are so frequent, so unobtrusive and, above all, so utterly unspectacular. Vaughan Williams's teacher once rather tactlessly (and, unfortunately, with some justification) rebuked Elgar for not having a 'fine body' of musical invention and sentiment in his *Banner of St George* to match the 'fine clothes' of his brilliant orchestral writing. With Vaughan Williams things are sometimes the other way round, but much more rarely than his detractors imagine.

His quiet rebellion against the implicit principle that 'Germanic is profound, oratorio is serious, Latin is frivolous and so is opera' was thus in itself suspect to some critics, even though the political development of the *entente cordiale* was beginning to lead to a reaction against matters Teutonic in favour of a rapprochement with the traditional foe across the Channel. The influence of French impressionism came at exactly the right time for him. The experience of service in the Royal Army Medical Corps on the Western Front in World War I affected him much more profoundly, I believe, than he was willing ever to disclose even to his most intimate friends. For there is an undeniable sinewy vigour and an abrasive, almost aggressive power in many of his works composed

---

[74] The theme of Paganini's A minor *Caprice* is clearly an exception, as Rachmaninoff was possibly the first to discover.

particularly in the inter-war years. I am thinking of works like *Sancta Civitas,* the Piano Concerto, parts of *Job* and the *Five Tudor Portraits* and, in particular, the fourth of his nine symphonies; but the expansion of his style comes first in a work where it is hardly to be expected, in the ostensibly placid and unruffled *Pastoral Symphony* of 1922.

This symphony is usually regarded as among the most 'English' of his works; and so it is. But it is also one of his most impressionistic. Without the 'Englishness', the themes would lack their peculiar reticence and remoteness. Without the impressionism of the scoring and the treatment of the material, they would simply be a meandering rhapsody forced to fit pre-arranged formal pattern-making. The lessons from Ravel have been wonderfully assimilated and are blended with the 'folky' elements of his style to distil in tranquillity the dark, disquieting emotions he felt as, evening after evening, he transported the wounded and the dying back from the front line to the base hospital against the backcloth of a battle-scarred landscape whose gentle rolling contours were not markedly dissimilar to those of the English downland where his family had made their home.

The opening of the work gives the game away at once, with its treatment of foreground and undulating background elements. First of all, the orchestration of each is constantly changing. Secondly, both main and subsidiary thematic lines are loaded with their own series of triads, so that the interplay is not of lines of music but of kaleidoscopically-scored blocks. Thirdly, the themes themselves are not tonal or chromatic, but modal or pentatonic. And fourthly, the rhythmic framework is supple and flexible, matching the ebb and flow of the melodic lines and the scoring, yet contrasting with the unyielding harmonic flow. It is as if the sonorous blocks of consecutive chords so effectively used by Debussy in a piece like *La cathédrale engloutie* had been given an extra dimension by treating them in counterpoint with another conflicting similarly harmonised line. The similarity of the harmonic charge added to each line softens the astringency of the contrapuntal clashes and yet instead of sentimentalising it lends it an eerie remoteness and a quietly and insistently throbbing melancholy. What is often mistaken for dullness and placidity in this work is really the outcome of feelings too hurtful to be given instant and direct expression; the question is not asked 'Why all this suffering?' so as to give a glib, immediate answer. In fact, no answer is attempted. The suffering is accepted as real, pondered on, and never taken for granted. But it is not just the individual, nor even the national community, that suffers; it is nature herself.

One of the most striking episodes in the work occurs in the second movement. It was inspired by the purely human accident of a bugler practising in the twilight and hitting the seventh partial of a note instead of the octave that he was aiming for. Vaughan Williams transmutes this magically into a passage of remote, haunting melancholy of a kind quite new in English or any other music; and it is worth examining how this passage is incorporated into the texture of the whole movement. The first time it occurs on a natural trumpet, against a pianissimo background of strings in octaves, that gradually settles on an unbarred E♭; there is a crescendo; and out of it – against it, perhaps – the full orchestra[75] bursts out for the only time in the movement in a kind of brief anguished protest based on the movement's main theme. The second time, right at the very end of the movement, the cadenza is heard on a natural horn. It is barred throughout and there is a counter-theme on the clarinet based on the movement's main theme. This time, the harmonic background is less static; a sequence of major chords, descending in a whole-tone tetrachord, F, E♭, D♭, C♭. The music fades away into the most delicate pianissimo and the strings round off the movement with a series of mysterious common chords that end up in a downward arching cadence: A♭ minor, F minor. The course of the music is easy to describe; to describe its effect is quite impossible. Suffice it to say that 'typically English' is a totally inadequate and quite useless phrase in this context. This music transcends any bounds of style or nationality, even indeed, one is tempted to say, of any human sorrow. It is as if the power behind the universe itself was in intensely poignant mourning.

Vaughan Williams's link with impressionism is often underplayed and even overlooked; but we should not overstate our case here. Just as

---

[75] Vaughan Williams dispenses with his heavy brass and percussion for this movement.

Elgar forged a truly personal idiom out of the Germanic and other influences to which he was subject as a young man, so did Vaughan Williams absorb what he needed from the great French (and Russian? His use of rhythm, while owing much to the English madrigalists, also owes much to the vitality of the later Russian romantics) pioneers and blend it with his English heritage. And this became the abstract expression in terms of ' putting black dots on paper', as he somewhat dismissively described his craft, of other, non-musical aspects of his personal and national heritage. These were: political radicalism and an intense sense of justice and fair play; a very strict and utterly sincere moral code, influenced by the puritan ethos, but by no means puritanical in itself; a kind of agnostic mysticism that persisted in trying to unravel the metaphysical secrets (the 'unknown region') of the universe; a powerful and intense lyric gift; a thorough knowledge of a wide range of English, continental European, classical and American literature; and – last, but not least – a ribald, at times Rabelaisian, sense of humour.

These qualities are reflected both in the texts he chose to set and in the manner in which he set them as well as in that music of his with which no specific text is associated. And even there, he sometimes gave the listener a clue. He told Michael Kennedy, for instance, that the end of his *London Symphony* was related to a phrase from H G Wells's *Tono-Bungay:* 'The river passes; London passes, England passes.' And of the ending of the Sixth, he remarked that he was trying to convey something of the flavour of the close of Shakespeare's *Tempest*:

> . . .We are such stuff
> As dreams are made on, and our little life
> Is rounded with a sleep.

But it is to William Blake rather than to Shakespeare that many people look when considering the visionary aspect of Vaughan Williams; and it is undoubtedly true that Vaughan Williams was a connoisseur of Blake's's art and that one of his greatest works owes its form and part of its vision to Blake. This is the 'Masque for Dancing' *Job*, in which RVW created what he hoped would be a new and characteristically English form of ballet for the Camargo Society, later to become first the Sadler's Wells and then the Royal Ballet. Actually, once again, the 'Englishness' of this superb work can easily be overestimated. True, the scenario was heavily influenced by Blake's engravings; but Vaughan Williams steered clear of interpreting the splendid Biblical story wholly in terms of Blake's interpretation of them. For him, the issues that underlay the Biblical account, not Blake's Swedenborgian theories about them (such as that Satan represented Job's material self and God his spiritual self) were what counted. And true, the great set-piece dances of the work are cast in archaic forms, such as the Pavane, the Galliard and the Sarabande. But though these dances were current at the English court, they were also current elsewhere, as a look at the titles of movements in many a baroque suite will confirm. Vaughan Williams must surely have chosen them, not merely for their associations with the Tudor and Stuart eras but also because they expressed for him the stately and stylised patterns that he wished to incorporate in his massive *Gesamtkunstwerk*. Moreover, such movements as Satan's Dance of Triumph, Job's Dream, The Dance of the Three Comforters, with its lachrymose saxophone, and even Elihu's Dance of Youth and Beauty have their roots quite a different age from that of any Elizabethan or Jacobean court festivity or pastoral. Furthermore, his version of the scenario of the 'Masque' cites stage pictures from foreign artists, such as Rubens and Botticelli, at least as much as it cites figures from traditional English dances such as 'Jenny pluck pears'.

Musically, the sheer eclecticism of *Job* can be very misleading. All the elements of Vaughan Williams's mature style are strongly represented. It is in fact a highly impressionist score. Along with the three great early Stravinsky ballets, it should form the pinnacle of the impressionist dance repertoire. Vaughan Williams's ability to give new life to old forms is shown not merely in his use of the archaic dances here, or in the way in which he so successfully blended impressionistic writing with the archaic part-writing of the Tudor fantasia in the *Fantasia on a Theme by Thomas Tallis*. He also developed innovations in symphonic forms: in his symphonies, from the *Pastoral* onwards, the themes are developed in a highly original and remarkably manner, evolving out of one another by a kind of musical osmosis and mutation highly suitable in the work of a composer who was, after all, related to Charles Darwin. This means that his approach to sonata form also differs from the

Teutonic norm. This process may or may not have been worked out consciously. It may even subconsciously owe something to the compositional procedures of Franz Liszt, a composer whose output Vaughan Williams cordially detested. The harmonic and melodic implications of his material required Vaughan Williams to develop and extend it in ways based on different precepts from those of classical sonata form and its contrasts and tensions of tonality. He also, after a number of early efforts that he later destroyed, eschewed the procedure of rhapsodising vaguely on the tune itself. His themes are often based on elements (usually tetrachords) taken from the modal scales, fusing them with Debussy's harmonic device of using the common chord of each note in a theme as an immutable harmonic support and with scoring procedures learnt from Ravel. Thus the first movements of the Sixth and Eighth Symphonies cunningly blend sonata and variation form, so that in the Sixth the Big Tune that emerges at the end of the movement has evolved out of various fragments of theme that have been jostling one another throughout the movement. In the Eighth, the 'seven variations in search of a theme' present the listener with a fascinating impressionistic kaleidoscope not just of sound but of thematic juxtaposition and evolution. The harmonies move and direct the shape of the material, but they do so, as in the pre-baroque fantasia, from *within the musical texture*, not as a result of the movement of the bass line. This again may be regarded as very English in its ability to absorb elements organically from different sources and make them its own, just as the English language itself does.

The final characteristic that we ought to consider of Vaughan Williams's musical personality is all of a piece with the rowdier aspects of Elgar's *Falstaff* and, in a way, of the rumbustious wit of Purcell. It is the earthiness that is found particularly in the *Five Tudor Portraits*. At a meeting of the Three Choirs' Festival, Elgar, Vaughan Williams and a friend were discussing the poet Skelton, who lived during the reigns of Henry VII and Henry VIII. Vaughan Williams admitted that his knowledge of the poet was limited to one or two majestic anthology pieces, one of which he had thought of setting (and later did, most effectively, as a *Prayer to the Father of Heaven*). Elgar responded: 'No, don't do that. You write an oratorio about Elinor Rumming.' This comment not only shows, incidentally, Elgar's understanding of the byways of English literature, but also represents a shrewd assessment of a side of his younger contemporary's musical personality that had been only sporadically revealed in his output so far.

Skelton was an East Anglian; and when a commission arose for Vaughan Williams to compose a choral piece for the Norwich Festival in 1936, he took five of Skelton's poems, three of them so pointedly ribald as to border on the scurrilous, and set them under the title of *Five Tudor Portraits*. They are all written in racy, semi-macaronic verse and are tributes, if that is the correct word, to characters that Skelton wished either to commemorate or to satirise.

Elinor Rumming was a disreputable alehouse-keeper of the 'honest gentlewoman' kind similar to those Elgar himself had portrayed in *Falstaff*, so the idea of composing even a short musical portrayal of such a character, let alone a whole oratorio about her, demonstrates a side of both Elgar's character and of Vaughan Williams's that puts Strauss's sanitised treatment of the folk-hero *Till Eulenspiegel* completely in the shade. Vaughan Williams's racy and pacy setting of the poem about her seems at first hearing to be simply a hearty, episodic and ribald romp for chorus and orchestra. It is, in fact, a remarkably well integrated piece, but the integration is rhythmic and metric rather than thematic or harmonic. The basic three-in-a-bar starts out with a heavy note-for-note change of chord on each beat; this quickens with hardly any perceptible change of tempo into a one-in-the-bar waltz. In the central section, devoted to the portrayal of the gossip Drunken Alice, the rhythmic fabric is distorted and fragmented by jazzy syncopations and a texture updating the march of Falstaff's scarecrow army, as if Elgar's music had been filtered through Shostakovich or Prokofiev; and in the final section the rhythm is re-integrated into a galumphing folk-dance measure, as if the assembled company were thumping their tankards on the table as they bawl out their song.

Vaughan Williams cannot be accused of being sexist. He provides us with an equally disreputable male counterpart to Elinor and her cronies – the cleric John Jayberd of Diss, whose music seems to spring from the same soil as that of Carl Orff's *Carmina Burana*[76]. He also mocks the pretensions of the epicene, self-absorbed dandies of his time in the brilliant finale of the suite. *Rutterkin* is a jazzy setting of Skelton's savage commentary on fashionable prancing courtly Tudor elegance and aping of foreign styles. The fact that the music might have been written by William Walton, whose music Vaughan Williams held in considerable regard, leads one to speculate that he might have been tilting at certain members of the circle in which Walton moved. It doesn't matter; what does matter is the unexpected brilliance and the cutting satire of the music.

To complement these cheerful but none the less quite savage caricatures, there are two gentler movements: the discreetly tender intermezzo *My Pretty Bess* and the charmingly pathetic and extended lament of little Jane Scroop for her pet sparrow, Philip, killed by her cat Gib. This is a piece that combines a tender, wide-eyed sympathy for a child bereft of its beloved pet and the sophisticated skill of a master-orchestrator in the impressionist vein. Once more, as we have seen with Elgar and as we shall also see when we come to consider Britten, we find a composer with the ability to empathise with the feelings of a child. But in Vaughan Williams's case, it is not nostalgia for lost innocence or a look back in regret to dreamier days, it is a matter of taking seriously a child's grief, keener, more bewildering and more vulnerable than that of an adult because the child is not sophisticated enough to understand the relative import of what has happened and why.

There are a number of comments that one might make on *Five Tudor Portraits*. First among them is that Vaughan Williams is not just having fun; he is using all the resources of his fully-developed musical idiom to mock and yet at the same time sympathise with aspects of the teeming vitality of English low life. If *Job* reminds us of Blake, *Five Tudor Portraits* surely reminds us of Hogarth or Rowlandson[77], or even

---

[76] There is no suggestion here of any influence of Orff on RVW. Both works probably have a common ancestor: Borodin's exuberant *Polovtsian Dances.*

[77] One of whose engravings had provided the inspiration for Walton's racy overture *Portsmouth Point.*

Dickens. Vaughan Williams might well be criticised in some of his more 'popular' works, such as the opera *Hugh the Drover,* of too readily accepting a picturesque or sanitised view of social orders other than those he knew best. In the *Tudor Portraits* he is an unblushing realist. There is no gentility here. The text is ancient, the targets are timeless and the moods are very English: pathos without sentimentality, vitality without coarseness and mockery without malice.

This is the side of Vaughan Williams that boldly claimed that a good music-hall song was worth any amount of off-scourings of the classics, the man who was prepared to admit impressionistic and lifelike portrayals of a cockney mouth-organ or barrel-organ into the scherzo of his *London Symphony.* It is also a side of his musical character that is seen in a rather different light in the Vanity Fair scene from *The Pilgrim's Progress.* Here, the Hogarthian vitality and fleeting vignettes of low-life Restoration London are part of a huge dream-pageant. But on the entry of Lord Hategood, the evil and corrupt judge who sentences Pilgrim to death on the flimsiest grounds, the whole atmosphere changes. Here is a real sense of the terrifying presence of an immanent vicious power that is reminiscent of – possibly even unconsciously cribbed from – Verdi's music for Iago's terrible, nihilistic credo in *Otello.* There are few musicians who have the imagination to portray the power of evil so vividly; and even they manage to do so only rarely. Vaughan Williams's music for Satan in *Job* is another instance of this; and certainly there is a whiff of it in the awesome energy of the F minor Symphony.

But the eclectic nature of Vaughan Williams's music can be seen by the very work from which the Vanity Fair episode is taken. When it finally reached the stage after almost half a century of germination, *The Pilgrim's Progress* was damned with faint praise, partly because of a production that was slated by all the critics. Semi-staged and student performances have since done something to rehabilitate it, but its visionary and ritualistic quality have found little favour with normal opera audiences, who can none the less sit through the first and third acts of *Parsifal* with little difficulty, it seems. He created here his own form of opera, just as he had created his own kind of symphony and his own version of the Elizabethan fantasia. He was not just a great Englishman; he was a great musician and a great experimenter with a protean outlook and a willingness to absorb whatever he fancied from whatever source. That one of the most important of these sources was English folk-song and another English poetry and literature should not blind us to the fact that he does not belong only to us but to the Europe of which he felt we were culturally a part and the common humanity from which, as one of his ancestors so cogently argued, we have all evolved.

11 – Kicking over the traces – well, sort of

The generation that came to maturity in England immediately after the First World War was faced with a whole host of ambiguities; and of no-one was this truer than of the musicians. In 1918 the country had emerged victorious from the most exhausting war in its history. But at least it had emerged victorious. Yet a nation that had been regarded as a people of thinkers, romantic poets and musicians had launched an aggressive war and had come within an ace of winning it. Three other huge polyglot empires had collapsed in defeat: one to be replaced by what promised to be an exciting new way of ordering society; one to be carved up into a number of new nation-states corresponding more – or less – to the wishes of those who spoke the dominant language of the area; and the third mainly to be allotted under a system of political tutelage to the control of one or other of the victorious European powers. In England, it was assumed that the Land Fit for Heroes could somehow remain the Land of Hope and Glory. Within five years of the victory of 1918, many of the heroes were unemployed, badly housed and poorly fed. Disillusion was rife and cynicism widespread.

As in so many matters, however, Britain was neither as badly off as some nor as well off as others. Horrendous though her casualties were, she had not seen her manhood bled white to the extent that France had. She did not have to endure the galloping inflation that rocked Germany in the early 1920s. Unlike Russia, she had not undergone the chaos of a revolution, the subsequent civil war and the turmoil of a series of miscalculated and hastily revised wholesale economic reforms. Nor did she inadvertently undermine the entire moral basis of her social order through applying the misguided idealism of prohibition, as the United States did. None the less, the 1920s were for many of her artists, as for those of most other countries in the European tradition, a period of reaction against a generation thought to be smug and out of touch with reality.

Yet it was also an exciting time. New styles, new fashions and new outlooks proliferated. The most interesting of these centred usually round some kind of rebellion against romanticism and the Germanic tradition. The novel aspects were the advent of jazz and the development of exciting new approaches to rhythm, harmony and subject matter. Technical advances in the sound film, the recording process and broadcasting offered access to a much wider audience than ever before. It might not be true to claim, as Cole Porter claimed, that anything went, but it was certainly true that the prospect of trying to satisfy the human appetite for novelty and the experimental was more open to musicians than ever before.

One of the earliest and most trenchant attempts to summarise how all this affected British musicians was provided by Arthur Bliss[78] in *What Modern Composition Is Aiming At,* a paper read to the Society of Women Musicians in July 1921. Fresh from his harrowing experiences in the trenches of the First World War, in which he served with considerable distinction, Bliss singles out and lists with some glee the following victims of the new music:

1. The oratorio composed especially for the provincial festival on the lines laid down by the Dean and Chapter.

2. The symphonic poem à la Strauss, with a soul sorely perplexed, but finally achieving freedom, not without much perspiring pathos.

3. The pseudo-intellectuality of the Brahms camp-followers, with their classical sonatas and concertos, and variations, and other 'stock-in-trade'.

4. The overpowering grand opera with its frothing Wotans and stupid King Marks.

This statement of principles was in fact a declaration of war on the Victorian and post-Victorian musical tradition of Germanic 'seriousness', complexity and intensity, which had for so long dominated

---

[78] See Bliss, *As I Remember* (London, 1989), pp 248–255.

English musical thinking at the universities and academies. Mendelssohn, Brahms, Wagner and Strauss were out; the French and the Russians were 'in'. English music, at its best always eclectic and cosmopolitan, was to become so again; and the influences it was to absorb were to come from even wider afield than Europe. This was in part an extra-musical reaction: how could a nation so devoted to earnestness in art and high ideals in musical craftsmanship have produced a political system that had, it was thought, plunged Europe into a cruel and ruinous war?

Bliss's own music of the time shows that he practised what he preached. Works such as *Rout, Madame Noy* and *Conversations* show an iconoclastic wit and a kind of conscious frivolity and flamboyant experimentation that drew on resources as deliberately different as he could exploit from the Germanic tradition in which he had been trained by his teacher Stanford. That Bliss later regressed, as some critics would have it, into a kind of Elgar/Vaughan Williams pastiche, spiced with unexceptionable dissonances and rhythmic irregularities, is neither here nor there. Nor is the fact that Bliss became Master of the Queen's Music, in effect the figure-head of the musical establishment he here castigated. His style expanded; it did not contract. The Elgar/Vaughan Williams pastiche – if such it were – was in itself a reaction against the prevalent academicism in favour of what was considered a more robust, 'vernacular' Englishness. Works such as the delightful pastoral *Lie strewn the white flocks* (dedicated to Elgar) and the much later imaginative and moving *Meditations on a theme of John Blow* indicate his sensitivity to his roots in a specifically English past[79].

More gifted and original as a composer and more cosmopolitan in his outlook was Constant Lambert. Perhaps unfortunately, Lambert was also a writer of encyclopaedic knowledge, not only of music but also of literature, painting and sculpture. He was a gifted conductor, especially of ballet, and a critical writer whose scintillating, often coruscating, wit matched his amazing erudition. He wore his immense

---

[79] As indeed does his collaboration with that most pugnaciously 'English' (and musically sensitive) of writers, J B Priestley, on his opera *The Olympians.*

learning very lightly, as his letters, his journalistic pieces and his book *Music Ho!* amply demonstrate. This meant, however, that he never really came to terms with the English musical establishment because he not only saw through the emotional flatulence, the earnest pedantry or the self-conscious frivolity of many an admired English (and continental) ikon of the age, but expressed his views trenchantly, amusingly and often more woundingly than he perhaps intended to. The very breadth of his interests and his knowledge somehow seemed to prevent his achieving a truly personal musical style, whether in jazz-influenced works like *The Rio Grande* – which owes almost as much to the vivacious and extrovert French tradition of composers like Chabrier as it does to jazz – or the dark-hued, much more introverted and at times emotionally and rhythmically obsessive Piano Concerto. But even in more ambitious and traditional works such as the turbulent, often morbid and disturbing *Summer's Last Will and Testament*, Lambert's idiom is essentially an urban one; and the townscape that it seems to reflect is sombre and somewhat indeterminate, resembling the set of a film where the action takes place in the small hours of the morning in some windswept modern dockyard. Except in one work, the exquisite and elegiac *Aubade héroique*, dedicated, significantly enough, to Vaughan Williams as a 70th-birthday tribute, he lies quite outside the accepted conventions of the English pastoral tradition. Yet there is both an energy and a melancholy about much of his music that set it apart from that of the continental masters that he most admired and he certainly could never be accused of teutonic stodginess and sterile academicism.

Lambert's friend and rival as a creative musician, William Walton, also started out as something of an iconoclast. Both he and Lambert were friends of the gifted and mildly eccentric Sitwell family, whose experiments with new, associative forms of poetic expression created something of a stir among the literati of the twenties. Unlike their two musical protégés, the three Sitwells, Osbert, Edith and Sacheverell, came from a wealthy background, against whose standards and philosophy they were in rebellion, but whose privileges they were quite prepared to continue to enjoy. They were also keen to support any artist who seemed to be in sympathy with their ideas on art; and it was as a result of a collaboration with them that Walton first came before the public. The result, *Façade*, was not merely a *jeu d'esprit,* as which it is sometimes dismissed. It was a witty parody of certain aspects of widely-held aesthetic beliefs, where the brilliant play on words and their associations was matched by attractive pastiche music that parodied or alluded to anything from the English and Scottish country dance[80] to the Viennese waltz, even the fox-trot and the popular music-hall tap-dance. The unmistakably English features of the work are its studied impertinence, witty, mocking convention without ever straying too far outside it, and the composer's willingness to absorb and assimilate music of a wide range of styles. Later on, Walton settled down to produce music that revealed his own individual brand of romantic melancholy and an ability, in certain of his ceremonial and larger-scale works like *Belshazzar's Feast,* the finale of the First Symphony, and a number of his film scores, to update the Elgarian blend of dignity and passion with elements of jazz and a harmonic asperity derived more from composers like Prokofiev and Bartók than Stravinsky.

Certain English musicians of the generations that had come to maturity before 1914 stood aloof from this. Elgar, for one, virtually turned his back[81] on serious composition after the death of his wife in 1920. Vaughan Williams absorbed the new influences and his wartime experiences, forging a style that remained rooted in English folk-song and the traditions of the Elizabethans, yet took creative account of early 20th-century reactions against the Germanic tradition in which he had been trained. Arnold Bax, a sympathiser with Irish national aspirations and a self-confessed 'brazen romantic', produced tone-poems and expansive symphonies in a highly personal and highly chromatic idiom and a luxuriant orchestral style somewhat redolent of the convoluted

---

[80] Frank Howes claimed that Walton's (English) *Country Dance* was one of the few movements in the work that showed no element of parody. In the words of a contemporary idiom: 'Who are you kidding?'

[81] Though Anthony Payne's imaginative and skilful reconstruction of his copious sketches for a third symphony have demonstrated beyond any doubt that his inspiration had not deserted him.

abstract designs of early Celtic art. Those of his works associated with Celtic legend or landscape, such as the fine tone poems *Tintagel* and *The Garden of Fand*, show a distinctly impressionistic touch and an ability to keep the momentum of a large span of music going, something not always evident in his seven symphonies. It is probably in his chamber music that he reveals more of that part of his personality that could be called 'English'. It is finely crafted, less exciting perhaps than his orchestral works, but also more terse; and he was one of the few major English composers of his time who was not just a pianist but a master of the keyboard. Bax, too, like Bliss, became (degenerated into, some might say) Master of the King's Musick and thus officially at any rate a member of the musical establishment. Frederick Delius continued to compose in his own cosmopolitan and highly individual way.

Each of these in his own way demonstrated his musical allegiances and his cultural origins. Delius in particular, of German extraction, an almost fanatical devotee of the philosophy of Nietzsche, exposed to the influence of American negro music in Florida and to the theories and practice of post-impressionist artists, writers, painters and and musicians alike in Paris as a young man, settled in the French countryside and with a Norwegian wife was possibly the most cosmopolitan of the three. Yet the poignant, often searing nostalgia that permeates his music, with its ever-frustrated yearning, its evanescent chromatic harmonies, its gently rippling rhythms and the pastoral atmosphere it often evokes, is of a kind quite different from that of, say, Mahler or the later Richard Strauss. The background may be teutonic, but the shape and ethos of the music is not. It lacks the onward drive of a work like *Ein Heldenleben* or the *Symphony of a Thousand* and the nostalgia it undoubtedly expresses is subtly different from that of Mahler's, as expressed in *The Song of the Earth* – more a memorial to, even a celebration of, the transience of life's bliss than a regretful farewell to life itself. Nor does any regret at the passing of the innocent wonders of childhood or the prospect of the bleak finality of death seem to concern Delius much. Even when he is at his most sensualist and Nietzschean, simultaneously celebrating both the joys and the pain of life, as in the exhilarating opening of *A Mass of Life*, Delius soon relaxes the reins in favour of a lush lyrical outpouring. The music loses momentum and subsides into an intense expression of the transitoriness of life and the beauty that, to him at any rate, alone gives it meaning. However hard Delius tries to evoke the German philosopher's vision of a vigorous, super-human race that will exult in its aesthetic superiority and will-power to the inferior creatures by whom it is surrounded and whom it is destined to dominate[82], it is Nietzsche's equally potent awareness of the brevity of life that really attracts him, not the prospect of accepting and transcending its ephemerality so as to make way by a conscious act of will for future and finer generations. Ruthless and egocentric, even cruel, in thought and action as he undoubtedly was, he was as a composer strangely delicate and tender.

It is in those passages where his music slips into a gently flowing pastoral dance-rhythm, such as the whole of *On hearing the first Cuckoo in Spring* or much of *Brigg Fair,* that Delius sounds most convincing and most English. At such times he also evokes for many listeners the calm and languor of the English countryside on a summer day and the idyllic, leisurely tempo of idealised English country life (seen through the eye of the urban poet who assumes that the countryside is in all respects the antithesis of the bustle and squalor of the town).

For all his steadfast atheism, his cosmopolitan outlook and his detestation of many aspects of English life, Delius insisted in being buried in an English churchyard. Yet, *per contra,* for all his Yorkshire accent, his forthrightness and his love of cricket, he was also stubbornly un-, even anti-, English. It is a mistake to think that his music is ever consciously English, as Elgar's or Vaughan Williams's is, but the qualities with which it is saturated often are considered so. Its understated, dreamy melancholy, its gentle fervour, its powerful yet controlled passion, its freedom in formal matters (which does not justify the stricture often levelled at him of formlessness) and its delight in the exquisitely-shaped miniature rather than the large-scale fresco: these are genuinely English rather than Germanic, Italianate or Gallic. But his

---

[82] It is important to remember that Nietzsche's *Übermensch* was an image of a superior type of *universal* humanity, and that he despised the German ruling classes of his day as vulgar, tasteless, insensitive, misguided and narrow-minded.

music is above all Delian, the expression of an individual, almost mannered personality. Even his 'American' and 'Scandinavian' music, such as *Appalachia, Sea-Drift*, or *The Song of the High Hills*, expresses his own attitude first and the sentiments of his subject or his text a long way afterwards. The late Deryck Cooke[83], as usual, put it both succinctly and accurately; and in so doing, he also puts his finger on the reasons why Delius's eclectic idiom failed to strike a wholly favourable response either with the English among whom he was born, the Germans from whom he descended, or the French among whom he made his home:

> In England, the English pastoral element was the main reason for the temporary response to Beecham's advocacy; real Delius-lovers in this country have chiefly been attracted by the music's power to evoke the open air and the English countryside; but the equally strong German and French elements always made him an exotic for the majority.

The composer of the 1920s most akin to Delius – indeed, one of his foremost critical protagonists, was Philip Heseltine (aka Peter Warlock). Warlock, like his idol, displayed a curious dichotomy between what he outwardly was and what his music expressed. Of all our song-writers, he showed the greatest empathy with the sounds, rhythms and verbal inflections of English verse. He also showed the most sophisticated literary taste. And, of course, virtually his whole output consisted of songs. If to be English is to be an exquisite miniaturist, then Warlock was surely the most English composer of any since the time of his beloved Elizabethans.

Warlock's emotional range is much wider than Delius's, just as his inspiration is much more restricted. He was also, in certain respects, more self-consciously 'English', both as a person and as a musician, than most of his fellow-composers. A small straw in this particular wind is his love of cricket, a love he shared with Delius, with his own slightly older contemporary, Arnold Bax, and with the greatest composer of the next

---

[83] In *Delius: A Centenary Evaluation* (*Vindications*, London 1982, p 118).

generation, Benjamin Britten[84]. He was in fact, both as a person and a composer, a curious split personality. One part of him was a would-be roistering Elizabethan man of action-cum-poet-cum-toper with a touch of the Restoration about his gallimaufry and his ribaldry. The other side showed him as a sensitive poet and critic as well as composer, with a black and melancholy side to his nature, almost as vehemently vindictive as he could be generous, as petty as he could be perceptive. Eventually he gassed himself at the early age of thirty-seven. But this is by the way. What was consciously English about Warlock's *musical* personality was his passionate love for the music of Purcell and the Elizabethans and his determination in his songs to match the inflections and rhythms of the poems he set with suitable melodic and harmonic illustrations.

He did not do this, though, using the Germanic method, perfected by Schubert, of consciously or unconsciously fixing on a key verbal image in the poem, finding a suitable musical motif to express it and then using this motif as a generating force for the accompaniment. He harked back to the lute-songs and ayres of the Elizabethans and the declamatory songs of the seventeenth-century Caroline composers such as Henry Lawes and blended with their methods the spicy harmonic devices of his own contemporaries.

Warlock's attitude to poetry is a curious blend of identification with the poem and aloofness from it. Stephen Banfield[85] in his perceptive critique of Warlock's songs, divides the latter into the archaic and the vernacular. The former is demonstrated in his deliberate choice and exploitation of the emotional and stylistic opportunities offered by texts from the sixteenth and seventeenth centuries. The latter, Banfield further subdivides into eight further categories, depending on the type of text set. Perhaps these could be summed up in two types – the 'low-life' (drinking-songs, bawdy songs, folk-ballads) and the 'ingenuous' (hymn- or carol-like, child-like). There are quite a number of the latter. There is, in fact, a strain of innocence that underlies Warlock's

---

[84] Neither Elgar nor Vaughan Williams seems to have been remotely interested in our national game.

[85] *Sensibility and English Song,* Cambridge, 1985, p 357

sophistication (the latter a quality that he seems to have absorbed both from Delius and from his cosmopolitan friend and mentor Bernard van Dieren). A further influence, Banfield points out, is that of the Anglican hymn-tune, skilfully disguised and often applied in the most unexpected places[86].

But Warlock's 'Englishness' (or perhaps better, his 'Elizabethanness') comes most notably to the fore in two of his best-known chamber works: the delightful and mainly extrovert *Capriol Suite* for string orchestra, in which a set of 16th-century dance-tunes are submitted – somewhat cautiously, let it be said – to a similar but less drastic kind of harmonic treatment as that meted out by Stravinsky to Pergolesi in *Pulcinella,* and the desolate settings of W B Yeats for voice and chamber ensemble called *The Curlew.* This displays almost throughout what French commentators referred to as 'le spleen anglais': a kind of bitter, resentful, destructive melancholy that can be at the same time both depressing and cathartic.

It was during the 1920s and 1930s that various attempts were made to develop the infra-structure of English musical life. Some of these were short-lived; others had a much longer-term effect. Organisations such as the British Symphony Orchestra and the City of Birmingham Orchestra, supported by a municipal subsidy, tried to inject at least some kind of stability into 'serious' musical life. The British National Opera Company struggled gallantly, and with some success, to develop a national opera, staging works such as Vaughan Williams's *Hugh the Drover* alongside Wagner and Mozart. The demise of Diaghilev's ballet company stirred certain influential English balletomanes to found a new company, the Camargo Society, drawing on the talented British dancers who had performed in Diaghilev's company, that was to become first the Sadler's Wells and later the Royal Ballet. It became common practice in state elementary schools run by enlightened authorities for children to be exposed to English folk-songs collected, arranged and published not so many decades previously by Cecil Sharp and others. There were also films for which music was required; it was the enterprise of British film

---

[86] Such as *Fair and True,* cited by Banfield.

companies and documentary film-makers, such as the GPO Film Unit, that enabled British composers such as Arthur Bliss, William Walton and above all Benjamin Britten to practise their craft in new and ingenious ways. Bliss's music to the Korda film of H G Wells's *The Shape of Things to Come* was a landmark in that Bliss was drawn into the very planning of the film itself instead of simply adding music as required after the film had been shot and edited. And finally, there was the BBC.

From its very first days the high-minded mandarins that controlled it (and it is significant that the title of 'controller' is still applied to the head of many BBC departments) were determined to raise public taste in the matter of music. This led in 1930 to the establishment of the Corporation's great symphony orchestra, which soon became one of the finest in Europe. Conscientiously trained by Adrian Boult, it acquired a versatility and a technical skill that far transcended anything that London had previously been used to, tackling works like Alban Berg's *Wozzeck* and exposing Vienna for the first time to Arnold Schoenberg's Orchestral Variations when it appeared there in 1936. Nor did it neglect the older repertoire of all kinds, from the baroque to the impressionist. And of course it enabled British composers to hear their music at least carefully rehearsed – often, indeed, brilliantly performed. The BBC also took over the administration of the Henry Wood Promenade Concerts, which have steadily expanded in scope and range until they now constitute a major eight-week London summer festival of music from the Middle Ages until whatever the current avant-garde happens to favour.

One significant composer who felt he had been rather shabbily treated by the Corporation was Stanford's pupil and Britten's teacher Frank Bridge. Bridge was not only an imaginative and exacting teacher and a gifted composer in the impressionist tradition; he was also a fine practical musician – good enough to become the viola player in an internationally famous quartet – and conductor. He never quite forgave the BBC for not appointing him as its director of music, a decision made on personal rather than musical grounds. Bridge had the reputation of having a somewhat fussy, stubborn and abrasive character (in these respects he was somewhat similar to his own teacher), which would certainly have led to friction with the Corporation's hierarchy. As a composer, however, the very faults that made him unsuitable for the BBC job ensured that his music was always superbly crafted, with every detail telling, and subtly imaginative in a manner lacking in some of his more 'establishment' colleagues. Certainly the young Britten responded to it with such enthusiasm that he was determined to study with Bridge. The tone poem *Enter Spring* and the symphonic suite *The Sea* are colourful examples of romantic impressionism with an English face, while the fine *Oration*, for solo cello and orchestra, his reaction to the loss of a favourite niece in a torpedoed ship during World War I, displays a depth of anguish and a sense of desolation that are as powerful as they are uncommon in English music. And as a first-class chamber-musician, he knew how to handle the string quartet in an original and efficient manner far in advance of that not only of many of his British contemporaries, but also of many continental masters. The third and fourth of his quartets in particular have a sinewy toughness that puts them in a class of their own in English chamber music; their mood and structure go far beyond impressionism. Constant Lambert said in *Music Ho!* that there was no musical equivalent of Paul Cézanne. Had Bridge's chamber music been better known abroad, he might have provided one. Bridge's music may not be 'English' in the narrower sense of the term, but it certainly has an eclectic yet very personal character. He has come down in history as Britten's teacher; he was also a creative musician worth remembering in his own right.

Though state support of music was nowhere near as lavish in Britain as it was in countries with a less democratic tradition; and though private support – 'plutocratic', if you will – of music was far less generous than it was in the United States, there was still a realisation in the country that music was something worth supporting. The great provincial festivals continued to commission substantial works from established and up-and-coming composers: Britten's *Our Hunting Fathers* and Walton's *Belshazzar's Feast,* to name only two examples, were first produced at Norwich and Leeds respectively.

The English composers prominent as the new generation of the inter-war years never quite kicked over the traces to the same extent as some of their continental contemporaries. For that reason, they sometimes tended, and still do tend, to be regarded as timid and reactionary. But they could equally well be accused of demonstrating that English sense of moderation that is prepared to hang on to the baby whilst throwing out the bath water. Fashions change; and so did they. But among their number was one young man whose precocity and brilliance made him immediately suspect in a society suspicious of both, yet who was to prove the first major British composer of opera for three hundred years and who managed to establish roots into and regenerate the English tradition that brought him an international audience as well as the haughty disapproval of – even outright dismissal by – the more Cartesian avant-garde continental luminaries. Appropriately enough, his surname was Britten.

12 – Britten:
Reading from Left to Right?

Many an English musician has shown immense talent as a child or an adolescent. In all too many, however, the flame has burned out quickly, leaving the historian with an all-too-familiar lament about what might have been. William Lawes, Pelham Humfrey, Purcell, Thomas Linley[87] and Warlock all died young. William Crotch, Mozart's respected pupil Attwood, Schumann's much-admired Sterndale Bennett and many others didn't quite die, either physically or musically: like the proverbial old soldier, they simply faded away. But in Benjamin Britten we find more and more, as his unpublished earlier works are unearthed and performed, a composer whose imagination matured at a remarkably early age, who matched his imagination with a dazzling technical command and who continued to mature and develop as a musical personality as he got older. Moreover, as he got older, he dug further and further into the English musical soil from which he sprang without losing touch either with the cosmopolitan and sophisticated musical world across the Channel and the Atlantic.

Britten was one of those infuriatingly talented people who excelled at practically everything he touched, both academically (his school reports have to be seen to be believed) and even athletically (he was a keen cricketer, sailor, swimmer and an apparently ruthlessly competitive tennis player). He was also, it goes without saying, a superb pianist, a fine conductor, both of his own music and that of other composers, including Mozart, Schubert, Purcell, Bach and Elgar, and a more than competent viola-player.

---

[87] One might mention here Stanford's gifted pupils William Hurlstone, Ivor Gurney, whom the First World War left bereft of his reason, and George Butterworth, killed on the Somme in 1916.

The musical environment in which he was brought up and worked spanned both World Wars; and his training as a musician took place, to all intents and purposes, during the inter-war period. He was also, to place him in his English musical environment, one of the post-impressionist, post-folksong[88] school of composers who had come to manhood during the 1930s when a reaction had set in all over Europe and in the USA against what was regarded as the hedonistic frivolity of the jazz age and the twenties.

In Europe, this was the Age of Hitler and of Stalinist collectivisation on the one hand and of the great industrial depression on the other. In America, it was the age of Roosevelt and the New Deal. In the arts, it saw the rise of the talking film from a gimmick to a genuine art form and a potent propaganda and educational vehicle. Art once more became what in previous ages it had already been: an arm of political propaganda in support of the prevalent social order, whether overtly, as in the totalitarian states, or more subtly, as in the democracies. For those in conflict with the status quo, it also became a vehicle of social protest. Thus Art for Art's Sake was submerged in many spheres by Art With A Message. Stylistically, the thirties saw the absorption and consolidation of the rather way-out experiments of the twenties and the emergence of a new generation of composers born and trained in the twentieth century.

Many 'progressive' artists – and Britten was certainly one of them – felt obliged to adopt some kind of political stance in their art towards current events; and in Britten's case that meant at least a sympathetic attitude towards the socialist experiment and a pacifist stance towards military aggression. In fact at one time Britten was dubbed 'Master of the Left's Music', mainly on the twin strengths of his own originality and his sympathetic treatment of poetic texts by left-wing writers such as W H Auden and Randall Swingler.

Britten was both precocious and prolific. His parents came from the professional middle classes (his father was a successful dentist in Lowestoft, his mother a talented amateur singer and pianist) and he was

---

[88] Or, to put it more crudely and less accurately, 'post-cowpat'.

also the youngest of four children. As a child, he began to compose quite early; and research into the boyhood manuscripts that he himself held back from publication shows that he had already acquired a fluent and reliable command of the nuts and bolts of composition at as early an age as had Mozart or the young Felix Mendelssohn. At prep school, he was a model pupil; and when he went on to boarding school at Gresham's School in Holt, Norfolk, he showed some of his efforts to the director of music, W W Greatorex[89]. Greatorex was somewhat disparaging of what he saw, but he encouraged Britten to appear at school concerts as a solo pianist. Having been bowled over by his first encounter with the music of Frank Bridge at a concert in Lowestoft, Britten went to him for private lessons in composition. He was determined, come what may, to be a creative rather than a merely interpretative musician.

At sixteen, Britten applied for a composition scholarship to the Royal College of Music; and two stories told of his application cast a revealing light both on the character of the kind of music he was writing and the attitude of the musical establishment to it. Vaughan Williams was on the interview board; and as the lad entered the room with a sheaf of manuscripts to show them, he asked ironically with a friendly grin: 'Is that all you've got to show us?', to which Britten replied in all seriousness, 'Oh no; I've got two more suitcases full outside'. After the board had looked at the music, another member of the board commented, 'What on earth is an English public-schoolboy doing writing music of this kind?' – ie, post-impressionist music showing the influence of Stravinsky when he should, it seems, have been writing respectable diatonic hymn-tune-like songs and piano pieces in four conventional parts. None the less, a scholarship was awarded; and Britten began his studies at the Royal College.

He felt that the teaching at the College was not satisfactory; his official teacher was John Ireland, another of Stanford's most promising pupils whose eclectic style has caused him, somewhat unfairly, to be included among the 'cow-pat' composers. Ireland was not a good teacher as far as Britten was concerned – if, that is, Britten was at all

---

[89] Famous (or notorious), as the composer of the hymn-tune 'Woodlands', usually sung to 'Tell out, my soul, the greatness of the Lord'.

concerned with the kind of teaching that the College provided. He missed lessons, carried a sizeable chip on his shoulder about what he felt to be lack of recognition of his own merits, and may well have been somewhat jealous of his brilliant pupil. Although Britten attended his lessons with him, he also continued privately with Frank Bridge. Bridge – the same age as Ireland – had, like Ireland, studied with Stanford; and something of his own teacher's pedagogical ruthlessness had rubbed off on him. He was a hard taskmaster, insisting from the start on a thoroughly professional approach to the job in hand. And one of the most revealing things about Britten's musical character is that while he expected the highest available standards from professional musicians, he also loved working with children and with dedicated amateurs. The professionals adored working with him because he had an acute ear, an almost intuitive sense of what needed to be done to improve an already high-class performance, forceful and well-thought-out ideas[90] about what the music should convey and infinite patience in getting what he wanted from them[91]. The amateurs felt, besides the privilege of working with an outstanding musician, that whether he was conducting his own music or somebody else's, his musicianship and personal charisma added something to the performance as nobody else could. But woe betide anyone who was not giving of his best: Britten's tongue also had a sharp edge to it; and he never forgot if he felt someone had let him – or, more importantly, the composer – down.

At one time in the 'thirties, he wanted to go to Vienna and study with Alban Berg, the most musically 'accessible' of Schoenberg's followers. His parents were persuaded by the College authorities on somewhat dubious grounds that there was something unhealthy about the kind of

---

[90] Not everyone agreed with him: Hans Keller, for example, one of his most ardent admirers as a composer, found some of his Bach performances aggressive and insensitive.

[91] When recording Elgar's *The Dream of Gerontius* with the LSO, he required no fewer than nine takes of the prelude before he was satisfied.

music that Berg composed[92] and that the young Britten would in some way be both morally and musically contaminated by contact with the world of serialism and dodecaphony. Britten, like many a brilliant young artist, had begun to question and react against the ideas and ideals held by some of his teachers. They were 'nationalist', trying to build up a specifically 'English' school of composition; he wanted to be cosmopolitan; they – or at any rate some of them – still treated the 'laws' of harmony[93] and counterpoint handed down as tablets from Vienna and Leipzig if not from Sinai, as if they were the Laws of the Medes and Persians; he felt he could flout them. They tended to be politically and socially conservative and conformist; he was, if not a bohemian, at any rate one of those who wished to reform society so that the arts had a greater role to play in it. And above all psychologically, he found himself quite by chance in a 'rebel' position: he was a homosexual in a society where his sexual tendencies were regarded as at best an unfortunate aberration and at worst a crime and a sin.

Besides his teacher Bridge, two other figures from outside the world of music influenced his outlook in these early days of maturity. The first was the poet W H Auden. The second was the documentary film-maker John Grierson. The influence of Auden is obvious both from Britten's letters and from the type of text he chose to set. By his own reckoning, the song-cycle for soprano and orchestra *Our Hunting Fathers* was his own real Opus 1: the work in which he felt he had at last achieved the

---

[92] To be fair to them, one can hardly regard the plots of *Wozzeck* and *Lulu* as examples of pristine gentlemanly or ladylike morality; but the fact that Adrian Boult, a pillar of the English musical establishment, was not only prepared to perform and broadcast *Wozzeck* in 1934 but to conduct it so convincingly as to receive a warm letter of congratulations from the composer himself, showed that he, at any rate, felt that it was musically worth it.

[93] What Vaughan Williams disparagingly referred to as 'stodge', though he was also uncompromisingly wary of any young iconoclast composer who 'didn't know his stodge'.

expression of his own individual musical personality. The choice of subject matter had been decided through and with Auden.

Grierson's influence was perhaps more subtle, but just as important at this stage in Britten's development. The documentary film movement was one of the great British contributions to popular art and the cinema in the 1930s; and John Grierson was the most celebrated director of documentary films. Grierson's attitude to documentary may be quoted in his own words:

> ... We believe that the cinema's capacity for getting around, for observing and selecting from life itself, can be exploited in a new and vital art form ... Documentary would photograph the living scene and the living actor ... beauty will come in good time to inhabit the statement which is honest and lucid and deeply felt and which fulfils the best ends of citizenship ... The opposite attempt to capture the by-product first (the self-conscious pursuit of beauty, the pursuit of art for art's sake to the exclusion of jobs of work and other pedestrian beginnings), was always a reflection of selfish wealth, selfish leisure, and aesthetic decadence.

Grierson and his disciple Cavalcanti, with whom Britten mainly worked as a film composer, thus held principles with which the young composer strongly sympathised throughout his career.

Britten regarded himself both as an artist and as a craftsman: more sensitive to the ultimate realities of life than the ordinary person and endowed with a special gift that enabled him to express what he felt about them, but there none the less in order to make those realities clear to his fellow-men and to express them as and when he was required to. He never considered the artist to inhabit an ivory tower of his own. He needed space, time and solitude to think out how to express what he felt, but he was also part of the community in which he lived and therefore responsible to it. He did not particularly like enjoy the actual film work, but he found writing to a strict deadline for carefully-calculated effects an excellent discipline; and one feels that the experience he gained with the GPO Film Unit writing for limited and unorthodox forces stood him in enormous stead much later in his life. And when he was asked if he could produce within four weeks a sizeable work for a virtuoso British string orchestra that had been asked to appear at the Salzburg Festival, he felt able to accept the commission and produced his brilliant

Variations on a Theme of Frank Bridge. In being Brittish, he also proved himself to be British, for the work was not only a tribute to Bridge and the Boyd Neel Orchestra, but also a worthy English contribution to a distinguished continental music festival.

These good intentions came at times into conflict with the facts of life as he experienced them; but he remained remarkably true to them throughout his career. At one time, it looked as if the frustrations of a creative musician's life in inter-war England were too great for him, for he was persuaded to join his friend, the tenor Peter Pears, Auden and a number of other artists who had settled in the United States in 1939 in a colony of like-minded artists who felt that life in Europe had no more to offer them. Despite the kindness of many patrons and friends in the States, Britten and Pears became disillusioned with the promiscuity and egotism of the colony, including Auden, and homesick for England in general and Suffolk in particular and decided to brave the Nazi submarines and return to their home country.

What had convinced him that his real roots lay in England was a chance reading of a poem by the early 19th-century Suffolk poet Crabbe called *The Borough* and an article on Crabbe in the BBC periodical *The Listener* by the great novelist E M Forster. His own account of the 'conversion' was simple:

> ... it was in California in the unhappy summer of 1941, that, coming across a copy of the Poetical Works of George Crabbe in a Los Angeles bookshop, I first read his poem, *Peter Grimes*; and, at the same time, reading a most perceptive and revealing article about it by E.M. Forster, I suddenly realized where I belonged and what I lacked.

It wasn't perhaps quite as simple as that: Britten for some time insisted on telling his American friends that his departure from the States was only temporary; and, like W H Auden, it seems that Pears was half-inclined to stay on there. But the decision was made, they returned to England and put down roots in Britten's native Suffolk, in the little town of Aldeburgh.

If the music of Elgar at its most characteristic summons up visions of the West Midlands, then the image that one derives again and again from Britten's music at its most poignant is that of the sea and of a small-town community dependent on it. Yet there is also the uneasy sense of

215

the one who would belong but always has to distance himself from the mores and behaviour of the community that he serves. The Suffolk or, should one perhaps say, the rural England that Britten evokes musically in his works is neither idealised nor sentimentalised. Its atmosphere is marvellously conveyed, yet its inhabitants are savagely pilloried as philistine and narrow-minded in works like his first opera, *Peter Grimes*, and more affectionately, but still with a certain arrogance, in the delightful comic opera *Albert Herring*. An English country house becomes the unexpected scene for hidden terrors in the two Henry James operas, *The Turn of the Screw* and *Owen Wingrave,* and projected as the background to child-exploitation and cruelty in *The Little Sweep.*

In all these works there is a constant exploration of the plight of the lonely idealistic individual yearning for security against a background of convention, self-satisfaction and lack of imagination. There is also the theme of innocence corrupted, one that recurs again and again in Britten. Sometimes, as in *The Turn of the Screw*, the corruption wins the field: the idealistic governess becomes in effect a meddling do-gooder. Commentators have traced this combination of factors to Britten's guilt about his sexual ambivalence, though Pears always dismissed this as nonsense. Auden, ever the domineering scoutmaster, tried to persuade Britten that he had to give way more to the bohemian streak that was undoubtedly part of his character. He must have been horrified when, as he grew older, Britten became more and more (but never entirely) associated with the British establishment, a friend of the royal family and a member of the House of Lords[94].

In a strange sense, Britten had regressed, socially if not musically, into a kind of updated Elgar. In this context it is not without interest that as a young man he detested Elgar's music, claiming that 'only in imperialistic Britain could a work like [the A flat Symphony] be tolerated', abandoning an attempt to listen to the Second after one minute (!) and likening the *Introduction and Allegro for Strings*, of which

---

[94] He never took his seat. He was already dying when he accepted the peerage, which he did, one suspects, more as a further official recognition of the value of music in the social order (he was already a Companion of Honour and one of the Order of Merit) than as a personal distinction.

in the 1960s he conducted a superbly vital recording, full of insight and power, to an Italian popular song. In later life, however, he greatly admired *For the Fallen* and was able to conduct *The Dream of Gerontius* with a commitment and insight, and with Pears singing the title-role, in a recording that underlines the drama and intensity of the music as few professional conductors have proved able to do.

It is in large part the kind of tensions that were at work in Britten's character that give his music its peculiarly English quality. Though he rebelled against the conventions of the social order in which he was brought up, he did so only up to a certain point. He believed in freedom, not license. He simply could not and would not give way to the laid-back bohemian standards that Auden thought would bring him to full self-realisation as an artist. Though there is violence a-plenty in his music, as there is so often beneath the surface in Shakespeare, Dickens and Hogarth, to mention three great English artists in other spheres, it is counterbalanced by a mischievous wit on the one hand and a nostalgia for a lost childhood happiness on the other that are equally redolent of the two great writers as they are of Elgar. But for Elgar, childhood was the land not so much of lost innocence as of lost wonder. For Britten, one gets the feeling the sophistication of adolescence and adulthood closed the gates, not to dreaming and freedom of fantasy but to a sense of security and innocent, uncorrupted affection.

Britten wrote a considerable number of works for children. Sometimes these were to enable young musicians to show off their skills. In others, they provided an opportunity for the enthusiastic music-makers of an entire community to participate. This is particularly so of his enchanting opera *Noye's Fludde*, in which the ingenuous text is matched with music whose sophistication is overlaid by a simplicity and a directness that make an immediate appeal. But Britten never wrote down to his young performers; it is as if the child in him had already reached the sophisticated level that he was able to turn to more adult themes.

This interest in – almost obsession with – childhood is a peculiarly English trait. Nowhere else in western culture are childhood and schooldays celebrated in literature as in England. Nor is it restricted to works composed with children in mind. It has, indeed, been argued that the opera *Billy Budd* is set not so much on an 18th-century man-of-war as in an English prep school[95], with Captain Vere as the headmaster, Claggart as the school bully and Billy himself as the innocent new boy destroyed by the corruption of the system.

But the 'system' did eventually claim at least part of him. In 1952 he had been discussing with some friends, who included Lord Harewood, cousin of Queen Elizabeth II, the topic of national operas, such as *The Bartered Bride, Boris Godunov, Aïda* and *Die Meistersinger.* Where, Britten wanted to know, was the English equivalent? 'You'd better write one', Harewood replied. And Britten did. The result was his most consciously 'English' and most consistently underrated opera: *Gloriana.* By the time he was commissioned to write this opera for the coronation of Elizabeth II, he was fast becoming our musical laureate. *Gloriana* and the great *War Requiem* of 1962, which was commissioned to commemorate the rebuilding of Coventry cathedral after its destruction in World War II, show him as the worthy successor of Handel and Elgar in this vein. In *Gloriana,* the pageantry that attends the outward trappings of power symbolises one aspect of the human being who is also a public figure. The love interest between the ageing queen and the Earl of Essex stands for the inner self-realisation that has to give place to it if the public figure's duty to the populace at large is to be fulfilled. Here, Britten takes Auden on full-face and comes down on the side of duty, not self-indulgence. At one time, as his letters and diaries show, he had been overawed by Auden's conversational brilliance and acute analytical mind. But he outgrew the bohemian view of how an artist should behave that Auden so frequently enjoined on him.

In Elizabeth and Essex, Britten also, consciously or unconsciously, created two ikons for late-twentieth-century Britain. She has a glorious past, both musically[96] and politically. But she has to come to terms with

---

[95] See, for example, Humphrey Carpenter's fascinating analysis of the work in his book on Britten (London, 1992, pp 292-6).

[96] The skilful pastiche-Elizabethan music that Britten creates here is just as *echt*-Britten as is his hilarious send-up of a clumsy amateur attempt to produce early 19th-century *bel canto* Italian opera at the end of *A Midsummer Night's Dream.*

her present. Her rulers have a sense of duty and a tradition of public service; but must human warmth and emotion always be emasculated in training her citizens to accept them? This ambivalence was rooted in affection: witness not only the working-out of the tension in *Gloriana,* but also Britten's treatment of folk- and popular melodies[97] and his very characteristic realisations of his much-admired Purcell. He could not totally submerge his own musical personality in any such tribute; he could not help doing so; and he would have felt it insincere to do so anyway.

The *War Requiem* is likewise polarised. The context of the Requiem Mass is vividly counterbalanced by the Wilfred Owen poems underlining the waste and futility of war that are inserted into the text at crucial points partly to underline, partly to undermine the message of the mass itself. The scepticism, even nihilism, of the poems chosen and the shrewdness with which Britten selects a fitting context for each of them render this public and ceremonial work one of his most personal and poignant confessions. They are confessions both of belief in eternal ideals on the one hand and of doubt and misgivings on the other. The blazing glory of the *Sanctus* and the measured, processional tread of the *Benedictus* are succeeded by the utter bleakness of Owen's doubts about any kind of resurrection. The terror of the Day of Judgment in the finale subsides into the numbness of the reconciliation in *Strange Meeting,* so that the eternal sleep of the two soldiers, English and German, is raised on to the plane of a procession into paradise.

The ambivalence of both *Gloriana* and the *War Requiem* matched the national mood at the time when they were composed: a nation conscious of her past glories and traditional values, and the sacrifices that their realisation would entail, yet also uneasily aware that they were fading and anxious about what would replace them. But their 'English' qualities lie deeper than those of mere pageantry, pastiche and association with poetry. Britten's extraordinary gift for evoking an

---

[97] Influenced, possibly, by his unique ability to emulate Schubert's technique of finding a suitable musical metaphor in the accompaniment to match the basic mood of the text.

atmosphere – even a visual image – in the listener's mind is given full play in both works; but in the *War Requiem* the atmosphere is tinged with that stoic, dogged emotion, that 'stiff-upper-lip' determination to endure, to hold out at all costs against adversity, that characterises the British reaction to overwhelming disaster that must somehow or other be met and defeated. This is as true of the apparently jaunty duet setting of Owen's 'Out there' as it is of the stern and measured setting of 'On seeing one of our heavy artillery pieces go into action' – surely one of Britten's most powerful movements in its restrained but none the less pent-up, seething anger. The rage expressed here is of the same tight-lipped, barely controlled order as that found in Vaughan Williams's Fourth Symphony, yet no two pieces of music could be superficially less similar. The *War Requiem* has been criticised for being derivative – some of its more dramatic and pathetic moments (the *Tuba mirum* and the *lacrymosa*, for example), certainly owe a good deal to Verdi on the one hand and Mozart on the other --, but the whole concept is strikingly original in its stark simplicity. This is perhaps most evident in the moving restraint of the *Agnus dei*, where the tenor soloist for once is actually allowed to be involved in the final prayer at the very end of the movement instead of simply declaiming Owen's poem drawing a stark contrast between the sycophantic belligerence of the priests and the calm resignation of the suffering Christ and the soldiers whom poet and composer identify with Him.

After the *War Requiem*, Britten concentrated on more intimate and personal works, composed for specific artists and sympathetic patrons. Yet his work retained right to the end of his days the spirit of exploration for which it had always been noted. The three Parables for Church Performance, for example, broke new ground in a number of ways. They took their point of departure from the traditional Japanese Nô drama, by which he had been fascinated on a tour to the far east in the 1950s. Yet they became peculiarly personal: the story of the first, *Curlew River,* was based on a Japanese story, but transferred to medieval England; the male actors became monks and the tiny orchestra was involved in the action in a manner that dated back far beyond even the days of Britten's beloved Purcell. The other two, one from the Old Testament (*The*

Burning Fiery Furnace) and one from the New *(The Prodigal Son)*, placed the form even more closely in a European framework, even though the stories were set in the Middle East.

Britten's continuing political commitment to causes in which he believed is further illustrated by such works as his cantatas *Voices for Today* and *Children's Crusade*, and the opera *Owen Wingrave*. His delight in writing for young people and his ability to turn a graceful compliment to respected authority can also be found in another of his very last works: the 'unpretentious, unpatronizing and unpompous[98]' *Welcome Ode*, designed to commemorate a visit by Queen Elizabeth II to the county of Suffolk. And in addition to his last and greatest tribute to the artistry of Peter Pears, the title role in *Death in Venice,* he also found time to write a very moving and powerful one to another much admired artist, Dame Janet Baker, in *Phaedra*. He was one who, artistically at any rate, could 'walk with kings, nor lose the common touch' – the common touch in his case being a loyalty to the basic views that he had held as a young man. Even as he retreated into his own private world in his final works, such as *Death in Venice* and the haunting and enigmatic Third String Quartet, so he also and at the same time dug deeper into his roots in English literature and English folk-song. And, strangely enough, the last work in which he did this, the suite *A Time there Was*, greatly moved a later Queen Elizabeth, as responsive to music, as respected and as admired in her day as the Virgin Queen had been in the days of the Oriana madrigals: 'the Queen Mum', a staunch friend and patron of the Aldeburgh Festival.

A Time there Was also reinforces his links with Mahler, whose influence Michael Kennedy rightly detects in the work, and with Thomas Hardy and the stoic, fatalistic rural tradition that he represents. The title comes from a poem of Hardy's that Britten had set in his song-cycle *Winter Words* and the shade of Hardy haunts the work, just as the shade of Britten's beloved Venice haunts his final opera and string quartet. The verse from which the title is taken runs as follows:

---

[98] Michael Kennedy, *Benjamin Britten,* Oxford, 1993 edition, p 247.

A time there was – as one may guess
And as, indeed, earth's testimonies tell –
Before the birth of consciousness
When all went well.

In this suite, Britten uses ten traditional tunes, a number of them collected by his admired Percy Grainger, to whose memory the work is dedicated and whose arrangements of English airs he had as a young man found infinitely preferable to those by composers such as Vaughan Williams.

There is no ambivalence here, no destructive tension between the 'English' and the 'cosmopolitan'. At its best, English art has always been eclectic and cosmopolitan. And Britten's music at its best – and what a best! – is both.

13 – Epilogue:
Is There Life After Britten?

By the time that Britten died in 1976, there already had been something of a reaction among young music-students against his music. It was not on any great scale, but it was noticeable. As Britten's friend and admirer, Professor Donald Mitchell[99], observed of his students at Sussex University in the 1970s:

> ... any mention of Britten would provoke a dismissive response: 'Old hat; we really don't want to listen to it' – or to think about it, I might add. He was absolutely 'out'. In the student generation I taught, fashion had gone totally against him ...

as it had in their turn against Elgar and Vaughan Williams, one might observe. After all, what suits the emotional needs of one generation does not necessarily satisfy the next one. Art may not 'progress', in the sense of continually changing for the better, but it does evolve, unless its techniques are deliberately maintained unmodified as part of a treasured and ossified tradition. Professor Mitchell continues:

> ... The only work that seemed to retain something of a reputation was the *War Requiem*, but that had been a popular success – even among students – just before the shift in critical opinion began; perhaps, ironically, its very success helped generate the shift. And the views of my students, of course, reflected those of a whole generation of young composers, not only in England but elsewhere.

That whole generation of young composers included at least three who had drunk at the fount of the new post-Schoenbergian serialism epitomised in particular by the music of Pierre Boulez. This is not the place to assess whether the widespread influence of this amazingly

---

[99] Humphrey Carpenter, *Benjamin Britten*, p 542

gifted, shrewdly analytical and highly articulate musician has been beneficial or simply fundamentally wrong-headed; it has certainly been widespread and in some cases stimulating. But it has not always met with wholesale acceptance. One of the most talented English commentators on music of this period summed up the dilemma of the serious musician as he saw it in these terms:

> . . . No musician likes living entirely in the past. He wants to follow the development of present-day music towards the future; and I've no quarrel with genuine followers of the Schoenberg-to-Stockhausen line. It's just that I can't breathe in a world where the common musical language evolved by humanity at large has been abandoned for the private language invented by a single individual.

Thus, Deryck Cooke[100], writing in 1968. Cooke was a fine musical scholar, though he would not have claimed to be anything of a composer[101]. His knowledge of music went far beyond the 'serious' field in which he was such a distinguished scholar: his repertoire of music-hall, jazz and other kinds of popular music of many ages was immense. Nor was he by any means a reactionary; and in his own field, he was far more learned, perceptive and sensitive than many of those who dismiss him and his theories without half his understanding and his clarity of vision (or his fine analytical ear). His interpretation of the language of western music[102] may not be anything like the whole story, any more than the doctrines of the serialists are[103] but it is a shrewd and scholarly attempt to argue that any piece of worth-while music has an effect far beyond the mere skill with which the composer has constructed the

---

[100] In *Vindications* (London, 1982) p 196.

[101] Yet his insight into the music of Mahler, as shown by his 'performing version' of Mahler's Tenth Symphony, shows creative imagination and insight of a very high order.

[102] *The Language of Music,* Oxford, 1961.

[103] Schoenberg himself said that there was still plenty of good music to be written in C major, as he put it.

pattern of sounds with which the listener is confronted. This is so, he argues cogently, because for hundreds of years, certain emotional states have been associated in musicians' and listeners' minds with certain melodic formulae, the effects of which are in turn based on the mathematical tensions between notes inherent in the harmonic series itself.

The most significant followers of total serialism were loosely known as the 'Manchester School' simply because three of them, Sir Peter Maxwell Davies, Sir Harrison Birtwistle and Professor Alexander Goehr, met as students and discussed one another's works at the Manchester College of Music. Their sources of inspiration and style ranged wide. Peter Maxwell Davies showed not merely an interest in traditional compositional styles, in his case even going back to the Middle Ages, but the ability to synthesise them into a personal style that communicates directly. Of his (so far) six symphonies it may well be said 'The symphony is dead; long live the symphony!'.

It is not without significance that, having conceived his third symphony as a purely abstract musical design, he suddenly realised when rehearsing it that it was also in fact a a powerful musical seascape: 'my most dynamic seascape to date'[104]. Whether this may be accounted as a sign of 'Englishness', he would probably dispute, but if we are in any sense still a seafaring race, then it should be possible for anyone belonging to a country with a maritime tradition to react to at any rate this particular work, regardless of how it is constructed.

Like Britten, 'Max' also rediscovered his roots in a seafaring community – that of the Orkney Islands – from whose physical background and way of life he has drawn powerful inspiration and to whose musical life he has contributed a great deal. And like a number of other English composers, notably Purcell, Sullivan, Walton and Britten, he has a strong sense of *musical* humour: witness the disarming and wittily brash orchestral variations *Mavis in Las Vegas*. Nor was he above quoting Lennon and McCartney's *Let it be* in his moving and powerful *Eight Songs for a Mad King*.

---

[104] See the composer's own note to his recording with the BBC Philharmonic Orchestra (Collins 1416-2).

Maxwell Davies has gradually moved back towards the central tradition of Western tonal music without ever compromising his musical integrity. As a young man, he worked for a time at Cirencester School and his open-minded attitude there enabled his pupils to appreciate and perform music of all traditions, from medieval to serialist. In many ways he is in fact the most eclectic of all our major composers – and that he *is* a major figure there can be no doubt: his ability to communicate with a far less specialist audience prepared to listen to what he has to say than that of most avant-garde composers is surely an indication of it. What has clearly been of importance to him is the ability to establish roots in a community, to absorb ideas from that community and the landscape in which they work and translate those ideas into musical terms and to work closely with a poet who also chose to establish his roots there. That these roots are Scottish[105] may well bring his music closer to Scots (and to Englishmen), but perhaps Sir Peter is in this respect an exception among modern British composers.

This same determination to write when asked to do so for a larger audience without compromising his musical beliefs is notable in Sir Harrison Birtwistle. One of Birtwistle's earlier commissions was for a piece for the Grimethorpe Colliery Band. He produced the *Grimethorpe Aria*, an impressive tone-picture of the mining area of Yorkshire. It is said that one of the miner-musicians encountering it for the first time dismissed it as 'bloody rubbish, not music', but admitted once the band had got to know it 'I still think it's not music – but it's bloody fascinating.' 'Music' or no, it was listened to in rapt attention by a Saturday-night Promenade audience that must have included hundreds of supporters of the band for which it was written and who had worked so diligently to master its intricate technical and musical challenges. Much less immediately approachable than Maxwell Davies and with a dour, tight-lipped earnestness and sense of the macabre and the uncanny that marks him off even from his contemporaries, Birtwistle is to my mind a 'serious' rather than a specifically English composer. But his seriousness commands respect, it has English resonances and his music

---

[105] His series of Strathclyde Concertos for the members of the Scottish Chamber Orchestra are further evidence of this.

has an almost uncomfortable toughness. But because the striking opera *Gawain* has a subject taken from a medieval English poem and is about one of the knights of the Round Table, that does not make it any more 'nationally' English than Wagner's choice of the Tristan legend. In neither his case nor Birtwistle's is there any compromise with musical 'Englishness'; Birtwistle is simply a richly-endowed and highly individual composer rather than a consciously English one.

Alexander Goehr's music is said to have fallen into the kind of academicism favoured by the English musical establishment since he went into the academic world, first as professor at Leeds and then, in 1976, at Cambridge. This crass misjudgment blandly overlooks the fact that of virtually all musical idioms that have evolved since the Middle Ages, serialism is one of the most academic of all, and like all strict academic disciplines can be as much a straitjacket to the unimaginative as it can be a stimulus to the original. Goehr's music has in fact progressed by absorption and refinement, not regressed through prejudice and stubbornness nor run into a predictable groove. He himself studied at the Royal Manchester College of Music at a time when there were at least two rival schools of composition[106]; and being not only broad-minded as well as youthfully iconoclastic, but cosmopolitan and widely-read (not just in music, either), has developed a post-Schoenbergian style of composition that is individual, solidly-based academically and certainly not narrowly national. In *Poetics of My Music*[107], he has explained his position with succinct clarity:

> . . . A piece of music is brought into being by a free act of the imagination. This single stroke, involving as it does the man, his beliefs and his memory, ensures something other than the result of choice. Take this irregular thing, and upon it make operations of one kind or another as elegantly as possible. This produces an order of brain following heart. But better still when the results of the brainwork themselves become new gestures and new images for development. A group of notes is transformed by the brain and a new image

---

[106] See 'Manchester Years' in *Finding the Key,* London and Boston, 1998, pp 27–41.

[107] *Finding the Key,* pp 42–57

fires the imagination: a *trouvaille*, or quotable gesture, in the sense that it suggests its own continuation. Suddenly a new association of harmonies or a new melodic tag interrupts the regular plan of a piece and sets everything out of joint. The composer must obey this ebb and flow, apparently exposing himself to the operations of chance as the painter reacts to the free movement of the paint that he himself has brought into play. Francis Bacon is quoted as saying 'What I really love is the way, of its own accord, paint makes things. The way that, in Constable, the flakes of paint as they happen to fall, make a horse.'

The operational aspects of the compositional process only make sense within such a hazardous and dynamic context, where a beginning image may suggest a conscious working-out, this in turn throwing up a new image and a new beginning . . .

In other words, he considers that composition is an interaction between the imagination, which may or, more probably, may not be controlled rationally, and the brain, each 'firing' the other, as Goehr puts it. But his reference to Bacon is interesting: ' . . . the flakes of paint as they happen to fall, make a horse.' Just, then, as in representational painting, the power of the medium forces the artist into creating an abstract visual pattern that also evokes the image of something recognisable in nature, so in abstract music the artist's mind and the patterns he creates through it interact. The artist's mind is not in consistent conscious control of the material, however carefully he tries to organise it. This is consistent with what Peter Maxwell Davies was pointing out when he suddenly realised that his Third Symphony was in fact a powerful seascape as well as a large-scale musical design.

Goehr's account of his own background shows him to be willing to try and find something to learn from in the enormous range of musical styles and attitudes that he has studied and absorbed. Brought up in a basically Germanic tradition, he was also influenced to a greater or lesser degree by teachers as different as his one-time predecessor C V Stanford, Hindemith, Olivier Messïaen, Krenek and Hauer, as well as his own teacher Richard Hall. He is not just English, not even just European; and although his Jewish background and ancestry have ensured that he is vitally interested in Israel and his own Jewish heritage, he is in no sense a nationalist Jewish composer either. He is a kind of modern Mahler, clear-headed and outspoken, but without the ruthlessness and the egocentric subjectivity that characterise Mahler: a cosmopolitan figure who has created his own musical identity and encourages his pupils to find theirs, too.

Other musicians have explored other traditions in an effort to integrate the music of the present with that of the past. One of the most notable is John Tavener. Tavener converted to Greek Orthodox Christianity in his thirties and has since composed using an idiom derived from that of the Greek church. Before his conversion, he had applied a combination of electronic techniques and those developed by Messïaen; his current compositions have a calm, static quality about them that might be described as updated Eric Satie with a solemn minimalist tinge to it. It is doubtful whether Tavener would like to be associated musically with some of the minimalists, yet the ethos of his music seems to place his later works, at any rate, in a similar category with, say, those of the Estonian Arvo Pärt rather than in any directly 'English' line of descent. The haunting atmosphere, however, of works such as *The Protecting Veil* marks Tavener out as a composer with something to say to those prepared to enter his world.

Another composer who has rejected outright serialism in favour of a more traditional approach is Nicholas Maw, whose vast one-movement *Odyssey* has been hailed[108] as 'one man's dogged journey away from 20th-century ideologies and back to the essence of music'. The leisurely pace at which his music unfolds has been likened by more than one commentator to that of Bruckner. It doesn't sound like it. Maw put his finger on one of the main musical objections to total serialism when he likened the kind of music it produced to 'scintillating pieces of sculpture which you walked round rather than travelled through'. His own music is an attempt to return to music that one can 'travel through' – a sincere and thoughtful attempt to come out at the other end of the serialist tunnel, as it were, armed with a new slant on traditional procedures.

Tavener and Maw have been selected out of many other late twentieth-century 'serious' composers of music who might have been

---

[108] Norman Lebrecht, *The Companion to 20th-Century Music,* London 1992, p 220.

mentioned because they are typical of musicians who wish to retain what they consider the basic expressive elements of the Western musical tradition rather than follow the paths once regarded as inevitable by the avant-garde of the sixties. They do not wish their music to communicate mainly via an intellectual process and to be appreciated basically as an intellectual exercise. Consciously or unconsciously, they hold a traditional view of aesthetic experience: it represents that link between thought and emotion that kindles the sense of the beautiful and the sublime. This is not primarily an intellectual matter, though the intellect plays a significant part. Associations play a great part in it as well as intellectual training. And a complete break with traditionally significant elements of association may result in an unprecedented experience, but not necessarily in something that can be applied as a future technique.

But if one kind of 'serious' music became more and more distant from the general musical public, in at least one field, the 'native woodnotes wild' of a group of young popular musicians seized the imagination of a whole generation of young people world-wide. That part of their appeal was undoubtedly due to modern hype and public relations they themselves (or at least the surviving members of the group) would probably be the first to admit. But that was by no means the whole story. The Beatles and the style of music that they represented were assessed and appreciated not only by Cooke but by the Schoenbergian Hans Keller, by performers such as the wayward genius pianist Glenn Gould and perceptive academic critics such as William Mann of *The Times* and Professor Wilfred Mellers.

Various reasons, not all of them musical, can be adduced for the success of the Beatles. Certainly, the group were superbly packaged; and they had a manager who knew how to exploit and project their image. But without their music and their lyrics, all the projection in the world would have been useless. Cooke's article on them[109] goes into considerable detail about the purely *musical* reasons for their success and ends with the following passage:

---

[109] See *Vindications*, pp 196 – 200.

Lennon and McCartney are genuine creators of a 'new music.' Strangely enough, a few 'serious' composers of 'new music' admire them, and some will say it shows you can enjoy the best of both worlds. Others will maintain it only shows that both types of music are rubbish. I myself wonder whether it isn't that the avant-garde are fascinated to find mere pop composers doing such things with the 'exhausted' vernacular.

McCartney has of late launched into the world of music on a larger scale and has also donated a considerable proportion of his immense royalties to the foundation of a music academy in his native Liverpool. The results of both ventures could be valuable, though it depends on his ability to hold the attention of the listener over long spans through sheer skill of musical construction as well as an ear for a good tune. It will be interesting to see what happens, especially in the light of the work done by rock musicians with an academic background, such as Pink Floyd.

The most unpredictable major English 'serious' composer of this age, whose life, if not his composing career, spanned almost the entire century, was Sir Michael Tippett (1905–1998). Tippett remained until the end of his days a seeker. Like Britten he loved the music of Purcell and the Elizabethans. Like Britten, he responded to English folk-music. Like Britten, he also admired the music of the baroque, but in his case it was the lighter, more elegant music of the Italians such as Corelli and Vivaldi and the melodic appeal of Handel rather than the powerful, intensely developed counterpoint of J S Bach. (Tippett's fondness for complexity in his own music probably precluded any attempts to take what was already complex and elaborate it further). But unlike Britten, he was an enthusiastic rather than an accomplished executant; unlike Britten, he made his first trip to the USA when already well into middle age. He responded very positively to American vitality and brash colourfulness, whereas Britten was never really at home in the States. And equally unlike Britten, he aimed not at the clarity and poise of Mozart but at the rugged visionary sublimity of Beethoven, a composer whom Britten as an adolescent admired greatly, but felt that any attempt to emulate him would result in the complete smothering of his own individual musical personality. Tippett was prepared to take the risk of not achieving the clarity and precision that was always Britten's aim, in the hope that he could communicate something deeply felt even if imperfectly realised. This meant that he tended to produce works that

231

might or might not hit the ambitious targets at which he aimed. It also meant that his vision was sometimes cloudy and his music extremely, some would say unnecessarily, complex, even clumsy.

Tippett was prepared to accept the challenge; and he was also prepared to take up the gauntlet thrown down a hundred years previously by Wagner. In musical structure and style, Tippett's five operas are not in the least Wagnerian; in psychological aim and in the challenge they offer the listener, they are. Similarly, his quartets and symphonies pay tribute to Beethoven in a number of ways, and cover similar ground, but inhabit quite another world, even if it is one that owes much to his great model.

Like Wagner, Tippett wrote his own libretti; and, again like Wagner, one might wish that his efforts in this direction were clearer and plainer. In one sense, indeed, he went further even than Wagner did. His libretti are not 'realistic'; like Wagner's, they deal in myths. But the myths in which they deal are neither classical (save perhaps in *King Priam*) nor traditional and legendary. Tippett was not content just to adapt ancient myths and the characters in them to his own ends. He even invented his own mythical situations and imagery, drawing on modern as well as traditional sources. And most unlike Wagner, he was prepared to chance his arm using modern popular verbal images and registers as well as modern vernacular musical idioms, from the blues and jazz in his earlier years to the rock and rap music of his later ones. Not for him the fustian, pseudo-medieval verse that Wagner so easily drops into in the chase for a truly 'German' style. Tippett's imagery draws on the vocabulary – the jargon, even – of 20th-century psychiatry and 'hip' slang. Not for him, either, the complex chromaticisms of Wagner's doom- and longing-laden music-dramas such as *Tristan* and *Parsifal.*

Tippett's eagerness, his vitality, his willingness to explore new paths and to expand his musical vocabulary, whether by adopting new 'serious' techniques or by borrowing from more popular musical idioms, apparent in his earliest works, remained with him throughout his long life. Throughout his career he was also concerned with the search for reconciliation between the darker, destructive and the creative, energetic, bustling, at times even manic aspects of the human psyche, always prepared to admit that he could be wrong, always the opponent of violence and destruction, yet always willing to admit that all

232

humanity, not least himself, had powerful, destructive as well as creative urges. Moreover, though his music has its dark sides, it is basically optimistic and life-enhancing. His psychological and philosophical mentor was mentor was not Schopenhauer but Carl Gustav Jung. What Nietzsche would have called the Dionysiac side of his character is always evident; but there is also a profound, tranquil, 'Apolline' side that is part of his Beethovenian heritage – derived from the pure radiant serenity of movements like the 'heiliger Dankgesang' of the great A minor Quartet. Yet even so, if the mantle of Wagner fell on anyone in the twentieth century it was on Michael Tippett. I personally think that the mantle of Beethoven the visionary fell on him as well.

Is Tippett's music 'English'? Certainly it was rooted in part in a great love for some of our profoundest musicians. The urgency and thrustful vigour of some of his fast movements is an updating into terms of twentieth-century hustle of the vigorous interplay of rhythms in the madrigal – madrigalian counterpoint galvanised by a dose of Beethovenian forcefulness. But the pensive melancholy of certain of his slow movements and the reflective calm of others has little to do with any evocation of an English pastoral or even urban landscape, or of any soliloquies in an English cloister. It derives at least as much from sources across the Atlantic as it does from anything English. Yet once more, the ability to generate a personal style and idiom from diverse and eclectic sources is an English trait. There were many traditions from which to pick and choose; there was only one unique and cheerful personality – gay in both the traditional and in the modern senses of the word – that could blend them into a whole. But he totally avoids either the ceremonial swagger of an Elgar, the self-imposed identification with our folk-culture of a Vaughan Williams, even the sense of personal involvement with a great national icon – the sea – of works like *Peter Grimes* and *Billy Budd*, or in the great ceremonial occasion[110] of the Britten of *Gloriana* or the *War Requiem*. Yet it is difficult to think of a

---

[110] His contribution to the Coronation festivities of 1953 was the splendidly virile and vigorous madrigal *Dance, clarion air* and his one piece of notable 'occasional' royal music was the delightful Suite in D, based on folk-tunes, composed for the birthday of Prince Charles.

French, German, or Russian Tippett. An American one, maybe[111]: if America was the melting-pot of Europe, then Tippett's art is a fascinating melting-pot of the Englisn, Germanic and American musical traditions.

No mention has been made in this book so far of the female creative artist. In the novel, in poetry, painting, sculpture, women have made a notable contribution to art in England in the nineteenth and twentieth centuries. Their contribution to music has featured less prominently. Yet it has been there, in the work of such composers as Elisabeth Lutyens and Elizabeth Maconchy, both of whose chamber music deserves wider recognition, Maconchy's daughter, Nicola LeFanu, and Thea Musgrave. It is not my intention to try to assess any of their output by any yardsticks of 'Englishness'. The contribution made to the art of music by creative women artists will surely grow in significance and will become part of the heritage left by the gifted younger generation of composers working in the full bloom of their maturity at the time of writing. This comment is intended to be neither patronising nor dismissive. This is not a history of English music, merely a series of scattered observations on certain 'English' aspects of the music of various composers whose music appeals to me and seems significant.

There has been a notable change in the country's position, though not perhaps in its image of itself, since the close of World War II. With the Empire gone, as has so often been noted, Britain's political leaders have seemed at times at a loss to know what role she should play in the modern world. The hollow pretensions of the Suez campaign and our immediate withdrawal from our commitment to the French and the Israelis when the pound came under attack were symptoms of this. The gradual decline of complacent British heavy industry in the face of resolute and innovative competition from overseas; the timidity of large British financial institutions in investing in the long-term development of striking new scientific and technological ideas; the blinkered, philistine insularity of the popular press; the emphasis on our ancient heritage and our quaintness rather than our sturdiness and enterprise;

---

[111] Charles Ives is an interesting parallel.

the cult, no longer of the 'gentleman' amateur but of the slipshod mercenary[112]; the continual search by government after government for the quick-fix economic solution, seem to have been matched by a corresponding increase in self-indulgence, violence, shallow and exploitative human relationships and a decline in courtesy and integrity. The chimera of a 'special relationship' with the United States[113] has always proved something of a one-way affair. The image of the 'law-abiding' Englishman, with his sense of fair play and tolerance, often seems to be giving way to that of the lager-lout, the spoilt-brat celebrity and the football hooligan. One could go on.

Is there any real pride in developing a specifically 'English' identity, when the reality so often seems to bear so little resemblance to the image? Does the Vision of Albion still count for anything, or is it a misguided nostalgic dream – one of the 'if-onlies' of art? Does what Hardy called the permanent moral character of an individual or a nation any longer have any place in art? It *is* clear that a supremely great and influential artist may be in many respects a despicably selfish and revolting human being: the case of Richard Wagner is only one of many such. But has the time gone for ever when a community's higher social, moral and individual values and aspirations are in some mysterious way reflected in the art that it produces and enjoys?

Despite the claims that we are one world, or even one Europe, linguistic, class and tribal identities still persist. They often express themselves in ways that are exclusive, arrogant, brutal or self-interested. Even if the feelings they engender are basically noble, they can easily be perverted in the interests of cunning political and financial manipulators. Perhaps the surfeit of information available thanks to the

---

[112] I see no reason to degrade the term 'professional' by applying it to those working in any field who are badly trained, lacking in true commitment and in it to get as much as they can for as little effort as is needed.

[113] Even when President Reagan gave discreet assistance to the Falklands campaign, it was surely an update of the Monroe doctrine with Britain fortuitously saving the USA the task of giving a troublesome Latin American military junta a well-needed bloody nose.

media and the Internet, useful or trivial, good or bad, truthful or economical with truth, will lead to an ever-increasing eclecticism of outlook. Or will the sheer power of the force that grips the artist when he is at work, as Professor Goehr and Sir Peter Maxwell Davies have hinted, still in some mysterious way be conditioned by his (or her, of course) native language, and the social environment, moral values and ideals prevalent among the national community in which he or she grew up and matured? Perhaps it is nearer the truth to claim that those artists who have been considered most in tune with the accepted national image and ethos at a given time were such powerful artistic personalities that they would have made their mark regardless of any status they may have achieved either here or abroad as national ikons. Perhaps it always has been.

Index of Names

Index of Works

Arne, Thomas Augustine: *Artaxerxes*, 86, 87; *Comus* incidental music, 43; *King Alfred*, 71; *Olimpiade*, 87; *Thomas and Sally*, 85

Arnold, Samuel: *The Banditti*, 85; *Castle of Andalusia*, 85; *The Children in the Wood*, 86

Attwood, Thomas: Coronation Anthems for George IV, 104

Bach, Johann Christian: Symphony No 53, 98

Bach, Johann Sebastian: B minor Mass, 145; G minor organ fugue, 149

Balfe, Michael: *The Bohemian Girl*, 134; *The Maid of Artois*, 134; *The Siege of Rochelle*, 134

Bax, Arnold: *The Garden of Fand*, 201; *Tintagel*, 201

Beethoven, Ludwig van: *Christ on the Mount of Olives*, 74; Quartet in A minor, Op 132, 233

Berg, Alban: *Wozzeck*, 206

Birtwistle, Harrison: *Gawain*, 227; *The Grimethorpe Aria*, 226

Bishop, Henry: Additions to Arne's *Artaxerxes* and *Comus*, adaptations of Mozart, Auber, Weber and Meyerbeer operas, 127; Music for Walter Scott adaptations: *Guy Mannering, Heart of Midlothian, The Antiquary*, 126

Bliss, Arthur: *Conversations*, 198; *Lie Strewn the White Flocks*, 198; *Madame Noy*, 198; *Things to Come*, 206

Boïeldieu, François: *La Dame Blanche*, 126

Boyce, William: *Heart of Oak*, 84; *Solomon*, 92; Trio Sonatas, 95

Brahms, Johannes: Symphony No 3, 32

Bridge, Frank: *Enter Spring*, 207; *Oration*, 207; *The Sea*, 207

Britten, Benjamin: *Albert Herring*, 216; *Billy Budd*, 218; *The Burning Fiery Furnace*, 221; *The Children's Crusade*, 221; *Curlew River*, 220; *Death in Venice*, 221; *First Canticle*, 45; *Gloriana*, 218; *The Little Sweep*, 216; *Noye's Fludde*, 217; *Our Hunting Fathers*, 213; *Peter Grimes*, 216; *Phaedra*, 221; *The Ploughboy*, 108; *The Prodigal Son*, 221; *A Time there Was*, 221; *The Turn of the Screw*, 216; *Variations on a Theme of Frank Bridge*, 215; *Voices for Today*, 221; *War Requiem*, 218; *Welcome Ode*, 221; *Winter Words*, 221